Hiking Waterfalls in Northern California

HELP US KEEP THIS GUIDE UP TO DATE

Every effort has been made by the author and editors to make this guide as accurate and useful as possible. However, many things can change after a guide is published—water levels vary, trails are rerouted, regulations change, facilities come under new management, and so forth.

We welcome your comments concerning your experiences with this guide and how you feel it could be improved and kept up to date. While we may not be able to respond to all comments and suggestions, we'll take them to heart, and we'll also make certain to share them with the author. Please send your comments and suggestions to the following address:

FalconGuides
Reader Response / Editorial Department
246 Goose Lane
Guilford, CT 06437

Or you may e-mail us at: editorial@falcon.com

Thanks for your input, and happy trails!

Hiking
Waterfalls in
Northern California

A Guide to the Region's Best Waterfall Hikes

Tracy Salcedo-Chourré

FALCONGUIDES

GUILFORD, CONNECTICUT
HELENA, MONTANA

FALCONGUIDES®

An imprint of Rowman & Littlefield
Falcon, FalconGuides, and Outfit Your Mind are registered trademarks of Rowman & Littlefield.

Distributed by NATIONAL BOOK NETWORK

British Library Cataloguing-in-Publication Information Available

Library of Congress Cataloging-in-Publication Data is available on file.
ISBN 978-0-7627-9457-7 (paperback)
ISBN 978-1-4930-1443-9 (e-book)

∞™ The paper used in this publication meets the minimum requirements of American National Standard for Information Sciences—Permanence of Paper for Printed Library Materials, ANSI / NISO Z39.48-1992.

Contents

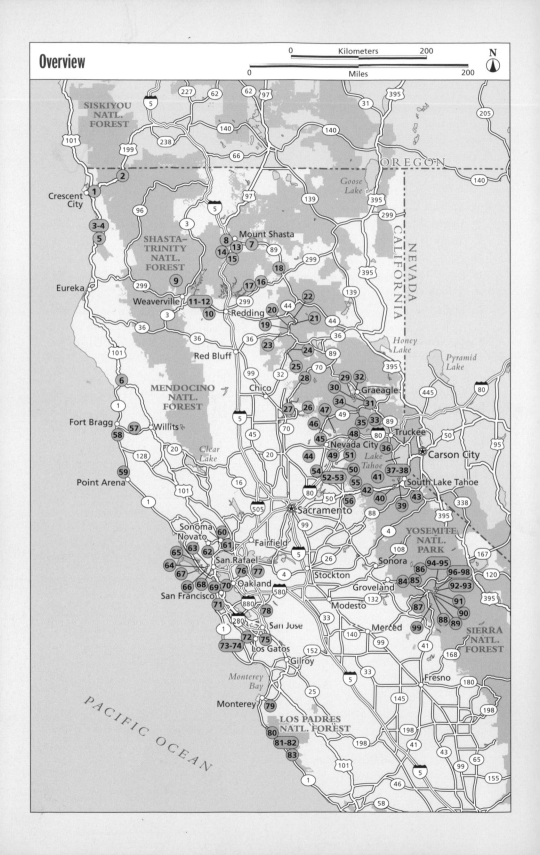

Acknowledgments

I must start by thanking the waterfall explorers and writers who've come before me. It turns out that a number of folks out there with waterfall obsessions have created fabulous resources for those who seek to find and explore Northern California's waterfalls. My hat is off to them: I cannot hope to catalogue what they already have. I have included their books and websites as resources in the appendix at the end of this guide.

Just as crucial to the production of this guide is the work and input of those who serve as stewards of public lands. The bulk of the waterfalls in this guide are accessible via trails on public lands, whether national forests, national parks, state parks, or local parks and open space. My thanks to the land managers who oversee these public resources, for the hard work they do every day, and for taking the time to review hike descriptions within this guide.

I am also grateful to the folks who supported me while I hiked and wrote, including my cohorts at Streetwise Reports. Thanks also to the editors and mapmakers at FalconGuides/Rowman & Littlefield, who ushered the guide through production. Finally, thanks to friends and family, including Alison Pimentel, Mike Witkowski, Julianne Roth, Bettina Hopkins, Kerin McTaggart, Mitchell and Karen Friedman, Rita Friedman, Deb and Kern Rodman, Tory Rodman, Samantha and Callie Friedman, Ned Farnkopf, Jesse and Judy Salcedo, Nick and Nancy Salcedo, Chris Salcedo and Angela Jones, Sarah Chourré, Martin Chourré, and last but never least, my sons, Jesse, Cruz, and Penn Chourré.

Mount Tamalpais and San Francisco Bay from the trail to Carson Falls (hike 64).

Introduction

I see now how hiking Northern California's waterfalls could become the obsession of a lifetime. One waterfall leads to another, and to another, and even as I put this guide to bed, my mind spins with the possibilities. By one waterfall blogger's count, more than 1,400 waterfalls await exploration in the state. This guide covers just a fraction of those: It represents a launch pad, both for you, the reader, and for me, the writer.

It turns out that hiking NorCal waterfalls is like sailing or skiing: You need the right conditions. California has a rainy season and a dry season, which means many falls are ephemeral, running for only a handful of months before evaporating. Thus, winter and spring are optimal for waterfall hiking, with watercourses filled by either rainfall or snowmelt.

But prime conditions for seeing waterfalls in full flow go deeper than that. Climate matters. And unfortunately, my window of research for this guidebook corresponded with a historic drought in the Golden State. Even in winter I found myself hiking NorCal's water-streaked cliffs. It was frustrating, but for the fact that I was hiking.

And hiking is what sets this guide apart from other waterfall compendiums. It is about the journey as much as the destination.

A hike to Carson Falls in Marin County, north of San Francisco, crystallized this for me: Sitting at the falls overlook, I gazed into a stagnant pool at the base of a black-streaked cliff, baking in an unseasonably warm winter sun. Waterfall? Ha! But on the hike back to the trailhead, I was met by a fabulous panorama, with Mount Tamalpais reclining on the southern horizon, a low wall of fog rolling over the wooded ridgelines to the west, and hills cloaked in golden grasses spreading east to the sprawling blue of San Francisco Bay. I paused, breathed deeply, and understood. I'd have to come again, to see the falls when the rain returned, but in the meantime I'd enjoy the path that I was on.

This revelation qualifies every hike in this guide. I've given each waterfall a beauty rating (up to five stars), but these are more than ratings of the falls themselves; they also take into account the quality of the hike.

The ninety-nine hikes in this guide are a drop in the proverbial bucket. I hope that they will inspire you, as they have inspired me, to head out on the route less traveled, and to use that as a springboard to a route less traveled still.

How to Use This Guide

Mileages

Original research for this guidebook was done in 2013, 2014, and the beginning of 2015. Trails were hiked using modern GPS technology, but exact mileages may differ from what appears on park maps. Distances listed on trail signs don't necessarily mesh with maps or GPS readings. I have recorded the mileages logged on my GPS unit for consistency's sake. Discrepancies seldom exceeded 0.5 mile and shouldn't affect a hiker's ability to gauge the difficulty or duration of a given hike.

Difficulty Ratings

The hikes are rated easy, moderate, or strenuous. In assigning a label, I took into account elevation gains and losses, hiking surfaces, and distances. Generally speaking, easy hikes are short and relatively flat. Moderate hikes involve greater distances and (perhaps) greater elevation changes. Strenuous hikes include steep ascents, long-distance loops, and routes that include challenging trail surfaces.

Keep in mind that every trail is only as difficult as you make it. If you keep a pace within your level of fitness, drink plenty of water, and stoke up on good, high-energy foods, you can make any trail easy.

Route Finding

Trails in this guide are generally well marked and maintained. On occasion, reaching a waterfall may require cross-country travel or a short bushwhack; I've tried to limit those instances. A handful of trails cross private property; be respectful by remaining on the designated trail.

Maps

The USGS topographic maps that pertain to each route are listed in hike descriptions. If a trail map is available from another source, either from the land management agency or online, that resource is listed. In the case of California State Parks, search for the park name on the agency website to go to the park home page. Click on "Brochures," then on "Park Brochure." A pdf of the printed brochure for each state park in this guide includes a basic, but adequate, map.

How the Hikes Were Chosen

All of the hikes in this guide are day hikes and, with only one exception, do not exceed 10 miles out and back or as a loop.

Creative trail construction makes crossing deadfall a snap on the trail to Chamberlain Falls (hike 57).

Additionally, all trailheads can be reached using passenger vehicles, though some of the roads are gravel or dirt. Conditions on unpaved roads vary with season, use, weather, and maintenance schedules; contact the land manager listed for each destination for the most current road status.

A few of the waterfalls described in the guide are drive-bys, in that a hike is not required to view the fall. Where applicable, I've included GPS coordinates for viewpoints.

Hiking Essentials

Hiking waterfalls in Northern California often means venturing into the backcountry.

While all of these excursions are day hikes, no matter the length of your hike, you should be prepared.

For starters, every hiker should carry survival and first-aid materials, layers of clothing for all kinds of weather, a compass, and a good topographic map—and know how to use them.

The next-best piece of safety advice is to hike with a partner or a party. If you chose to hike alone, tell somebody where you're going and when you plan to return.

Finally, before you set out on any hike, consider physical conditioning. Being fit makes wilderness travel more fun and much safer.

Here are a few more tips:

- Check the weather forecast. Be careful not to get caught at high altitude in a bad storm or along a stream in a flash flood. Watch cloud formations so you don't get stranded on a ridgeline during a lightning storm. Avoid traveling during prolonged periods of cold weather.

- Keep your party together; move only as fast as your slowest companion.

- Before you leave for the trailhead, find out as much as you can about the route, especially the potential hazards.

- Don't wait until you're confused to look at your maps. Follow them as you go, maintaining a continual fix on your location.

- If you get lost, don't panic. Sit down, relax, check your map, and get your bearings. Confidently plan your next move. If necessary, retrace your steps until you find familiar ground, even if you think that might lengthen your trip. If you calmly and rationally determine a plan of action, you'll be fine.

- If you are genuinely lost, stay put. It is easier for authorities to locate a lost hiker when that hiker is not on the move.

- Your pack should contain backcountry essentials, including water,

The Merced River churns below the bridge atop Nevada Fall (hike 98).

an emergency blanket, and an emergency whistle, which will help ensure your safety if you become lost or can't make it back to the trailhead for another reason.

- Stay clear of all wild animals. Make sure you know how best to deal with encounters with a black bear, mountain lion, or other animal in the backcountry.

Play It Safe

Hiking is generally a safe endeavor, but common sense dictates that when venturing into the wild, travelers should take precautions. Education is the best protection, but a day pack loaded with everything you need to stay safe if you get held up on the trail, for whatever reason, is good insurance.

Carry a good first-aid kit that includes, at a minimum: aspirin or over-the-counter pain reliever, antibacterial ointment, antiseptic swabs, butterfly bandages, adhesive tape, adhesive strips, two triangular bandages, two inflatable splints, moleskin or Second Skin for blisters, 3-inch gauze, CPR shield, rubber gloves, a snakebite kit, a sewing needle and thread, and lightweight first-aid instructions.

Pack a survival kit that includes, at a minimum: compass and map (a GPS unit will do, but be sure to carry extra batteries), whistle, matches in a waterproof container, cigarette lighter, candle, signal mirror, flashlight, fire starter, aluminum foil, water purification tablets, space blanket, and flare.

Critters

You will share most trails in Northern California with a variety of wild creatures, many of which will go unseen and undetected. Some will come right up to you, including that adorable ground squirrel that wants to share your granola bar. Some will pester you, including horseflies, bees, and wasps. Some you may only catch fleeting glimpses of, such as mule deer and pileated woodpeckers. And some you may only encounter by way of what they leave behind: footprints and scat.

For the most part, animal encounters on the trail are benign. Abide by two basic rules for both your safety and that of the animals:

- Do not feed any wild animal, no matter how cute or how much it begs. Acclimating chipmunks, deer, birds, and larger mammals like bears is not only dangerous for humans, but also reduces the animals' ability to survive when the humans have gone home.

- Keep your distance. Approaching a wild creature not only increases the chance that you might get bitten (or worse), it also increases anxiety levels for the animals.

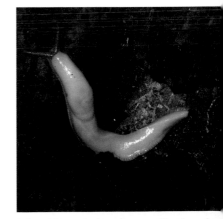

The ultimate in harmless woodland creatures: the banana slug.

Black Bears

Though generally black bears stay clear of humans, they can be encountered just about anywhere in Northern California, but especially in the Sierra Nevada, in the foothills and Gold Country, and in the redwood forests of the North Coast.

Black bears do not, as a rule, attack humans, but they may pose a danger if you handle food improperly, if you startle them, or if you get between a mother bear and her cub.

Food is the primary instigator of bear-human interactions. Keep in mind that letting a bear get human food is contributing—directly—to the eventual destruction of that bear. Think of proper bear etiquette as protecting the bears as much as yourself.

Avoid bear encounters while hiking by making noise. If you travel with a group, talking is an effective bear deterrent. If traveling alone, carry a bear bell or make noise by singing or talking … even if no person is around to hear.

If you encounter a black bear, remember the following:

- Keep your distance. Maintain a separation of at least 300 feet from any black bear.
- Do not run. Running may initiate a predatory response from the bear.
- Back away. Turning your back may trigger a predatory response.
- Don't climb a tree, as black bears can climb them too.
- If you are with small children, pick them up without bending over. If you are a group, band together.
- If attacked, defend yourself. Try to remain standing. Do not feign death. Use bear spray if you have it.
- Respect any warning signs posted by agencies.
- Teach others in your group how to behave in case of a black bear encounter. Report encounters, including location, to park rangers, who may want to post education/warning signs.
- If physical injury occurs, leave the area. Do not disturb the site of an attack. Black bears that have attacked people must be killed, and an undisturbed site is critical for effectively locating the dangerous animal.

Mountain Lions

Mountain lion sightings are relatively rare, and attacks on humans are extremely rare, but it's wise to educate yourself before heading into mountain lion habitat—which includes most of the territory covered in this guide.

To stay as safe as possible when hiking in mountain lion country, follow this advice:

- Travel with a friend or in a group, and stay together.
- Don't let small children wander away by themselves.
- Avoid hiking at dawn and dusk, when mountain lions are most active.

- Know how to behave if you encounter a mountain lion.

The vast majority of mountain lions exhibit avoidance, indifference, or curiosity that never results in human injury. But it is natural to be alarmed if you have an encounter of any kind. Keep your cool by remembering the following:

- If a mountain lion is more than 50 yards away and directs its attention to you, it may be only curious. You should back away, keeping the animal in your peripheral vision. Look for rocks, sticks, or something to use as a weapon, just in case. Keep small children close. Mountain lions are not known to attack humans to defend young or a kill, but they have been reported to "charge" in rare instances. It's best to choose another route or time to hike through the area.

- If a mountain lion is crouched less than 50 yards away and staring at you, it may be assessing the chances of a successful attack. Slowly back away, but maintain eye contact. Do not run; running may stimulate a predatory response. Make noise, talking and yelling loudly and regularly. Try not to panic. Shout to make others in the area aware of the situation. Raise your arms above your head and make steady waving motions, or raise your jacket or another object above your head to make yourself appear larger. Do not bend over, as this will make you appear smaller and more prey-like.

- If you are with small children, pick them up without bending over. If you are a group, band together.

- Defend yourself and others. If attacked, fight back. Try to remain standing. Do not feign death. Pick up a branch or rock; pull out a knife, pepper spray, or other deterrent device. Individuals have fended off mountain lions with rocks, tree limbs, and even cameras.

- Respect any warning signs posted by agencies.

- Teach others in your group how to behave in the event of a mountain lion encounter. Report encounters, including location, to park rangers, who may want to visit the site and, if appropriate, post education/warning signs.

- If physical injury occurs, leave the area. Do not disturb the site of an attack. Mountain lions that have attacked people must be killed, and an undisturbed site is critical for effectively locating the dangerous mountain lion.

Rattlesnakes
Most regions covered in this guide are rattlesnake country. Sightings are relatively rare, and the snakes are an important component of the ecosystem. Rattlesnakes typically are not aggressive toward humans—we are simply too big to be prey. Most snakebites occur when hikers startle or attempt to handle a rattlesnake. To avoid a nasty encounter, watch where you put your hands and feet when you are stepping over logs or climbing on rocks. If you see a rattler, back away and let it pass.

The same sun that parches California's annual grasses also may parch hikers. Stay hydrated.

Ticks

Hiking waterfalls means hiking in tick season. Though not all species are carriers, some ticks in Northern California can transmit Lyme disease. After traveling through brush, check your clothing for the arachnids. If one latches on, remove it carefully, making sure to get the mouthparts. You can have the creature tested to see if it might have transmitted the disease.

Weather

Let's face it: If you hike all of these waterfalls, you are going to encounter every kind of weather, from snow to blistering sunshine. Insulate yourself from the potential consequences of weather extremes by keeping yourself properly hydrated, carrying high-energy snacks, wearing a hat, applying sunscreen, and packing layers of clothing that you can add or shed depending on the conditions.

Hypothermia

Hypothermia is a condition in which the body's internal temperature drops below normal. It is caused by exposure to cold; is aggravated by wetness, wind, and exhaustion; and can be life-threatening.

To defend against hypothermia, stay dry. Choose rain clothes that cover the head, neck, body, and legs and provide good protection against wind-driven rain. Most hypothermia cases develop in air temperatures between 30 and 50°F, but hypothermia can develop in warmer temperatures.

If your party is exposed to wind, cold, and wet, watch yourself and others for uncontrollable fits of shivering; vague, slow, slurred speech; memory lapses; incoherence; fumbling hands; frequent stumbling or a lurching gait; drowsiness; exhaustion; and inability to get up after a rest. When a member of your party has hypothermia, he or she may deny any problem. Believe the symptoms, not the victim. Even mild symptoms demand the following treatment:

- Get the victim out of the wind and rain.
- Strip off all wet clothes and get the victim into warm clothes.
- If the victim is mildly impaired, provide warm drinks.
- Get off the trail and seek medical attention as quickly as possible.

Heat-Related Illnesses

Hikers can avoid heat-related illness by avoiding activity in the heat of the day and staying hydrated. Selecting clothing that breathes, which allows perspiration to evaporate and cool the skin, and wearing a lightweight, brimmed hat will help. Applying sunscreen to all exposed parts of the body is always a good idea.

Watch for warning signs of heat-related illness, both in yourself and members of your party. These include nausea and/or vomiting; headache, light-headedness, and/or fainting; weakness, fatigue, and/or a lack of coordination; loss of concentration; and flushed skin.

Symptoms of heat exhaustion include all of the above, coupled with low blood pressure, heavy sweating, and a rapid pulse. If you or a member of your party exhibits these symptoms, seek shade, lie down and elevate the feet and legs, apply a wet cloth to the head and neck (and other parts of the body, if you can), and drink cool liquids.

Heatstroke is life-threatening. Hikers who lose consciousness; vomit; have red, hot skin (moist or dry); and have a weak pulse and shallow breathing are in danger of convulsions, coma, and death. Cool the victim by any means possible, as quickly as possible, and call for emergency medical aid.

Sunset burnishes the Merced River copper.

Hydration

Hydration is important for hikers regardless of weather conditions. Hydrate before, during, and after your hike. Hydration bladders carried in backpacks are fabulous for maintaining hydration on the trail, as there is no need to stop and fish a water bottle out of your pack.

As far as quantity, there are no hard-and-fast rules. Drink as much as you can. Drink even when you are not thirsty. But at a minimum, plan on consuming 32 ounces of water for every 2 hours on the trail. That may mean carrying a filter or purification tablets so that you can refill water bottles or bladders from streams and lakes, even on day hikes (all backpackers should carry these).

Unless it's an emergency, do not drink untreated or unfiltered water from any water source.

Leave No Trace

Most of us know better than to litter—in or out of the backcountry. Be sure you leave nothing, regardless how small, along the trail or at a campsite. Pack everything

Looking at the back side of Half Dome from the Panorama Trail to Illilouette Fall in Yosemite National Park (hike 93).

out, including orange peels, flip tops, cigarette butts, and gum wrappers. Pick up any trash that others leave behind.

Follow the main trail. Avoid cutting switchbacks and walking on vegetation beside the trail.

Don't pick up "souvenirs," such as rocks, antlers, or wildflowers. The next person wants to see them too, and collecting souvenirs violates park regulations.

Avoid making loud noises on the trail (unless you are in bear country) or in camp. Be courteous—remember, sound travels easily in the backcountry, especially across water.

Carry a lightweight trowel to bury human waste 6 to 8 inches deep and at least 200 feet from any water source. Pack out used toilet paper in a ziplock bag.

Go without a campfire if you can't find an established fire pit. Carry a stove for cooking and a flashlight, candle lantern, or headlamp for light. For emergencies, learn how to build a no-trace fire.

Camp in obviously used sites when they are available. Otherwise, camp and cook on durable surfaces such as bedrock, sand, gravel bars, or bare ground.

Leave no trace—and put your ear to the ground and listen carefully. Thousands of people coming behind you are thanking you for your courtesy and good sense.

For more information visit https://LNT.org.

Map Legend

80	Interstate Highway	■	Building/Point of Interest
101	US Highway	▲	Campground
93	State Highway	▲	Campsite
D2 / FR 21N35Y	County/Forest Road	✪	Capital
	Local Road	∩	Cave
	Unpaved Road	⌒⌒⌒	Cliffs
	Railroad	—	Dam
	Featured Trail	╎	Gate
	Trail	▬	Lodging
	Paved Trail	🅿	Parking
‖‖‖‖‖	Boardwalk	⊃⊂	Pass/Gap
	State Line	▲	Peak/Summit
	Small River/Creek	🅰	Picnic Area
	Intermittent Stream	×	Point Elevation
	Body of Water	🄱	Ranger Station
	Marsh/Swamp	🚻	Restrooms
	Sand	🔍	Scenic View/Viewpoint
	National/State Forest/Park	⟋	Spring
	National Wilderness/Reserve/Preserve	🐎	Stables
	State/County Park	☏	Telephone
	Recreation Area	○	Town
	Miscellaneous Area	10	Trailhead
▬	Bench	⊢══⊣	Tunnel
	Boat Ramp	❓	Visitor/Information Center
⊃⊂	Bridge	≋	Waterfall
		♿	Wheelchair Accessible

Eureka and Crescent City

This region stretches south along the California coastline from the Oregon border to the southern Humboldt county line and covers waterfalls located outside Eureka, Arcata, Orick, and Crescent City. The landscape is rugged from coastline to coastal mountains, and stands of old-growth coast redwoods, the signature species of the North Coast, tower over each of these trails. Be prepared for fog, wind, and rain: You're not in sunny California at this latitude.

On the trail to Fern Falls in Jedediah Smith Redwoods State Park (hike 1).

1 Fern Falls

Ramble through a stunning old-growth redwood forest to a small, perennial waterfall on Jordan Creek.

Height: About 30 feet
Beauty rating: ★★★★★
Distance: 5.8 miles out and back
Difficulty: Moderate due only to distance
Best season: Year-round
County: Del Norte
Trailhead amenities: None
Land status: Jedediah Smith Redwoods State Park. *Note:* When Redwood National and State Parks was created in 1968, the boundary encircled three California state parks. Jedediah Smith, Del Norte Coast, and Prairie Creek Redwoods are embedded inside the national park. The state of California and the federal government operate the parks in a partnership as a single entity.
Maps: USGS Hiouchi CA and Crescent City CA; park map available at the visitor center and online
Trail contact: Jedediah Smith Redwoods State Park, 1111 2nd St., Crescent City, CA 95531; (707) 458-3018 (entrance station) or (707) 458-3496 (visitor center); www.parks.ca.gov

Finding the trailhead: From CA 1 in Crescent City, take Elk Valley Road east for 1.1 mile to the junction with Howland Hill Road. Turn right onto Howland Hill Road and follow the narrow road for 3.5 miles, winding through tremendous redwood groves, to the signed Boy Scout Tree Trail parking pullout. The one-lane road is paved for the first mile and is a good gravel road after that. There is parking for about twenty-five cars. If you must park outside the pullout, be sure you are safely clear of Howland Hill Road. GPS: N41 46.139' / W124 06.602'

The Hike

From the second you set out on the Boy Scout Tree Trail, you will be enchanted. Lit by the slanting rays of a midwinter sun, the furrowed bark of the massive redwoods along-side the trail shimmers gray and green. Touch the bark: It feels light and alive, its pores open to the mist and the filtered sunshine. Yes, the term "magical" is overused in the voluminous literature praising California's redwoods, but really, there's no more accurate way to describe the old-growth forests of the North Coast. And this one is quintessential.

Thankfully, you'll have ample time to reset the awe meter, because Fern Falls lies far down a winding path. With plenty of opportunities to contemplate the girths of the trunks, crick your neck gazing into the canopy, and sneak a hug or two, by the time you reach the waterfall, with its flanking ferns and shallow pool, you should be primed and open to yet another sublime setting.

To begin, the Boy Scout Tree Trail climbs gently away from the trailhead. The trees along this stretch are stunning—among the largest you'll see along the route. Perhaps it is the orientation of the slope, perhaps the angle of the sun, but the huge silvery trunks are illuminated with artistic perfection. The trail is artful as well, winding easily up the slope through fern gardens, under fallen giants, and over picturesque footbridges.

Fern Falls (Jedediah Smith)

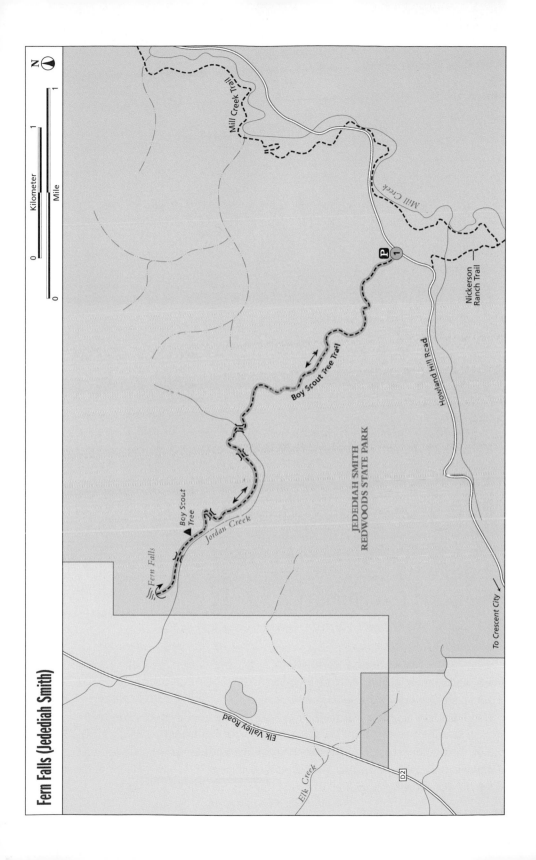

Fern Falls tumbles into a clear pool at trail's end.

The other remarkable thing about the outset of the trail is how sounds of the sea, far out of sight, filter into the woods. The lonesome sigh of a buoy, the cry of a gull, the moans of foghorns all drift up into the stillness. The resonant quietness seeps into the bones.

Climb over a sloping ridge and begin to drop; the trees here are slightly—only slightly—diminished in size and grandeur. A long, rolling descent leads into a creek drainage; use the bridge to ford the nameless stream, and then climb out of the ravine. The route drops through several more drainages as it rolls through the forest, with bridges spanning the clear waterways. Watch carefully for the spur trail to the Boy Scout Tree, which breaks right at about the 2.5-mile mark.

Fern Falls is at trail's end. The waterfall fans out across a short, low-angle rock face and drops into a clear pool, with a gravel beach of sorts on the far side of the creek at its base. Refresh, refuel, and then return as you came.

Miles and Directions

0.0   Start by heading gently uphill on the signed Boy Scout Tree Trail.

0.2   Cross a footbridge.

0.6   Crest the ridge and begin a gentle descent.

1.6   Drop down switchbacks and cross a footbridge.

1.9   A set of stairs leads through another stream drainage and to a second footbridge.

2.5   Switchback down to a bridge over a streamlet. The easily missed side trail to the Boy Scout Tree breaks right from the traversing trail beyond the drainage.

2.6   Cross another bridge surrounded by willow; the trail parallels the clear stream.

2.9   Reach Fern Falls. Turn around here and retrace your steps.

5.8   Arrive back at the trailhead.

2 Smith River Falls

The rains that soak California's North Coast fuel a number of waterfalls in the Smith River drainage. While a trail, of sorts, leads down to a thunderous fall on the Middle Fork of the Smith River, most of these falls can be viewed from scenic CA 199.

Height: Variable
Beauty rating: ★★★
Distance: Variable
Difficulty: Easy
Best season: Year-round
County: Del Norte
Trailhead amenities: None

Land status: Smith River National Recreation Area
Maps: USGS Gasquet CA and Hiouchi CA
Trail contact: Six Rivers National Forest, Smith River National Recreation Area, 1330 Bayshore Way, Eureka, CA 95501; (707) 442-1721; www.fs.usda.gov/recarea/srnf/recarea/?recid=11440

Finding the trailhead: CA 199 heads east from Crescent City, paralleling the Smith River through its scenic canyon. To access the Middle Fork Smith River from Gasquet follow CA 199 east for 16.5 miles to the junction with Knopki Creek Road. Follow Knopki Creek Road, a good gravel road easily negotiated by a passenger vehicle, along the Middle Fork drainage for about 2 miles until the road begins to climb.

The falls on the Middle Fork of the Smith River.

DEFENDING THE NORTH COAST REDWOODS

The complex of public lands that stretches from just north of Eureka and Arcata to the Oregon border protects 45 percent of the remaining old-growth redwood forest in California, according to the California State Parks department. Three state parks—Prairie Creek Redwoods, Del Norte Coast, and Jedediah Smith–Redwoods—along with Redwood National Park, make up what has been designated a National Heritage Site and an International Biosphere Reserve.

Within these boundaries remnants of a coast redwood forest that once sprawled over 2 million acres towers into the clouds.

Protection of these ancient, massive trees has been no small feat, as the durable heartwood is highly valued as a building material and fuels a timber industry that has supported towns and cities along the North Coast for more than a century. The preservation of old-growth redwoods spurred passion and conflict throughout the region in the latter part of the twentieth century, and my father was a warrior in several nonviolent skirmishes between loggers and environmentalists. He traveled into redwood country on numerous occasions in those years, working to preserve the Headwaters Redwood Grove, an old-growth stand slated for harvest by the Pacific Lumber Company. He was, on one occasion, arrested for his defiance—along with so many other peaceful protestors that buses were needed to transport them away from the site. As he tells the story, officers used zip ties in lieu of handcuffs, because there weren't enough of the real thing to go around.

That battle to preserve the old-growth stands has died down. Lumber companies still operate in redwood country, but the focus of the economy has shifted to, of all the unlikely possibilities, cultivation of marijuana. Though growing weed for recreational purposes was still illegal in California as of 2015, medical marijuana is legal in the state, and the battleground has shifted from saving redwoods from loggers to securing marijuana's legalization via popular vote.

But a battle to save the grand old trees remains. The threat: climate change. Redwoods thrive on the fog that perennially blankets the North Coast, able to siphon moisture from the marine layer. Indeed, scientists theorize that the redwood's symbiosis with fog has resulted in the trees' attaining such spectacular heights, as being tall enables them to take advantage of all the moisture in a fog bank. But with climate change has come a decrease in the height and density of coastal fog, which in turn threatens the ability of the redwoods to survive. This battle is being engaged on a number of fronts ... and I have no doubt my father would again submit to a zip-tie arrest if that would make a difference.

Viewing the Falls

A number of waterfalls spill down the steep slopes along CA 199 in the Smith River canyon. Most drop right next to the highway and don't require a hike to view; many are seasonal, so travel in late winter and spring will ensure the best flow. One of the prettiest is located east of Gasquet and is best viewed from the westbound lane; it tumbles about 70 feet down an exposed talus slope on the left (south). The curves along CA 199 should slow you down enough to see what can be seen, but be sure not to hold up traffic for the sake of viewing. Be courteous and use turnouts and pullouts.

A marginal "hike" to falls on the Middle Fork of the Smith River can be reached off Knopki Creek Road. The unmaintained path is short and, for those who don't like exposure, a little scary. The trail skitters down a steep hillside, vaguely traversing and then switching back to an "overlook" on the root ball of a moss-draped oak perched on the side of a cliff. The furious and enervating 40-foot cascade, heavily screened by trees, is split by a buttress of dark rock, and debris is scattered both in the flow and alongside the pool below. A pair of ropes suspended from the trees may beckon the foolhardy: If they are in place, do not use them! Safer to experience the thunder of the falls from above.

3 Fern Canyon

In the height of the rainy season, you can spy waterfalls running down between the ferns of this remarkable canyon.

Height: Varying; about 50 feet
Beauty rating: ★★★★
Distance: 1.0 mile out and back
Difficulty: Easy
Best season: Winter and spring
County: Humboldt
Trailhead amenities: Restrooms, trash cans, and information signboards
Land status: Prairie Creek Redwoods State Park. *Note:* When Redwood National and State Parks was created in 1968, the boundary encircled three California state parks. Jedediah Smith, Del Norte Coast, and Prairie Creek Redwoods are embedded inside the national park. The state of California and the federal government operate the parks into a partnership as a single entity.

Special considerations: The floor of Fern Canyon is the bed of Home Creek. Appropriate footwear—shoes that are waterproof and/or water shoes and wool socks—will make enjoying the canyon and its seasonal waterfalls much more pleasant.

Maps: USGS Fern Canyon CA; park map available at the entrance station or online

Trail contact: Prairie Creek Redwoods State Park, 127011 Newton B. Drury Pkwy., Orick, CA 95555; (707) 465-7335; www.parks.ca.gov

Finding the trailhead: From Eureka head north on US 101 for about 45 miles, through the hamlet of Orick, to the signed junction with Davison Road (also signed for Gold Bluffs Beach). The junction is about 3 miles north of Orick, with Elk Meadow sprawling along the west side of the highway. Turn left onto Davison Road and travel a total of 6.6 miles to the trailhead (at the end of the road). The entrance station, where fees are paid, is at 3.5 miles; pass a gate that closes at sunset at 5.5 miles. The gravel road is negotiable by passenger cars, but several stream crossings and the overall roughness of the surface are easier to navigate in a high-clearance vehicle. GPS: N41 24.039' / W124 03.949'

The Hike

Fern Canyon is a major draw in Prairie Creek Redwoods State Park, for good reason. As a waterfall hike it's a bit of a stretch: Any ephemeral waterfalls you may see in the canyon play second fiddle to the wallpaper of ferns that flocks the cliffs from floor to top. It's a fairy tale in the wilderness—a realm of forest sprites and wood nymphs.

Seven varieties of fern can be found here, per park literature, including sword, deer, lady, chain, and five-finger ferns. The narrow chasm is remarkably still, though the sounds of the surf, the burbling of Home Creek flowing over its gravelly bed, and the occasional low voice of a visitor expressing awe or catching her breath as icy water flows over her boot-tops may break the spell.

Getting to the canyon is easy. The wide, gravel Coastal Trail leads up to the canyon mouth. Home Creek flows out of the canyon, sometimes snaking placidly down its

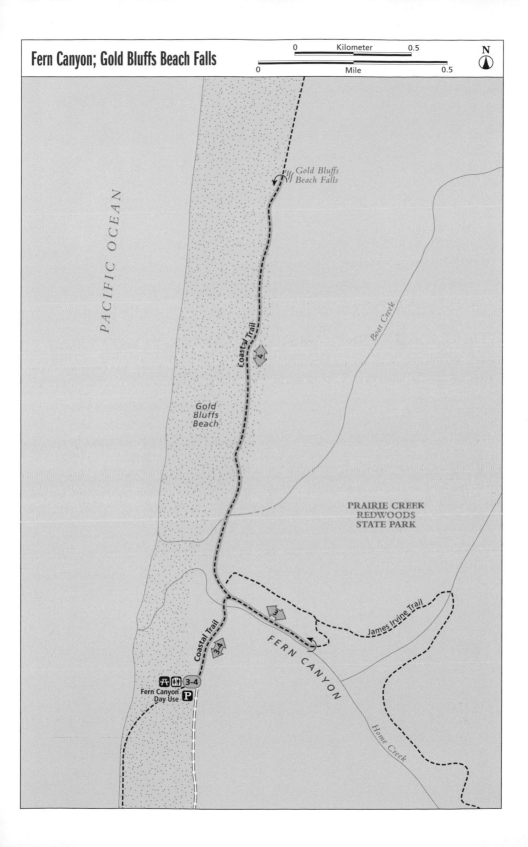

Fern Canyon; Gold Bluffs Beach Falls

Gold Bluffs Beach Falls

PACIFIC OCEAN

Boat Creek

Coastal Trail

4

Gold Bluffs Beach

PRAIRIE CREEK REDWOODS STATE PARK

James Irvine Trail

3

FERN CANYON

Coastal Trail

3-4

3-4

Fern Canyon Day Use

Home Creek

gravel bed, sometimes swelling into pools, sometimes gaining velocity as it is funneled into channels. Proceed up the canyon as you can—an endeavor made easier if you are prepared to get wet (seasonal bridges are installed). Depending on rainfall, small waterfalls thread through the ferns on the canyon walls into the stream. Follow the canyon out and back, or make a loop by hitching up with the John Irvine Trail to return along the top of the canyon to the mouth of Home Creek.

Miles and Directions

0.0 Start by walking up the wide, flat Coastal Trail toward Fern Canyon.

0.2 Ford Home Creek at the mouth of Fern Canyon. At the signed junction with the James Irvine Trail on the far side of the creek, stay right and head up into the deep dark greenery. After a healthy rain, falling water can be heard and spied.

0.5 After you've explored, retrace your steps.

1.0 Arrive back at the trailhead.

◀ *In the rainy season small falls flow down the walls of Fern Canyon.*

4 Gold Bluffs Beach Falls

Follow a spectacular stretch of California's Coastal Trail to a hidden waterfall.

See map on page 21.
Height: About 250 feet
Beauty rating: ★★★★
Distance: 3.2 miles out and back
Difficulty: Easy
Best season: Winter and spring
County: Humboldt
Trailhead amenities: Restrooms, trash cans, and information signboards
Land status: Prairie Creek Redwoods State Park. *Note:* When Redwood National and State Parks was created in 1968, the boundary encircled three California state parks. Jedediah Smith, Del Norte Coast, and Prairie Creek Redwoods are embedded inside the national park. The state of California and the federal government operate the parks into a partnership as a single entity.
Maps: USGS Fern Canyon CA; park map available at the entrance station or online
Trail contact: Prairie Creek Redwoods State Park, 127011 Newton B. Drury Pkwy., Orick, CA 95555; (707) 465-7335; www.parks.ca.gov

Finding the trailhead: From Eureka head north on US 101 for about 45 miles, through the hamlet of Orick, to the signed junction with Davison Road (also signed for Gold Bluffs Beach). The junction is about 3 miles north of Orick, with Elk Meadow sprawling along the west side of the highway. Turn left onto Davison Road and travel a total of 6.6 miles to the trailhead (at the end of the road). The entrance station, where fees are paid, is at 3.5 miles; pass a gate that closes at sunset at 5.5 miles. The gravel road is negotiable by passenger cars, but several stream crossings and the overall roughness of the surface are easier to navigate in a high-clearance vehicle. GPS: N41 24.039' / W124 03.949'

The Hike

It takes some sleuthing to locate Gold Bluffs Beach Falls. The waterfall is actually distant from the beach itself, tumbling over a high bluff on the east side of the Coastal Trail and screened by a thick wall of sedge, willow, and the interlocking boughs of evergreens. You will hear it before you see it, and the viewing will require a short bushwhack through the sedge and into the overgrown grotto at the base of the bluff.

The waterfall is a slender but significant horsetail, arcing hundreds of feet from the tree-topped summit of the gold-hued bluff. Enveloped in the dense shade and surrounded on three sides by the steep cliffs, with the sound of falling water muffling the beat of the surf on the shore, the site seems distant from the beach.

The short first section of the Coastal Trail, to the mouth of Fern Canyon, is easy. Home Creek, which spills out of the canyon, is the major obstacle along the route. Depending on the season and the amount of recent rainfall, the crossing can be tricky, and finding the continuation of the Coastal Trail might involve a few false starts (all this is easier when seasonal bridges are installed). The trail is left of the signed junction with

The scenic Coastal Trail leads north to Gold Bluffs Beach Falls.

the James Irvine Trail on the north side of the creek and continues through the thick willow and alder stands flourishing in the riparian zone. This patch of trail can be profoundly mucky: In one wild moment my boot was completely sucked off my foot by sticky mud. Wet feet precluding the need to find rocks to hop or logs to follow across soggy patches, staying on the trail became much more straightforward after that misstep.

After a half mile in the woods, the Coastal Trail breaks out into a narrow swath of meadowland between towering bluffs on the east and a break of dunes on the west. The steady thumping of surf crashing onto Gold Bluffs Beach forms a backbeat for the next easy mile of hiking. The bluffs are truly impressive, in places more than 500 feet high, capped with flattop of forests. In places you might spy (or hear) ephemeral cascades tumbling down toward the sea. Seabirds and raptors soar overhead, riding columns of air that rise up the vertical faces.

The falls are the turnaround point, though the Coastal Trail continues northward to the Oregon border. From the falls reverse course and return as you came.

Miles and Directions

0.0   Start by walking up the wide, flat Coastal Trail toward Fern Canyon.

0.2   Ford Home Creek at the mouth of Fern Canyon. At the signed junction with the James Irvine Trail on the far side of the creek, stay left, following the sign for the Coastal Trail.

0.8   Break out of the woods. The trail winds through grasses at the base of the bluffs.

1.6   Reach the wall of sedge, brush, and trees that fences off access to the base of Gold Bluffs Beach Falls. Punch through the foliage to check out the plunge, and then retrace your steps.

3.2   Arrive back at the trailhead.

5 Trillium Falls

A shady loop links the bridge overlooking Trillium Falls to Elk Meadow, where odds are good you'll see a member of the California's largest herd of Roosevelt elk.

Height: 25 feet
Beauty rating: ★★★
Distance: 2.7-mile lollipop
Difficulty: Easy
Best season: Winter and early spring
County: Humboldt
Trailhead amenities: Restrooms, picnic sites, trash cans, and information signboards
Land status: Prairie Creek Redwoods State Park. *Note:* When Redwood National and State Parks was created in 1968, the boundary encircled three California state parks. Jedediah Smith, Del Norte Coast, and Prairie Creek Redwoods are embedded inside the national park. The state of California and the federal government operate the parks into a partnership as a single entity.
Maps: USGS Orick CA; park map available at the entrance station or online
Trail contact: Prairie Creek Redwoods State Park, 127011 Newton B. Drury Pkwy., Orick, CA 95555; (707) 465-7335; www.parks.ca.gov

Finding the trailhead: From Eureka head north on US 101 for about 45 miles, through the hamlet of Orick, to the signed junction with Davison Road (also signed for Gold Bluffs Beach). The junction is about 3 miles north of Orick, with Elk Meadow sprawling along the west side of the highway. Turn left onto Davison Road and travel 0.2 mile to a left turn into the paved Elk Meadow parking lot and trailhead. GPS: N41 19.387' / W124 02.732'

The Hike

Trillium Falls, a cascade not more than 25 feet high in a redwood-shaded canyon, lies only a half mile from the trailhead, but the loop that winds through the surrounding forest, with views across the valley to the east and brief passage alongside Elk Meadow, is worth following all the way around.

Not the least of the attractions are the Roosevelt elk that frequent the meadow. These giant creatures were once nearly extinct in the state, along with the tule elk found farther south. Conservation efforts have resulted in the return of both subspecies in protected areas of their former ranges. Don't approach the elk; view from a distance, and take only pictures.

Trillium, on the other hand, you can examine up close. It's a striking, low-growing member of the lily family, with three bracts that look like leaves and flowers with three petals. The flowers can be red, purple, white, or yellow, depending on the species. They bloom along the trail from midwinter through spring.

To reach the falls that bear the flower's name, drop out of the parking lot on the paved path. At the junction go right on the paved, multiuse Davison Trail toward the signed junction with the Trillium Falls Trail. A large signboard marks the start of the trail proper; climb away from the open meadowlands into the redwood forest above.

Trillium Falls.

At the half-mile mark, cross the bridge spanning the creek below the falls. It's the perfect vantage point, with the modest cataract tumbling down and under the span. You can return as you came, but this route continues beyond the falls, following a modest traversing climb along the base of the coastal ridge, winding in and out of ravines thick with ferns and shaded by redwoods.

Pass a number of named groves as the path begins to descend and then hooks back north toward the trailhead above Elk Meadow. Views open along this stretch; in the afternoon, while the trail is in deep shadow, the ridgetops across the valley glow in the light of the sinking sun.

The route finally drops back onto the paved Davison Trail, which traces the west side of Elk Meadow as it heads north toward the trailhead. If the willows are bare, you can see into the meadow, where Roosevelt elk may be grazing. Follow the Davison Trail back to the trailhead.

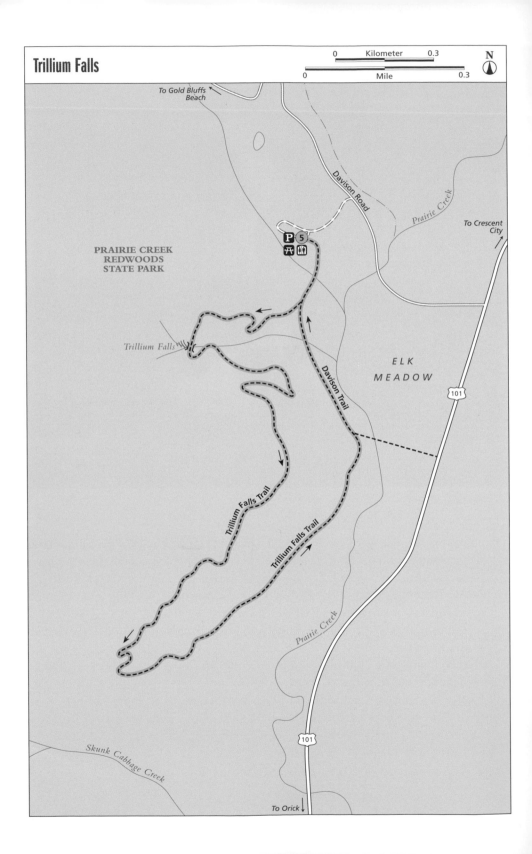

Trillium Falls

To Gold Bluffs
Beach

Davison Road

Prairie Creek

To Crescent
City

PRAIRIE CREEK
REDWOODS
STATE PARK

P 5

Trillium Falls

ELK
MEADOW

Davison Trail

101

Trillium Falls Trail

Trillium Falls Trail

Prairie Creek

Skunk Cabbage Creek

101

To Orick

Miles and Directions

0.0 Begin by following the paved path down to the paved Davison Trail. Turn right on the Davison Trail.

0.1 The Trillium Falls Trail, marked with a large signboard, breaks right. Follow the footpath up into the woods.

0.4 Switchbacks lead up to the Redwood Volunteers Grove.

0.5 Reach Trillium Falls. Cross the bridge and continue climbing.

0.9 Arc westward into a fern-lined alley, and then climb a threesome of switchbacks.

1.1 Pass a bench in the first of several named groves to follow; this is the Doris and Richard Leonard Grove.

1.4 Cross a roadway, following the trail signs. A series of named redwood groves follows, with the trail winding down through carpets of fern.

2.1 Cross a bridge that was demolished by a fallen tree in 2014. The trail continues north, stretching back toward the trailhead.

2.5 Back alongside Elk Meadow pass two trail junctions, staying left at each and following the flat, wide Davison Trail.

2.6 Close the loop at the junction with the Trillium Falls Trail. Retrace your steps.

2.7 Arrive back at the trailhead.

6 Dora Falls

A short walk leads to the base of a tucked-away waterfall.

Height: 60 feet
Beauty rating: ★★★
Distance: 0.2 mile out and back
Difficulty: Easy. Use caution descending from the redwood grove to the river, as the path is washed out and can be slippery.
Best season: Winter and early spring
County: Mendocino

Trailhead amenities: None
Land status: Smithe Redwoods State Natural Reserve
Maps: USGS Piercy CA
Trail contact: Smithe Redwoods State Natural Reserve, California State Parks; (707) 247-3318 (Richardson Grove State Park); www.parks.ca.gov

Finding the trailhead: From US 101 in Leggett, drive about 4 miles north to a pullout on the left (west) side of the highway signed for the Frank and Bess Smithe Grove. The site is about 11 miles south of the entrance station for Richardson Grove State Park and 18 miles south of Garberville. There is parking for about twenty-five cars. GPS: N39 53.904' / W123 45.066'

The Hike

Located just north of the Standish-Hickey State Recreation Area, styled the "gateway to tall trees country," Smithe Redwoods State Natural Reserve protects a stand of coast redwoods on the site of a former resort. The redwood grove is on the banks of the South Fork Eel River, throwing a blanket of shade onto the cleared forest floor. Step out of the trees onto the riverbanks, and the sunlight can be blinding … if the fog hasn't rolled up the river valley.

Dora Falls is across the highway from the redwood grove. Carefully cross the two-lane roadway, hop over the guardrail near the bridge spanning Dora Creek, and pick up the narrow footpath that climbs along the right (south) side of the stream. It doesn't look like much from the road: The waterway is funneled out of a giant culvert into a concrete channel that flows under the highway, and upstream a tangle of broom and saplings looks less than inviting. But bushwhack up along the obvious, if unmaintained, route for just over a tenth of a mile to the base of the fall, and you'll find an unexpected reward.

The waterfall, which is seasonal and best when fed by copious winter rains, begins as split streams and then fans down the cliff face, forming a curtain about 20 feet wide before settling into a pool and feeding into the mouth of the culvert (the culvert's tail is at the highway bridge). The site feels secret and secluded, boxed into the narrow canyon and overgrown with alder and brush. There's room at the base, however, to sit and enjoy. Return as you came.

The redwoods of the Frank and Bess Smithe Grove, downstream of Dora Falls, grow alongside the South Fork Eel River.

Miles and Directions

0.0 Begin in the parking area for the Frank and Bess Smithe Grove. Cross the highway to the bridge spanning Dora Creek and head up the overgrown path on the right (south) as you face the ravine.

0.1 Reach the base of the falls. Return as you came.

0.2 Arrive back at the trailhead.

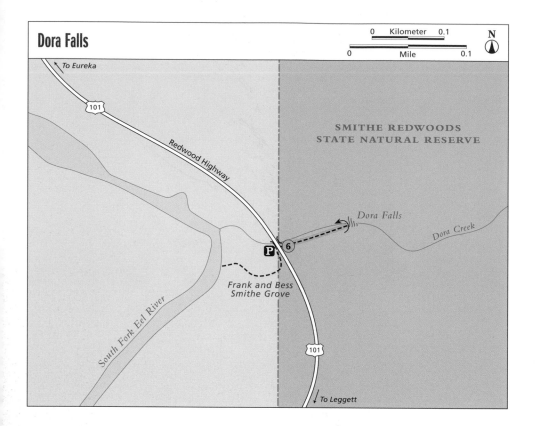

Option: Stretch a visit to the waterfall by meandering through the stunning Smithe redwood grove. Likely because of its history as a resort site, the trees in the grove are well spaced and parklike, with plenty of open ground between the massive trunks. Several paths lead from the grove down to the pebbly banks of the South Fork Eel River, flowing fast and milky green in winter. In summer the confluence with Dora Creek is an inviting swimming hole. A tour of both the falls and the grove totals about 0.5 mile.

Shasta-Trinity

Between the remote and lovely Trinity Alps and Mount Shasta, a composite volcano that, at more than 14,000 feet, dominates the upper Sacramento River valley, recreational opportunities in the north-central part of the state abound. These waterfall hikes are found in the watersheds surrounding Redding, Dunsmuir, Mount Shasta City, and Weaverville.

Middle Falls on the McCloud River (hike 7).

7 McCloud Falls

A lovely trail through woodland and canyon links three distinctive falls on the McCloud River.

Height: 15 feet for Lower Falls; 50 feet for Middle Falls; 30 feet (plus cascades) for Upper Falls
Beauty rating: ★★★★★
Distance: 4.2 miles out and back
Difficulty: Moderate due only to distance and the climb from Middle Falls to the overlook above
Best season: Spring and fall
County: Siskiyou

Trailhead amenities: Restrooms, picnic sites, trash cans, and information signboards; Fowlers Campground with additional facilities nearby
Land status: Shasta-Trinity National Forest
Maps: USGS Lake McCloud CA
Trail contact: US Forest Service, Shasta-Trinity National Forest, McCloud Ranger Station, PO Box 1620, McCloud, CA 96057; (530) 964-2184; www.fs.usda.gov/main/stnf

Finding the trailhead: From I-5 as it passes Mount Shasta City, follow CA 89 east for about 14.7 miles, past the town of McCloud, to the McCloud River Loop Road/FR 40N44 (signed for Fowlers Camp and Lower Falls). Turn right onto the McCloud River Loop Road and go 0.6 mile to a signed junction. Stay right, following signs for Lower Falls. Continue 0.5 mile to the Lower Falls picnic area and trailhead. GPS: N41 14.422' / W122 01.490'

The Hike

A tour of the three falls on the McCloud River begins at Lower Falls, which is literally steps from the picnic area at the trailhead. The waterfall can be viewed either from the picnic area itself or by walking down short staircases to the riverside, where a shelf of water-sculpted rock provides a viewing platform. Lower Falls is diminutive compared to what lies upstream, but it makes a lovely starting and ending point.

From the Lower Falls a paved trail leads through the mixed evergreen woodland that thrives alongside the McCloud River, rounding easy switchbacks into Fowlers Campground. Interpretive signs describe how the indigenous people, the Winnemem Wintu, called these "the Falls Where the Salmon Turn Back," as well as the more modern history of the area, which has served as a tourist attraction since the 1800s. Locals have long hunted and fished near the McCloud, and the river also provided water for the nearby town that shares its name.

The trail turns to dirt as it leaves the camp; a sign points the way to Middle Falls. Follow the easy route along the river to the second waterfall, where the McCloud River pours over a 50-foot rock escarpment into a broad pool, feathering across a face that stretches about 100 feet from canyon wall to canyon wall. This substantial block of whitewater would definitely turn a salmon back.

Middle McCloud Falls is inarguably the most spectacular of the three waterfalls on the McCloud River.

Climb switchbacks out of the canyon—the most strenuous part of the hike, but nicely graded, and with views of Middle Falls to mitigate the ascent. The path becomes paved on the canyon rim, with railings protecting overviews of the falls below.

The route becomes dirt again as it continues upstream, now high above the river. Slip under a mossy cliff face that overhangs on the north, and then cross a slide, where the path is narrow and exposed. The route ends at the overlooks near Upper Falls, a tiered waterfall with cascades above a final horsetail that shoots clear of the rock before plunging into a pool below. Upstream of the final drop, the whorls and eddies of the waterway have sculpted huecos in the bedrock; those that are empty are polished and dark, while the river pools and cycles in others, deepening them before moving on. When it's time for you to do the same, backtrack to the trailhead.

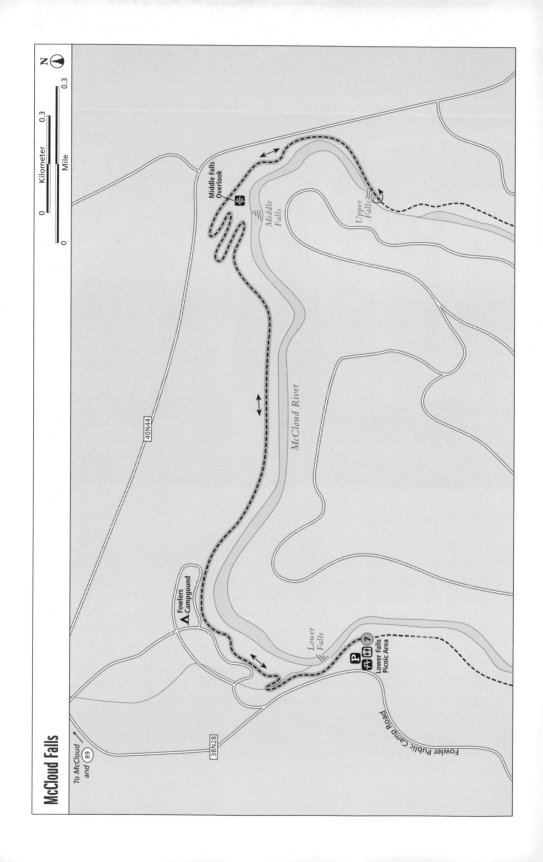

McCloud Falls

To McCloud and (89)

38N28

40N44

Fowlers Campgound

McCloud River

Middle Falls
Overlook

Middle Falls

Upper Falls

Lower Falls

Lower Falls
Picnic Area

P

7

Fowler Public Camp Road

N

Kilometer
0   0.3

Mile
0   0.3

The McCloud River churns in a hueco above the Upper Falls.

Miles and Directions

0.0 Begin by heading through the picnic area toward the river. Take the staircase down to the riverside, enjoying views of Lower Falls. Follow the paved path upstream.

0.3 Reach the Fowlers Campground. Stay right (riverside) on the paved River Trail, ignoring spur trails leading left into the camp.

0.6 Leave the camp at the sign for Middle Falls; the trail turns to dirt.

1.3 Reach Middle Falls. Climb switchbacks up toward the rim.

1.6 Climb a wooden staircase onto the canyon rim. Follow the trail, now paved, past an overlook of Middle Falls.

2.1 Reach the overlooks of Upper Falls. Retrace your steps.

4.2 Arrive back at the trailhead.

8 Faery Falls

Follow a remote forest road that parallels Ney Springs Creek to a secluded waterfall.

Height: About 40 feet
Beauty rating: ★★★★
Distance: 2.0 miles out and back
Difficulty: Easy, with one short, steep pitch
Best season: Spring
County: Siskiyou
Trailhead amenities: None

Land status: Shasta-Trinity National Forest
Maps: USGS City of Mount Shasta CA
Trail contact: US Forest Service, Mount Shasta Ranger Station, 204 West Alma St., Mount Shasta, CA 96067; (530) 926-4511; www.fs.usda.gov/main/stnf

Finding the trailhead: From I-5 in the city of Mount Shasta, take the Central Mount Shasta exit and head west on Hatchery Lane for 0.3 mile. Turn left onto Old Stage Road and go 0.2 mile to the Y-junction with W A Barr Road. Go right on W A Barr Road for 2.2 miles, over the Box Canyon Dam on Lake Siskiyou, to the junction with Castle Lake Road. Turn left onto Castle Lake Road and drive 0.1 mile to the intersection with Ney Springs Road. Stay left onto Ney Springs Road, a graded gravel road, and drive 1.3 miles to a clearing at the junction with an unsigned road that climbs to the right (about 0.3 mile beyond the Cantara-Ney Springs Wildlife Area sign). Park in the clearing. If you round a sharp bend, cross Ney Springs Creek, and reach a gate, you've gone too far. GPS: N41 15.949' / W122 19.453'

The Hike

The setting at the trailhead doesn't promise much: a walk in a dark woodland, with no views of Mount Shasta or the surrounding peaks of the Shasta-Trinity mountains. But two intriguing destinations, the ruins of the Ney Springs Resort and Faery Falls, lie not far up the unsigned forest road.

Faery Falls is tucked in a narrow gorge and perpetually screened from the sun by the heavy canopy of encroaching evergreens. The waterfall descends in two tiers, the first shorter, and the second fanning across the bulk of the dark rock face before landing in a shallow pool at the base. Cascades spill down the watercourse below the falls, also inviting exploration. The moss-obscured ruins of the late-nineteenth-century resort, which grew up around mineral springs purported to have health benefits, lie downstream of the cascades, where the creek mellows.

The route follows a nice forest road for most of the distance (the road is passable by high-clearance vehicles to a barricade not far from the falls, but makes for a nice walk). Side trails break left off the roadway to the creekside—the well-traveled path that diverges just above the trailhead leads to a line of camp/picnic sites with fire pits and stonework designs on the forest floor. The main route climbs to a barricade: There is parking here for folks with hardier cars who want a shorter hike. A nice camping/picnic spot is on the right.

Faery Falls tumbles down Ney Springs Creek above the ruins of a resort.

Beyond the barricade the route narrows and steepens. Look down and left, toward the creek, to the ruins of the Ney Springs Resort; a short side trip on social paths allows exploration of the streamside site. Given the narrowness, steepness, and wildness of the canyon in its present state, it's hard to imagine that the place once hosted a hotel and other resort amenities. But the foundations, overgrown and draped in moss but obvious once they're identified, testify to John Ney's vision.

Not far above the disintegrating remnants of the resort, a second unsigned social path departs to the left, dropping to cascades on the creek, where you can check out the whitewater as it tumbles from pool to pool. The pitch of the roadway steepens sharply before the next unmarked trail that breaks left, this one leading to the waterfall proper. Head down the narrow path to its end and pull up a perch on the steep, shaded side of the canyon. There's no easy way to the base of the falls, but scramble around at will, and then return as you came.

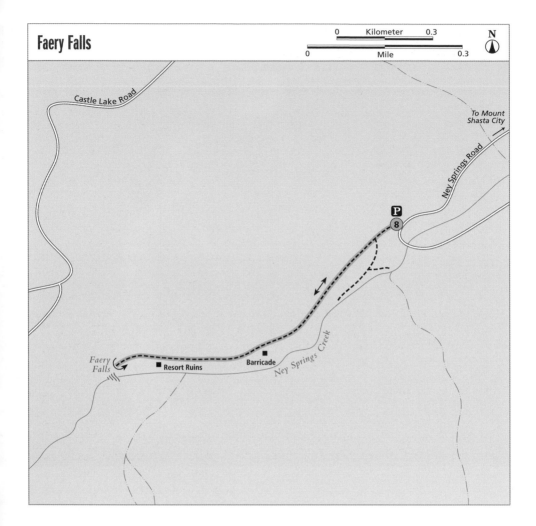

Miles and Directions

0.0 Start on the dirt forest road that breaks right and uphill from the clearing.

0.2 Pass a well-worn use trail that breaks left to creekside camp/picnic sites. Stay right on the forest road.

0.5 Pass a barricade. Use the social trails that break to the left, toward the creek, to explore the ruins of the Ney Springs resort.

0.7 A social path leads right to a series of nice cataracts on Ney Springs Creek.

0.9 As the forest road steepens, take the clear but unsigned path that breaks left toward the waterfall.

1.0 Reach Faery Falls. Retrace your steps.

2.0 Arrive back at the trailhead.

9 Canyon Creek Falls

Follow a popular trail into the Trinity Alps Wilderness to the lowest of a series of waterfalls on Canyon Creek.

Height: About 100 feet
Beauty rating: ★★★★★
Distance: 8.3 miles out and back
Difficulty: Strenuous
Best season: Spring and early summer
County: Trinity
Trailhead amenities: Restrooms, trash cans, and information signboards
Land status: Trinity Alps Wilderness

Maps: USGS Mount Hilton CA
Trail contact: US Forest Service, Shasta-Trinity National Forest, Weaverville Ranger Station, 360 Main St., PO Box 1190, Weaverville, CA 96093; (530) 623-2121; www.fs.usda.gov/main/stnf. Portions of the wilderness area also fall under the purview of the Klamath National Forest and the Six Rivers National Forest.

Finding the trailhead: From Weaverville head west on CA 299 for 8 miles to Junction City. Take Canyon Creek Road to the right, before crossing the bridge. Follow Canyon Creek Road north for 13 scenic miles to the road's end at the Canyon Creek trailhead and parking area. GPS: N40 53.234' / W123 01.447'

The Hike

Reading about the falls along Canyon Creek in the Trinity Alps, it becomes clear that proper names are an issue. The spectacular waterfall visible from the trail as you climb out of the woods nearly 4 miles from the trailhead appears to be widely regarded as "the" Canyon Creek Falls, with the cascades in the gorge above labeled Lower Canyon Creek Falls, Middle Canyon Creek Falls, and Upper Canyon Creek Falls. This day hike takes you up to view the lowest falls, with the remainder better explored as part of an overnight trip in the wilderness.

The hike to the lower falls follows one of the most well-used trails in the Trinity Alps, though the route feels remote. Though the bulk of the trail passes under cover of trees—oaks down low, and pines and firs above—the naked ridges and peaks of the high Alps come into view now and again, craggy and pocked with snow, sometimes bleeding ephemeral falls down narrow folds on their stony slopes. The path breaks out of the woods near the turnaround point, switchbacking up bare rock with views opening across the Canyon Creek drainage to the falls. The waterfall is a provocative sight, as the creek is jettisoned out of a tree-trimmed chute, starkly white against the dark greens and grays that surround it. Then the water plummets out of sight.

Begin by climbing from the parking lot to the junction of the Bear Creek and Canyon Creek Trails; head left on the signed Canyon Creek Trail. This drops to cross Bear Creek in a steep ravine, a crossing that can be a bit gnarly in high water. The path

Canyon Creek Falls is the first in a series of cataracts in this spectacular Trinity Alps drainage.

then climbs over a low, forested ridge into the Canyon Creek drainage and begins a long, easy climb through mixed woods. Not much breaks the monotony of the first few miles: a stand of madrones with smooth trunks glowing red amid the various shades of green; brief openings in the canopy that allow you to play peek-a-boo with crag and creek views as the moderate ascent continues.

Round a couple of switchbacks up a scrubby slope; the trail then drops into a camp, with views across the valley to the stony lower reaches of the Mount Hilton massif. An ephemeral fall courses down the far slope in season. The trail to the Sinks,

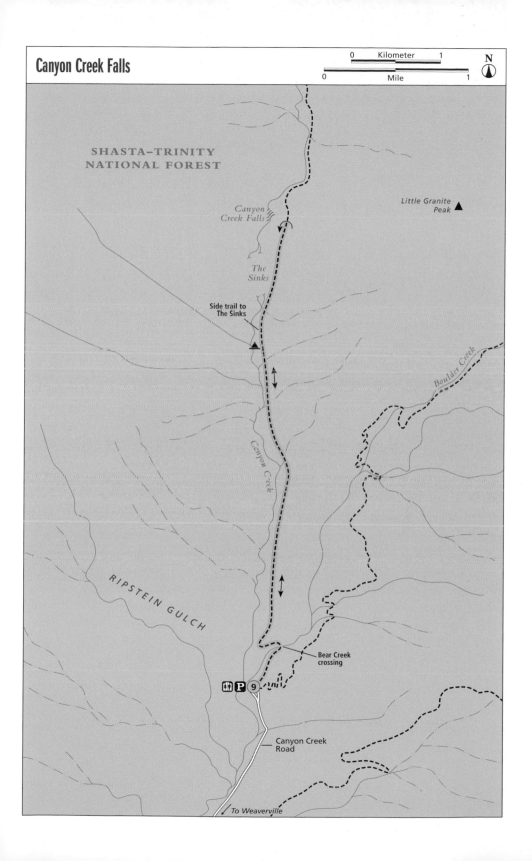

Canyon Creek Falls

0 — Kilometer — 1
0 — Mile — 1

N

SHASTA–TRINITY
NATIONAL FOREST

Little Granite
Peak ▲

Canyon
Creek Falls

The
Sinks

Side trail to
The Sinks

Boulder Creek

Canyon Creek

RIPSTEIN GULCH

Bear Creek
crossing

P 9

Canyon Creek
Road

To Weaverville

where the creek may pool in a rockslide or sink below it, depending on water levels, breaks off to the left not far beyond the camp; stay right on the Canyon Creek Trail.

The views get better and better as you climb, the trail eventually leaving the forest to switchback up exposed slopes on the east side of the creek. Ephemeral falls may flitter down the steep slopes that hem in the west side of the valley, but when the whitewater plunge of Canyon Creek Falls comes into view, its superiority is clear. The best views of the waterfall are from the traverses and switchbacks at this point.

The turnaround for a comfortable day hike is another half mile or so up the trail from the switchback views. Cross a seasonal stream and climb to a trail sign that points to the right—the Middle and Upper Canyon Creek Falls lie upstream, as does the lovely Canyon Lake basin, a popular backpacking destination located 7 miles from the trailhead. From the sign, return as you came.

Miles and Directions

0.0 Start by climbing to the junction of the Bear Creek Trail and Canyon Creek Trails. Go left on the signed Canyon Creek Trail.

0.4 Ford Bear Creek.

1.5 Pass a stand of red-trunked madrones.

2.6 Round a pair of switchbacks that lead up a scrub-covered slope.

3.1 Reach the campsite alongside the creek. The trail skirts the camp to the right.

3.3 At the junction with the signed trail to the Sinks, stay right on the Canyon Creek Trail.

3.8 The trail leaves the woods behind, climbing switchbacks built into the bare stone of the mountainside. Canyon Creek Falls comes into view; this is the best view you'll have of the biggest plunge.

4.1 Cross a streamlet and reach a trail sign. This is the turnaround; if you bear right, following the arrow, the trail continues to the cataracts on Canyon Creek above. Retrace your steps.

8.3 Arrive back at the trailhead.

10 Brandy Creek Falls

Climb an old logging road to a series of short falls on Brandy Creek.

Height: Varying from 10 to 20 feet
Beauty rating: ★★★★
Distance: 3.0 miles out and back
Difficulty: Moderate
Best season: Spring, early summer, and fall
County: Shasta
Trailhead amenities: Restrooms and information signboard. A fee is charged; pay at the Whiskeytown National Recreation Area visitor center.

Land status: Whiskeytown National Recreation Area
Maps: USGS Igo CA; trail guides and maps available on the Whiskeytown National Recreation Area website
Trail contact: Whiskeytown National Recreation Area, 14412 Kennedy Memorial Dr., PO Box 188, Whiskeytown, CA 96095; (530) 242-3400; www.nps.gov/whis/planyourvisit/waterfalls-of-whiskeytown.htm

Finding the trailhead: From Redding follow CA 299 west for 8.2 miles to the junction with John F. Kennedy Memorial Drive, signed for the Whiskeytown National Recreation Area. Turn left onto Kennedy Memorial Drive; the visitor center is on the right (pay the fee here). From the visitor center continue on Kennedy Memorial Drive for 1.3 miles to a sharp right turn, heading across the dam on South Shore Drive. Continue to the junction with Brandy Creek Road, a total of 3.1 miles from the visitor center. Turn left onto Brandy Creek Road and follow the winding dirt road for 1.4 miles to the signed junction to Sheep Camp. Stay straight on Brandy Creek Road. At the junction at 2.2 miles, stay left toward the Brandy Creek Falls trailhead. The parking area and trailhead is at the end of the road, 3.2 miles from the junction with South Shore Drive. GPS: N40 35.816' / W122 36.017'

The Hike

Brandy Creek Falls descend in low-angled stair steps, fanning over slick, shiny slabs and weaving through boulder-choked channels. The path that explores the falls wanders over footbridges and tangles of tree roots that can be slippery in wet weather or when soaked by mist. The complexity of the walking and the different faces of the falls make for an enlivening end-of-trail experience—a nice conclusion to an otherwise straightforward climb through a dark, dense woodland.

A steady traversing ascent on an eroding but well-defined logging road leads to the falls. It's a meditative hike through a mixed forest, with pockets of oak and maple mixing with the conifers. Brandy Creek rumbles in the steep ravine below, sometimes visible and always audible. There are few distractions: A bridge spans a fern-filled tributary partway up the hill, the riparian foliage turning a startling gold in autumn; and there is one trail junction, with the Rich Gulch Trail, as you approach the falls.

A bench overlooking the lower falls, a 15-foot tumble into a dark pool with a cataract below, heralds the start of the sequence of cascades. Continue up the trail,

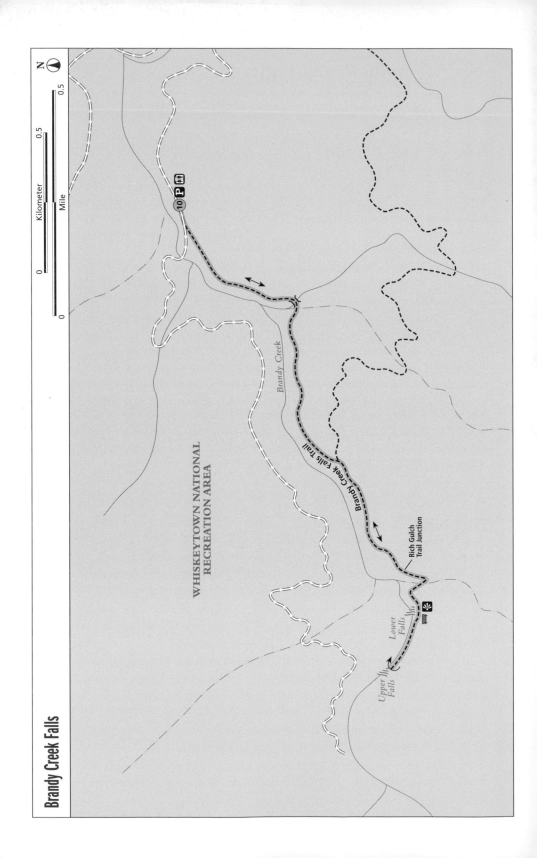

Brandy Creek Falls

Bridges link the several tiers of Brandy Creek Falls.

now a singletrack path, to the upper falls, using the rails where provided, as sections of the path are uneven and slick. A set of bridges provides excellent view platforms for the upper falls—one above and one below a long, broken slide of whitewater, with another series of short falls spilling from pool to pool above. The surrounding rocks offer places to sit and enjoy the show. Return as you came.

Miles and Directions

0.0 Start by climbing the old logging road, staying left at the fork just above the trailhead (the right-hand road leads down to the side of Brandy Creek). The route is straightforward; stay on the eroding road, avoiding the game trails that occasionally branch right, down toward the creek, or left, up into the woods.

1.1 At the junction with the Rich Gulch Trail, stay right on the signed Brandy Creek Falls Trail.

1.3 Pass the bench overlooking the lower falls.

1.5 Reach the upper falls, linked with bridges and paths outfitted with rails. Explore and relax, then retrace your steps.

3.0 Arrive back at the trailhead.

11 Crystal Creek Falls

A paved, wheelchair–accessible path leads to a sprawling waterfall on Crystal Creek.

Height: About 50 feet
Beauty rating: ★★★
Distance: 0.6 mile out and back
Difficulty: Easy
Best season: Spring and early summer
County: Shasta
Trailhead amenities: Restrooms, information signboard, picnic sites, and trash cans. Picnic facilities and trash cans are also at the base of the falls. A fee is charged; pay at the Whiskeytown National Recreation Area visitor center.

Land status: Whiskeytown National Recreation Area
Maps: USGS French Gulch CA; trail guide and map available on the Whiskeytown National Recreation Area website
Trail contact: Whiskeytown National Recreation Area, 14412 Kennedy Memorial Dr., PO Box 188, Whiskeytown, CA 96095; (530) 242-3400; www.nps.gov/whis/planyourvisit/waterfalls-of-whiskeytown.htm

Finding the trailhead: From Redding follow CA 299 west for 8.2 miles to the junction with John F. Kennedy Memorial Drive, signed for the Whiskeytown National Recreation Area. Turn left onto Kennedy Memorial Drive; the visitor center is on the right (pay the fee here). From the visitor center return to CA 299 and drive 8.5 miles to the junction with Crystal Creek Road. Turn left onto Crystal Creek Road and go 2 miles to the open rocky area on the left. Turn left and follow the access road to the paved parking lot and picnic area. GPS: N40 38.964' / W122 40.080'

The Hike

The falls on Crystal Creek are newly come to the landscape, a lovely little addition to a massive construct of water diversion and storage facilities known as the Central Valley Project. The project, built to control flooding and provide water for agriculture in the Great Valley, consists of reservoirs and canals that stretch from the alpine watersheds surrounding Redding to the thirsty agricultural lowlands surrounding Bakersfield, more than 400 miles to the south.

The dams that impound water in the Whiskeytown, Shasta, and Trinity reservoirs are the most obvious man-made structures on the landscape, with the lakes behind them the grandest "natural" features. Crystal Creek Falls, created when Crystal Creek was diverted to make room for a bypass structure, is tiny by comparison, but mighty as a scenic waypoint within the Whiskeytown National Recreation Area.

The barren landscape on the approach to the Crystal Creek picnic area is another remnant of the water diversion project: The tailings from excavation of

Crystal Creek Falls is man-made and ▶
wheelchair accessible.

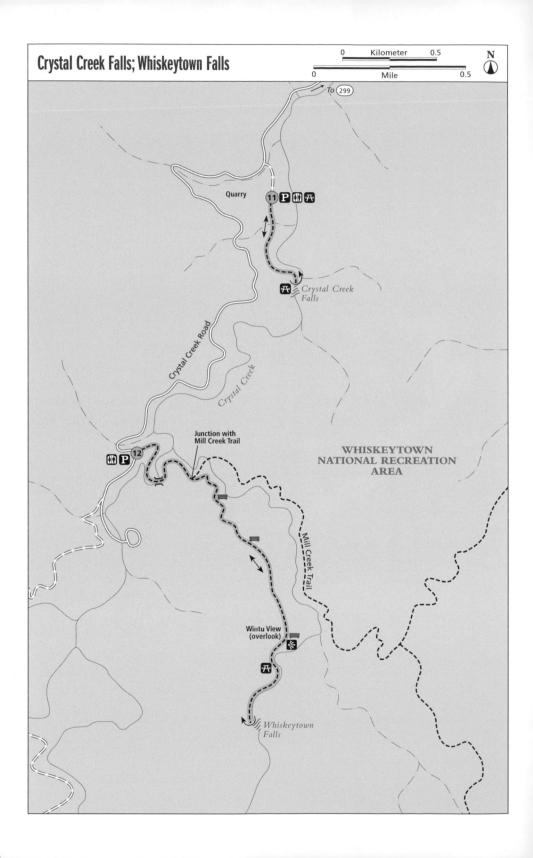

Crystal Creek Falls; Whiskeytown Falls

To (299)

0 Kilometer 0.5

0 Mile 0.5

N

Quarry

11 P 🚻 🏕

Crystal Creek Falls

🏕 ℹ

Crystal Creek Road

Crystal Creek

Junction with
Mill Creek Trail

🚻 P 12

WHISKEYTOWN
NATIONAL RECREATION
AREA

Mill Creek Trail

Wintu View
(overlook)

🏕

Whiskeytown
Falls

an 11-mile-long tunnel that runs from Lewiston Lake to Whiskeytown Lake were deposited here (an estimated 250,000 cubic yards of granite). If the main parking lot is full, a walk on the pale crushed rock leads to the trailhead.

The trail proper is a wide, paved, wheelchair-friendly lane that winds alongside a meadow and then curls into the mouth of a wooded canyon, with Crystal Creek flowing below and to the left. Pass a picnic site and the falls open before you, covering the sloping face of a short cliff. The bypass building is to the right; when the valve is open, the water spills into Crystal Creek. A spread of sun-warmed slabs opposite the falls is a great viewing platform; a narrow path (not wheelchair accessible) leads down onto the rocks. Return as you came.

Miles and Directions

0.0 Start on the paved path, which skirts a meadow.

0.3 Pass the picnic site and take the side path down to view the falls. Return as you came.

0.6 Arrive back at the trailhead.

12 Whiskeytown Falls

A relentless climb up an old logging road leads to a waterfall that once was a well-kept secret.

See map on page 50.
Height: 220 feet
Beauty rating: ★★★★
Distance: 3.4 miles out and back
Difficulty: Strenuous
Best season: Spring and early summer
County: Shasta
Trailhead amenities: Restrooms, information signboard, and trash cans. A fee is charged; pay at the Whiskeytown National Recreation Area visitor center.

Land status: Whiskeytown National Recreation Area
Maps: USGS French Gulch CA; trail guide and map available on the Whiskeytown National Recreation Area website
Trail contact: Whiskeytown National Recreation Area, 14412 Kennedy Memorial Dr., PO Box 188, Whiskeytown, CA 96095; (530) 242-3400; www.nps.gov/whis/planyourvisit/waterfalls-of-whiskeytown.htm

Finding the trailhead: From Redding follow CA 299 west for 8.2 miles to the junction with John F. Kennedy Memorial Drive, signed for the Whiskeytown National Recreation Area. Turn left onto Kennedy Memorial Drive; the visitor center is on the right (pay the fee here). From the visitor center return to CA 299 and drive 8.5 miles to the junction with Crystal Creek Road. Turn left onto Crystal Creek Road and drive 3.5 miles to the Mill Creek trailhead and parking area on the left. GPS: N40 38.292' / W122 40.577'

The Hike

As you make your way up the unforgiving trail to Whiskeytown Falls, you may assume that the nonstop climbing was what screened this waterfall from common knowledge for more than 40 years. Not so, according to park literature: Loggers working in the rugged forest when it was in private hands undoubtedly knew of the falls, as did rangers in the 1960s, when the land was preserved as a national recreation area. But the desire of early park managers to protect the area from overuse prevented the area's development and resulted in the falls being "forgotten" until 2004, when a pair of park service employees—a biologist and a geologist—studied a map, ventured into the backcountry, and rediscovered them.

The trail leading to the falls follows a logging road used in the 1950s by the Northern California Logging Company, which harvested Douglas fir, ponderosa pine, and incense cedar from the steep slopes. The hike begins with a fairly steep descent on a crushed stone path into the bottomlands surrounding the west fork of Crystal Creek. Cross the creek on a footbridge and settle into a comfortable gear for the climb. There is a brief respite as the trail rounds the bend to the junction with the Mill Creek Trail, but beyond the junction the climbing is persistent, with sections that will wind even the fittest. Thoughtfully, the park has placed benches (breath catchers) at intervals along the climb.

Spurs break left and right as the trail ascends Steep Ravine and then tops out (briefly) at Wintu View. A bench at the overlook faces the steep, forested ridges of Whiskeytown's backcountry. The route is flat for a stretch and then meets up with the creek. Pass the trail camp with picnic sites (bikers and equestrians must leave their steeds here and continue on foot); at this point the path becomes a singletrack and traces the creek into a box canyon crowded with alders and maples, which provide fabulous color in the fall. Cross a footbridge, climb a set of stone stairs, and you've arrived at the base of the secret falls. You can see about 70 feet of whitewater from the base, which features viewing platforms sculpted into the rock, as well as the waterfall's trail register. Use the stone steps protected with a rail to climb to a pair of viewpoints above, dubbed

A stiff climb up an old logging road leads to Whiskeytown Falls.

the Photographer's Ledge and the Artist's Ledge. Return as you came.

Miles and Directions

0.0 Start by passing the restrooms and dropping into the West Fork Crystal Creek drainage.

0.3 Cross the creek on a footbridge. The climbing begins.

0.5 At the junction with the Mill Creek Trail, stay right on the trail to Whiskeytown Falls.

0.7 Pass the first of a number of benches placed alongside the steep, eroded logging road. The benches are roughly 0.2 mile apart.

1.3 Reach the bench and overlook at Wintu View.

1.4 Pass the picnic sites and benches at the mouth of the narrowing box canyon.

1.5 Cross a footbridge.

1.7 Reach the base of the falls. Use the steps to climb to viewing platforms above. Retrace your steps.

3.4 Arrive back at the trailhead.

13 Hedge Creek Falls

A trail leads down to, and then under, the waterfall on Hedge Creek.

Height: About 30 feet
Beauty rating: ★★★★
Distance: 0.8 mile out and back
Difficulty: Easy
Best season: Late winter and spring
County: Siskiyou
Trailhead amenities: Picnic facilities, trash cans, and water
Land status: City park

Maps: USGS Dunsmuir CA; no map is needed.
Trail contact: City of Dunsmuir, 5915 Dunsmuir Ave., Dunsmuir, CA 96025; (530) 235-4822; www.ci.dunsmuir.ca.us. Dunsmuir Chamber of Commerce & Visitor's Center, 5915 Dunsmuir Ave., PO Box 122, Dunsmuir, CA 96025; (530) 235-2177 or (800) DUNSMUIR; www.dunsmuir.com/hikes-waterfalls

Finding the trailhead: From northbound I-5 in Dunsmuir (toward the north end of town), take the Siskiyou Avenue exit. Go left, under the freeway, and then immediately right onto the frontage road (Mott Road). The parking area is a pullout on the corner; the park is across the street. GPS: N41 14.179' / W122 16.178'

The Hike

Mossbrae Falls may be Dunsmuir's reclusive waterfall star (see sidebar on page 56), but Hedge Creek Falls has what it takes to be a scene stealer. The clincher: passing through the alcove that opens behind the fall. Between the brevity and ease of the trail, the pass-around (a perfect place to repeat the tale told on the Dunsmuir Chamber of Commerce website that outlaw Black Bart used the "cave" as a hideout), and the overlook of the Sacramento River at trail's end, Hedge Creek Falls is a great hike for families with children.

The trail begins in Hedge Creek Park, with picnic sites and great views of the narrow Dunsmuir valley and Mount Shasta towering above. Pass through the picnic area to the signed trail above the creek. Three switchbacks drop easily and quickly to Hedge Creek and the falls, with the noise of the nearby highway overcome by the noise of falling water as you descend. Follow the path behind the 15-foot free-falling portion of the plume, hunching below the overhanging basalt.

From the falls the trail continues downstream alongside Hedge Creek, which forms cataracts as it completes its run into the Sacramento River. The turnaround at trail's end is a wooden platform overlooking the mighty Sacramento, with the Union Pacific rail line on the opposite bank. Take in the sights; then return as you came.

A pass-through alcove is tucked behind Hedge Creek Falls. ▶

Miles and Directions

0.0 Start in Hedge Creek Park, heading down the switchbacks into the drainage.

0.2 Reach the falls and follow the path behind the water through the alcove.

0.4 Reach the overlook of the Sacramento River. Retrace your steps.

0.8 Arrive back at the trailhead.

MOSSBRAE FALLS

Dubbed by Jefferson Public Radio the "Forbidden Falls of Dunsmuir," fabled Mossbrae Falls remains off-limits to hikers. The reason: The falls can only be reached by trespassing on the Union Pacific Railroad right-of-way, posing an immediate danger to hikers who might be on or near the tracks when a train passes through. "If a train comes, your options are to run, press against the canyon wall, or jump into the Sacramento River below," wrote Victoria Reed in a piece she prepared on the conundrum of Mossbrae Falls for the public radio station.

While the danger doesn't deter all hikers from venturing to the falls, I won't guide you there. In fact, I won't go there myself. There is no parking at the "trailhead," and No Trespassing signs festoon the tracks. Having read Reed's September 2014 piece, I also knew I could be fined for sneaking down the tracks. And Reed recounts the tale of an unfortunate hiker who was struck (but thankfully not killed) by a train while attempting to get to the falls. I'm not a trespasser by nature, and while I've done my share of tempting fate for the sake of a good hike, I've got no desire to add a narrow miss with a locomotive to the list.

The city of Dunsmuir, a local trail group, and the Union Pacific have been working for years to provide safe access to the spring-fed falls, which are 50 feet high and 150 feet across, and look spectacular in photos published in books and posted on various websites (including the City of Dunsmuir's). "Dozens of small cascades fall from the springs above over a wide, moss-covered rock face, into a deep pool. Large rocks on the bank offer a front row seat," wrote Reed; she also quoted a city official who called a visit to the falls "the most beautiful experience of my life."

The hope is to link Hedge Creek Falls with Mossbrae Falls via a public trail, but exactly when that might happen is unclear. Meantime, the famous Forbidden Falls of Dunsmuir remains just that: famous and forbidden.

14 Lower Burstarse Falls

Carve two notches in the hiking stick for this route, one for reaching the seasonal waterfall and the second for completing a short section of the storied Pacific Crest Trail.

Height: About 40 feet
Beauty rating: ★★★
Distance: 5.2 miles out and back
Difficulty: Strenuous
Best season: Spring and early summer
County: Siskiyou
Trailhead amenities: None. Though the trail is technically outside Castle Crags State Park, it is good form to pay the fee at the entry station before proceeding to the trailhead.
Land status: Castle Crags Wilderness

Maps: USGS Dunsmuir CA and Seven Lakes Basin CA
Trail contact: US Forest Service, Mount Shasta Ranger Station, 204 West Alma St., Mount Shasta, CA 96067; (530) 926-4511; www .fs.usda.gov/main/stnf. Castle Crags State Park, 20022 Castle Creek Rd., Castella, CA 96017; (530) 235-2684; www.parks.ca.gov; www.fs.usda.gov/Internet/FSE_DOCUMENTS/ fsm9_008098.pdf

Finding the trailhead: From I-5 in Castella (south of Dunsmuir), take the Castella/Castle Crags exit. Head west for 0.3 mile to the Castle Crags State Park entrance; pay the fee, and then head back to Castle Crags Road and turn right. Continue west for .3 miles to Dog trailhead on the right, at the blue-and-white Pacific Crest Trail sign. You'll leave the park and enter the Shasta-Trinity National Forest at the 2.3-mile mark. The trailhead is on the left side of the huge clearing as you drive in. GPS: N41 09.739' / W122 22.176'

The Hike

The Pacific Crest Trail (PCT), which rides the ridges of California, Oregon, and Washington for more than 2,600 miles from Mexico to Canada, incorporates plenty of challenging terrain. Fear not the forbidding surroundings: Though the piece of the PCT to Burstarse Falls is enveloped in steep, wooded mountainsides and shadowed by jagged crags and an imposing volcano, it's an easy ride. The Dog Trail leading to the PCT? Not so easy, but it's over relatively quickly …

The falls themselves are ephemeral, so timing is everything. The setting is surreal on misty days after the rainy season starts (but before the snow flies), with the mosses blooming fluorescent green, the Castle Crags feathered in clouds a paler shade of gray, and the falls beginning to show their vigor. Otherwise this is a springtime trek, with the window opening after the snow melts and closing when the sun parches the landscape, dries up the destination, and transforms the first stretch, up the Dog Trail, into a moisture-sucking slog.

Some might argue that hiking up the Dog Trail to the PCT is a slog no matter the weather. The path leads uphill over uneven terrain for just over a half mile, incorporating switchbacks and long traverses. The scant tree cover allows great views up and

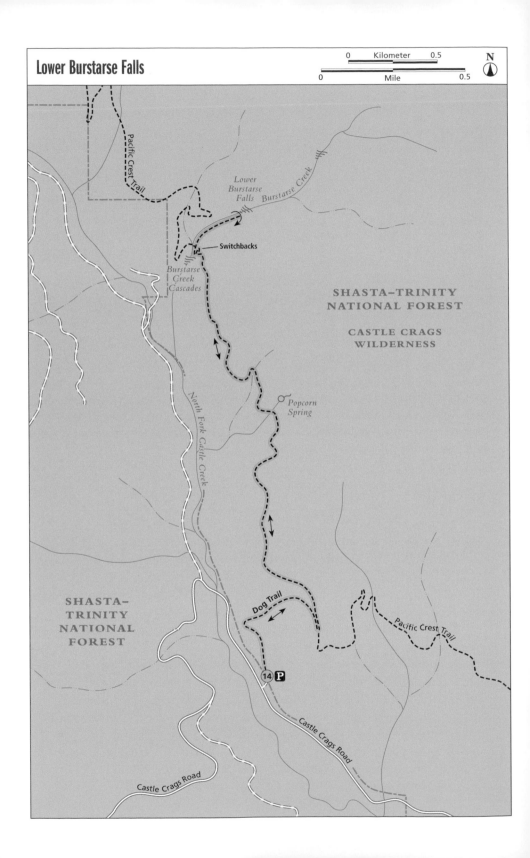

Lower Burstarse Falls

0   Kilometer   0.5

0   Mile   0.5

N

Pacific Crest Trail

Lower
Burstarse
Falls

Burstarse Creek

Switchbacks

Burstarse
Creek
Cascades

North Fork Castle Creek

Popcorn
Spring

SHASTA–TRINITY
NATIONAL FOREST

CASTLE CRAGS
WILDERNESS

SHASTA–
TRINITY
NATIONAL
FOREST

Dog Trail

Pacific Crest Trail

14 P

Castle Crags Road

Castle Crags Road

The Castle Crags loom above the Pacific Crest Trail leading to Burstarse Falls.

down the steep Castle Creek valley, with occasional road noise drifting up or across through the woods.

But once you're on the PCT, the walking and the viewing are easy. The trail makes a long traverse of the mountainside above the north fork of Castle Creek and below Castle Crags, tucking in and out of drainages and shaded by a mixed forest of pines, firs, and oaks. There are several seasonal streams to cross before reaching the more substantial Burstarse Creek (big enough to warrant a sign); none of the fords are difficult, and the sound of falling water above and below the path is soothing.

Burstarse Creek can be heard before it is seen. A pair of switchbacks drops into the ravine, where the waterway braids through rocky channels under the dense green canopy. Social trails lead upstream to the right; pick one of these up and climb alongside the stream, past the confluence with a side stream, to a series of cascades. Full disclosure: I made my trip in the aftermath of a Pineapple Express, and there was so much water in Burstarse Creek that it was unsafe for me to ford or scramble alongside. But given the cataracts at the trail crossing, the falls above and beyond could only have been amazing. If you encounter the same, the cascades are the turnaround.

Miles and Directions

0.0 Start climbing the Dog Trail, which is unsigned as such. But you'll pass wilderness signage within a few hundred feet, proving you are on the right track.

0.6 Finish the hardest climbing at the junction with the PCT. Turn left on the signed trail.

1.3 Views of the Castle Crags peek over the treetops. The vistas are better on the return trek.

1.6 Cross a seasonal stream; a cascade is on the right and above.

1.9 Cross another seasonal streamlet with a cascade.

2.3 Cross the more substantial streamlet dropping down from Popcorn Spring (unsigned).

2.6 Ford another streamlet, and then descend two switchbacks to the signed crossing of Burstarse Creek. Explore the cascades and waterfall; then retrace your steps.

5.2 Arrive back at the trailhead.

15 Sweetbrier Falls

This short tumble from road to river is a nice little tag as you tick off the waterfall hikes in the Dunsmuir/Mount Shasta area.

Height: About 20 feet
Beauty rating: ★★★
Distance: 0.4 mile out and back
Difficulty: Easy
Best season: Winter and spring
County: Shasta
Trailhead amenities: None. Please respect local property owners by parking on the west side of the railroad tracks in the parking pullout.

Land status: Shasta-Trinity National Forest
Maps: USGS Tombstone Mountain CA; no map is needed.
Trail contact: Shasta-Trinity National Forest Headquarters, 3644 Avtech Pkwy., Redding, CA 96002; (530) 226-2500; www.fs.usda.gov/main/stnf

Finding the trailhead: From Dunsmuir follow I-5 south for about 7.5 miles to the Sweetbrier Avenue exit. Go left on Sweetbrier Avenue, passing under the freeway, and then follow Sweetbrier Avenue for about 0.5 mile to where the road curves sharply right, becoming Falls Avenue and crossing the railroad tracks. A large parking area is on the north side of the curve before the tracks. GPS: N41 07.840' / W122 19.288'

A short walk leads to little Sweetbrier Falls.

Viewing the Falls

This neighborhood waterfall is literally in the neighborhood, mere yards from the nearest cabin in the tiny community of Sweetbrier. It is more a stroll than a hike—getting to the falls requires following Falls Avenue across the Union Pacific rail line. Pass among the charming mountain cabins clustered along the banks of the deep, green Sacramento River, then across the arcing bridge spanning the waterway. Where Falls Avenue bends sharply left on the far side of the bridge, go right (upstream) on the unsigned riverside trail, passing a handmade bench outfitted with saw blades. Walk about 25 yards down the path to the bridge below the falls, which spill from the mossy roadway above, and then pass under the trail bridge and into the Sacramento. The combination of the railroad tracks, the bridge and river, the falls, and the massive volcano that looms above makes this an ideal short hike for families with children.

16 Lion Slide Falls on Hatchet Creek

A short path weaves through the willow and oak alongside Hatchet Creek to a block waterfall and swimming hole.

Height: 25 feet
Beauty rating: ★★★
Distance: 0.4 mile out and back
Difficulty: Easy
Best season: Spring, summer, and fall

County: Shasta
Trailhead amenities: None
Land status: Unknown
Maps: USGS Montgomery Creek CA
Trail contact: None

Finding the trailhead: From Redding head east on CA 299 for 34.4 miles to Big Bend Road. Turn left onto Big Bend Road and drive 0.8 mile to the pullout adjacent to Hatchet Creek, just before the bridge. The trailhead is a bit obscured by willow. GPS: N40 52.350' / W121 53.725'

Lion Slide Falls thunders into a pool on Hatchet Creek.

Viewing the Falls

Lion Slide Falls (aka Hatchet Creek Falls) is a neighborhood waterfall. Homes aren't clustered nearby as in more populated areas of Northern California, but for folks who live in the surrounding countryside, or in Redding, less than an hour's drive to the west, the falls and swimming hole are a popular destination on a hot day in spring or summer. The fall, as broad as it is high, splits into two sheets around a huge fallen tree that tips from cliff top into the pool at the base. Social paths lead down to the creek and to the border of the main pool. An easy, unmaintained trail leads about 0.2 mile from the parking area to the fall.

17 Potem Falls

This elegant, secluded horsetail waterfall graces a canyon embossed in mosses and ferns.

Height: 70 feet
Beauty rating: ★★★★★
Distance: 0.8 mile out and back
Difficulty: Easy
Best season: Winter, spring, and summer
County: Shasta
Trailhead amenities: None. Parking is limited alongside FR 27.

Land status: Shasta-Trinity National Forest
Maps: USGS Devils Rock CA
Trail contact: Shasta-Trinity National Forest Headquarters, 3644 Avtech Pkwy., Redding, CA 96002; (530) 226-2500; www.fs.usda.gov/main/stnf

Finding the trailhead: From Redding follow CA 299 east for 30 miles to the junction with Fenders Ferry Road. Turn left onto Fenders Ferry Road and continue for 3.5 miles to FR 27, a good gravel road that passenger cars can manage easily. Continue on FR 27, staying left at 8.1 miles to stay on the forest road. Continue down to, and then across, the narrow bridge overlooking the dam on the Pit River (Pit Seven Reservoir), at this point a thickening arm leading into Shasta Lake. Climb up the other side of the canyon to the unmarked parking pullout on the left side of the dirt road at the 9.5-mile mark. GPS: N40 50.332' / W122 01.620'

The Hike

The setting of Potem Falls is almost tropical. When the rains come, swelling the mosses and waking the ferns, brushstrokes in a varied palette of green enliven the ravine enveloping the classic waterfall. A fabulous pool wells at the base of the long, unbroken whitewater spill. Swimming on a rainy winter's day may be out of the question, but come warm days in spring and early summer, the cool, deep water invites.

The upside-down hike to the base of the falls, while moderately steep, is short. Three sweeping, easy switchbacks mitigate the incline. The waterfall comes into view at the second switchback: Though the trail swings away at that point on the descent, the falls are in sight for a portion of the ascent. The last switchback deposits you near Potem Creek, which forms low-key cataracts as it rolls down the ravine. The turnaround point is poolside; return as you came.

Even in a rainstorm Potem Falls has a tropical flair.

Miles and Directions

0.0 Start on the narrow, unsigned trail that departs from the parking pullout alongside FR 27.

0.1 Drop around the first of three sweeping switchbacks.

0.4 Reach the base of Potem Falls. Retrace your steps.

0.8 Arrive back at the trailhead.

Lassen

Lassen Volcanic National Park is the fulcrum around which these waterfall trails revolve, with a pair of significant outliers at Burney Falls and along Deer Creek. The region is rural and spectacular. Major towns include Burney, Chester, and Mineral; plan on long, lovely drives through the woods to get from waterfall trailhead to waterfall trailhead.

Burney Falls (hike 18).

18 Burney Falls

An entire rock face spills water at Burney Falls, with the creek pouring over the top and seepage from an underground reservoir seething through cracks in the volcanic matrix.

Height: 129 feet
Beauty rating: ★★★★★
Distance: 1.3-mile loop
Difficulty: Easy
Best season: Year-round
County: Shasta
Trail amenities: Restrooms, visitor center, gift shop and store, picnic areas, campground, fishing, and boating. A fee is charged. The visitor center and store are open in the summer season only. Dogs and bicycles are not allowed on hiking trails in the park.
Land status: McArthur-Burney Falls Memorial State Park
Maps: USGS Burney Falls CA; map in the park brochure (also available on the park website)
Trail contact: McArthur-Burney Falls Memorial State Park, 24898 CA 89, Burney, CA 96013; (530) 335-2777; www.parks.ca.gov

Finding the trailhead: From the junction of CA 89 and CA 299 about 4 miles northeast of the town of Burney, continue north on CA 89 for 5.7 miles to the signed entrance to McArthur-Burney Falls Memorial State Park. Continue on the park road for 0.1 mile, past the entrance station, to the trailhead parking area. GPS: N41 00.789' / W121 39.039'

The Hike

Burney Falls never fails. The massive spill—more than 100 million gallons per day—is perennial: Whatever snow falls in winter feeds both the creek and spring-fed reservoir that fuel Burney, whether it is enough to bury nearby Lassen Peak in 40-foot drifts or the feeble quantities that California may see in a drought season. The falls are the centerpiece of a premier park and recreational area in the north-central part of the state, in the southernmost reaches of the Cascade Range. Lake Britton, opening just downstream, and the recreational opportunities of the Pit River add to the region's allure.

Before setting off on the easy day hike that tours the falls, take in the views from the overlook at the trailhead. There's the proper spill—that of Burney Creek

PIT RIVER FALLS

While in this region of NorCal, you can also check out the Pit River Falls, which can be viewed from an overlook about 15.3 miles east of the junction of CA 89 and CA 299 on CA 299 (west of Fall River Mills; GPS: N40 59.544' / W121 28.464'). With no easily accessible designated trail or trailhead, the most direct route to the falls is a cross-country trek through scrub, and it is not recommended.

Burney Falls is fed by both Burney Creek and an underground reservoir.

tumbling over the 129-foot wall—but the wall also weeps, with streams of white seeping down over basalt and moss to help fill the huge, 22-foot-deep, blue-green pool at the waterfall's base. Interpretive signs describe how the falls have migrated about 1 mile upstream over the course of 3 million years, every drop of water eroding the volcanic base away.

The trail, built by the Civilian Conservation Corps, is a breeze, descending easily via a stone staircase, a switchback, and long traverses to the base of the falls. There are several spots along the route that invite walkers to pause and enjoy the sight, and the base of the initial downhill is likely the best.

Headed downstream, information signs offer advice to the angler, who can find rainbow, brook, and brown trout in the clear waters above and below the falls. The trail courses between the creek and talus slopes to Rainbow Bridge, which offers safe

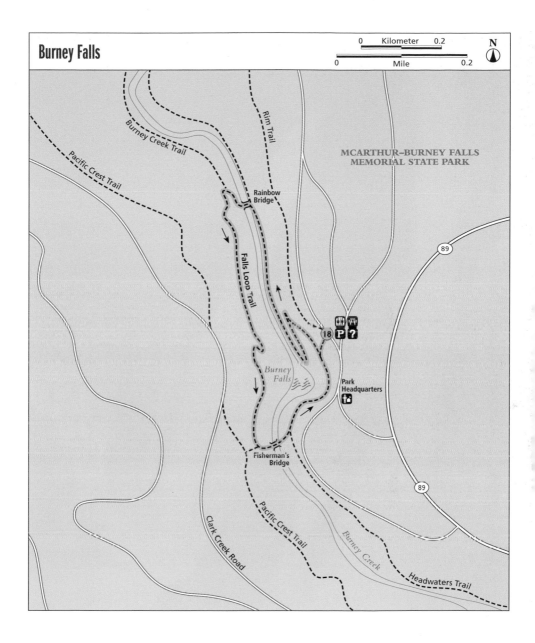

0   Kilometer   0.2

0   Mile   0.2

N

Rim Trail

Burney Creek Trail

Pacific Crest Trail

MCARTHUR–BURNEY FALLS
MEMORIAL STATE PARK

Rainbow
Bridge

Falls Loop Trail

89

18

Burney
Falls

Park
Headquarters

Fisherman's
Bridge

Pacific Crest Trail

Clark Creek Road

89

Burney Creek

Headwaters Trail

passage across the creek. On the far side head left and uphill on an easy traverse, passing through thick woodland toward the top of the falls.

Two switchbacks and easy staircases later, arrive at the top of the falls, and then continue upstream alongside the creek. Cross back to the east side via the Fisherman's Bridge, passing benches bearing plaques inscribed with inspirational quotes, and then loop back downstream. The falls aren't a presence at this point; if you were headed downstream without a scout, you'd have no clue of the spectacular drop

not far ahead. The route, now paved, winds up through open woodland back to the overlook and trailhead.

Miles and Directions

0.0 Start at the trailhead near the overlook on the signed Falls Trail, which descends a rock staircase.

0.3 Round a switchback near the base of the hillside and the base of the falls. Take the signed Falls Loop Trail to the right, headed downstream alongside Burney Creek.

0.6 Reach Rainbow Bridge. Turn left, cross the bridge, and turn left again, heading upstream and uphill on the signed Falls Loop Trail.

0.9 Pass the first switchback, with a falls view. Two more switchbacks and a pair of short staircases lead to the top of the falls.

1.1 Pass the junction with a connector to the Pacific Crest Trail, and then go left across the Fisherman's Bridge. After crossing, stay on the paved path that heads back toward the developed areas of the park. The Headwaters Trail continues upstream.

1.2 Reach the developed parking lots and overlooks surrounding the trailhead. Stay left on the signed gravel path.

1.3 Arrive back at the trailhead.

Options: More than 5 miles of trails are available for exploration in McArthur–Burney Falls Memorial State Park. Continue downstream from the falls on the Burney Creek Trail to reach Lake Britton. The Headwaters Pool is a mile upstream from the falls via the Headwaters Trail.

◀ *The Falls Loop Trail offers a number of views of massive Burney Falls.*

19 Bluff Falls

This seasonal waterfall spills over a broken bluff above CA 89 near Lassen Volcanic National Park's Southwest Entrance.

Height: 40 feet
Beauty rating: ★★★
Distance: About 0.4 mile out and back
Difficulty: Easy, but requires cross-country travel across talus
Best season: Late winter and early spring (during and right after snowmelt)
County: Tehama

Trailhead amenities: A dirt parking pullout
Land status: Lassen National Forest
Maps: USGS Bluff Falls CA
Trail contact: Lassen Volcanic National Forest, Almanor Ranger District, 900 CA 36, PO Box 767, Chester, CA 96020; (530) 258-2141; www.fs.usda.gov/lassen/

Finding the trailhead: From Mineral head west on CA 36 for about 4.3 miles to the junction with CA 89, signed for Lassen Volcanic National Park. Turn left onto CA 89/Lassen National Park Highway and go about 3.6 miles to the parking pullout opposite Bluff Falls. GPS: N40 24.817' / W121 31.915'

Viewing the Falls

Reaching the base of Bluff Falls is more bushwhack than hike. In fact, most visitors stay alongside the roadway, looking upward at the spill. But you can climb closer if you choose, picking a route through willow and across talus to the base of the falls.

The waterfall is ephemeral: You'll need to catch it during or right after snowmelt. A nameless stream tumbles over a section of a broken gray cliff wall that stretches across the western skyline along CA 89, the road leading into Lassen Volcanic National Park. The spill originates in a willow thicket on the bluff top and ends in a talus field, with another willow thicket dropping from the talus to the roadside. That willow presents

Bluff Falls spills down a short cliff face outside Lassen Volcanic National Park.

a formidable barrier to a direct assault on the base of the fall; better to skirt it by following the roadway south from the roadside parking area for 150 yards to where the woods meet the willow. Climb up along the edge of the forest to where you can cut north above the thicket and then scramble uphill. The destination is always in sight; you won't lose your way. Return as you came.

20 Mill Creek Falls

Follow a roller-coaster trail out to Mill Creek Falls, a ribbon that drops over a tiered cliff at the confluence of East Sulphur Creek and Bumpass Creek.

Height: 72 feet
Beauty rating: ★★★★
Distance: 3.8 miles out and back
Difficulty: Moderate
Best season: Late spring and summer
County: Tehama
Trailhead amenities: Restrooms and water at the Southwest Walk-in Campground; restrooms, information, food, and other amenities in the Kohm Yah-mah-nee Visitor Center
Land status: Lassen Volcanic National Park
Maps: USGS Lassen Peak CA; Lassen Volcanic National Park map
Trail contact: Lassen Volcanic National Park, PO Box 100, Mineral, CA 96063; (530) 595-4480; www.nps.gov/lavo

Finding the trailhead: From the park's Southwest Entrance, follow the Lassen National Park Highway less than 0.1 mile to the Southwest Walk-in Campground and Kohm Yah-mah-nee Visitor Center. The signed trailhead is on the east side of the parking lot near the visitor center's amphitheater. GPS: N40 26.231' / W121 31.974'

The Hike

Mill Creek Falls is a narrow whitewater plunge at the confluence of East Sulphur Creek and Bumpass Creek. Spray from the 72-foot fall darkens the cream-and-gold-colored cliff over which it cascades, and the narrow gorge of East Sulphur Creek resonates with its splendid roar. The falls can be enjoyed from a shady overlook on the Mill Creek Falls trail or from a perch on one of the footbridges at the very brink, where the creeks gather in a frothy fury before taking the plunge.

The trail begins by dropping down stairs behind the Kohm Yah-mah-nee Visitor Center and the Southwest Walk-in Campground. Switchback down through big pines and firs to a bridge crossing West Sulphur Creek, which meets with East Sulphur Creek downstream to form Mill Creek. Climb up onto the hillside on the north side of the drainage and traverse southward through the knee-high mule ear that flourishes on the sunny slope.

The trail dips into a dense fir forest as it bends east, then northeast, into the East Sulphur Creek drainage. Like a ride on a roller coaster, the route bucks in and out of gullies as it follows the contours of the East Sulphur ravine, but the trend is generally upward. A gentle roar accompanies you up the canyon, but it can be hard to discern whether what you hear is the falls, the creek, or the wind in the trees. Regardless, it's a sweet, wild sound.

East Sulphur Creek and Bumpass Creek collide to form Mill Creek Falls.

Rock-hop across a side stream at the 1-mile mark, and then begin a relatively stiff climb, followed by a short, rather steep descent, to the overlook of Mill Creek Falls. From this shady viewpoint you can enjoy the waterfall as it rockets down terraces into the shadowy creek bed below, with the rock on either side of the cascade streaked orange with mineral deposits and green with moss. Continue down the trail (stay right at the spur that leads left at a switchback) to the twin footbridges that span the creeks feeding the falls. From the top of the falls, you can look down into the void and feel the rush. There are a few safe places to step off the bridges and settle on a rocky perch to enjoy a picnic before you return as you came.

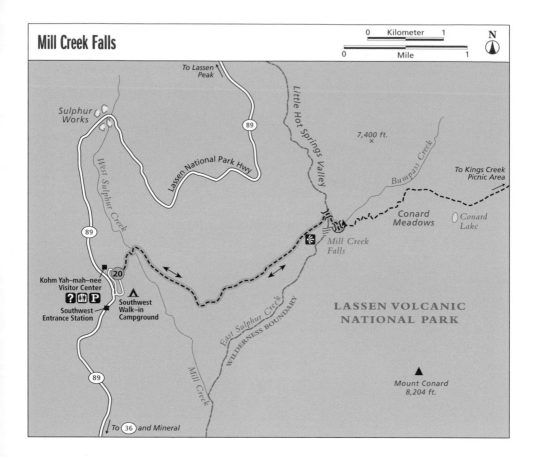

Miles and Directions

0.0 Start at the signed Mill Creek Falls trailhead.

0.3 Cross West Sulphur Creek.

0.5 Enter the East Sulphur Creek drainage.

1.0 Rock-hop across a side stream.

1.75 Arrive at the Mill Creek Falls overlook.

1.9 Descend to the footbridges that span the top of the spill. Retrace your steps from here.

3.8 Arrive back at the trailhead.

Option: The trail continues on the other side of the bridges that span the top of the falls, climbing steeply to Conard Meadow and then on to Crumbaugh Lake, Cold Boiling Lake, and the Kings Creek Picnic Area trailhead.

21 Kings Creek Falls

After tumbling down a steepening gorge, Kings Creek streaks over a vertical cliff and plummets into a hidden creek bed.

Height: 70 feet
Beauty rating: ★★★★★
Distance: 3.0 miles out and back
Difficulty: Moderate
Best season: Late spring and early summer
County: Shasta
Trailhead amenities: Parking pullouts on either side of the Lassen National Park Highway; information signboards and trash cans

Land status: Lassen Volcanic National Park
Maps: USGS Reading Peak CA; Lassen Volcanic National Park map
Trail contact: Lassen Volcanic National Park, PO Box 100, Mineral, CA 96063; (530) 595-4480; www.nps.gov/lavo

Finding the trailhead: The Kings Creek Falls trailhead is located on the Lassen National Park Highway/CA 89, about 15.5 miles from the Manzanita Lake entrance station and 12.5 miles from the Southwest Entrance Station. It is on the southeast side of the road. GPS: N40 27.635' / W121 27.564'

The Hike

The premier waterfall in a spectacular, often overlooked national park, Kings Creek Falls is a cooling interlude amid a fury of volcanism. Lassen Peak looms overhead and out of sight, but on the narrow ledge above the waterfall, with a thin wire railing guarding the daring vantage point, it's water, not fire, that invigorates the senses.

A hike to the fall begins with a pleasant meander along the edge of the Lower Meadow, with a gentler incarnation of Kings Creek winding through it. A brief hitch through red firs leads to a trail fork near the east edge of the meadow. Go left (northeast) on the signed trail to Kings Creek Falls; the right (southeast) trail leads to Sifford Lake. The horse trail departs from the cascade overlook trail at the next sign, which states that the cascade view is 0.1 mile distant. Stick to the horse trail, as the trail that parallels the Kings Creek cascades has been closed due to hazardous hiking conditions in recent hiking seasons. Check with park rangers about the trail's status at the time of your visit.

The horse trail climbs to an open area offering views of the Kings Creek drainage and down toward Warner Valley, and then begins a fairly steep, rocky, switchbacking descent. How horses negotiate this stretch is a mystery; it's difficult for an able-bodied human. At the base of the descent, navigate a haphazard walkway of mud-covered boards and rocks through a marshy area before the horse trail meets the base of the cascade trail.

Kings Creek Falls is the premier waterfall in Lassen Volcanic National Park.

Turn left onto the well-worn path leading to the falls. Stay left again at a log bridge spanning the relatively calm creek to the right (south), where a signed trail leads up to Bench Lake, Sifford Lake, and points beyond.

The creek drops over the falls about 100 yards downstream from the bridge. The trail forks before the falls, with the right (lower and streamside) path leading to the overlook. A single cable guards the steep drop; from this perch you can safely observe the splintered white veil spun by the 70-foot drop of Kings Creek. From the overlook you can try to look down to the base of the falls and the creek bed below—but that's a vertigo-inducing challenge. After you've swallowed your awe and taken your photographs, return as you came.

Kings Creek Falls

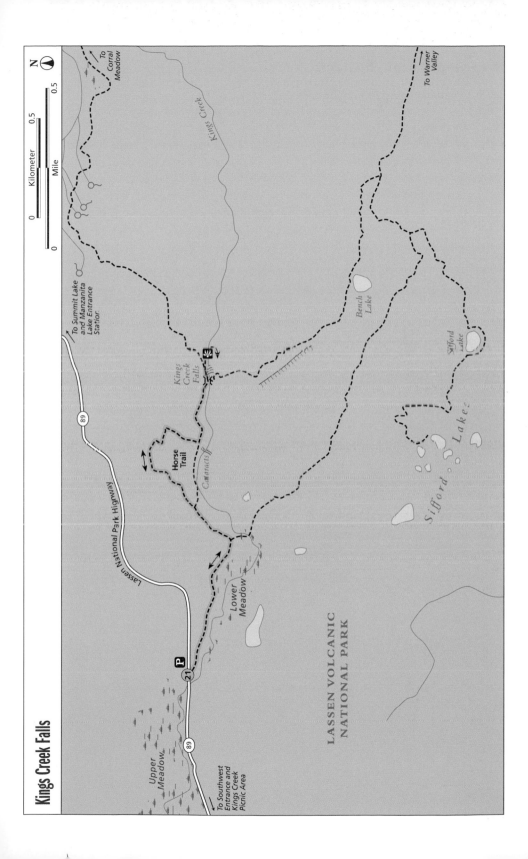

N

Kilometer
0   0.5

Mile
0   0.5

To Corral Meadow

Kings Creek

To Summit Lake
and Manzanita
Lake Entrance
Station

Kings Creek Falls

Bench Lake

Sifford Lake

Sifford Lakes

To Warner Valley

89

Lassen National Park Highway

Horse Trail

Cataracts

Lower Meadow

P
21

89

Upper Meadow

To Southwest
Entrance and
Kings Creek
Picnic Area

LASSEN VOLCANIC NATIONAL PARK

Miles and Directions

0.0   Start at the Kings Creek Falls trailhead.

0.5   Reach the trail intersection in the Lower Meadow and go left on the signed path for Kings Creek Falls.

0.7   At the junction of the closed Kings Creek cascade trail, the spur to the cascade view, and the horse trail, go left on the horse trail.

1.25 The horse trail meets the Kings Creek Falls trail at the base of the cascade trail. Go left, tracing the creek downstream.

1.4   Pass the signed trail to Sifford and Bench Lakes. Stay left toward Kings Creek Falls.

1.5   Reach the falls overlook. Take in the spill; then retrace your steps.

3.0   Arrive back at the trailhead.

Option: If trail conditions permit (check with park rangers, and respect closure signs if they are present), you can follow the path alongside the cascades to reach the falls. This trims about 0.2 mile one-way off the journey, but does not negate any of the challenge. Rock stairs lead down a steep pitch alongside the cataract, which becomes more vigorous as it drops. Watch your step. Below the cataracts the noise subsides, the pitch subsides, and the entertainment subsides as well, as forest envelops the trail. The cascade trail hitches up with the bottom of the horse trail at 1.25 miles; head downhill from the junction to Kings Creek Falls.

You can also use Kings Creek Falls as the first stop on longer day hikes in Lassen Volcanic National Park, including a fine loop that encompasses Sifford Lake or a shuttle hike that ends at Summit Lake.

22 Hat Creek Falls

A series of cascades capped by a short, tiered fall lies along the trail to Paradise Meadow.

Height: 20 feet, with cascades flowing below
Beauty rating: ★★★★
Distance: 3.2 miles out and back to Paradise Meadow
Difficulty: Moderate; the route is steep.
Best season: Late spring and early summer
County: Shasta
Trailhead amenities: None. The nearest restrooms are located 0.5 mile north on the

Lassen National Park Highway at the Devastated Area Interpretive Trailhead.
Land status: Lassen Volcanic National Park
Maps: USGS West Prospect Peak CA and Reading Peak CA
Trail contact: Lassen Volcanic National Park, PO Box 100, Mineral, CA 96063; (530) 595-4480; www.nps.gov/lavo

Finding the trailhead: From the Manzanita Lake entrance station, follow the Lassen National Park Highway/CA 89 for 9 miles to the parking area, which is on the left (north) side of the highway. The trailhead is 19 miles from the Southwest Entrance Station via the Lassen National Park highway. GPS: N40 30.563' / W121 27.904'

The Hike

Most people who set off on the trail from Hat Lake are bound for Paradise Meadow, which boasts both a spectacular setting and a lush wildflower display in the spring. But along the way hikers are treated to a cataract and short waterfall that, in high season, are as delightful as the meadow. Because the cataracts and waterfall are so close to the meadow, the grassland is included as the final destination.

The hike begins across the park road from the parking area. The path is wide and flat to begin with, nicely shaded, with Lassen Peak looming above and Hat Creek rollicking in its bed to the right (west). The site of Hat Lake also lies to the right of the trail; the lake is small and slowly filling with meadow grasses, but still a tempting roadside attraction.

The route begins to climb almost immediately, passing through dips that may hold water in early season and bordered with a thick, unruly hedge of willow, mule ear, and other riparian plants. Yellow dots on the trees denote the route.

At about the 0.5-mile mark, climb into a narrowing ravine that cradles a tributary of the West Fork Hat Creek. Stream crossings are made via small footbridges until the path settles in on the south side of the first cataract.

Cross another tributary stream, then the trail steepens abruptly, with the cataract growing larger and louder as the pitch of the path increases. The trees thin and the walls of the ravine open as the stream tumbles over the short, frothy falls. Descend from the marked route to the streamside via a use trail, which leads almost to the base of the waterfall.

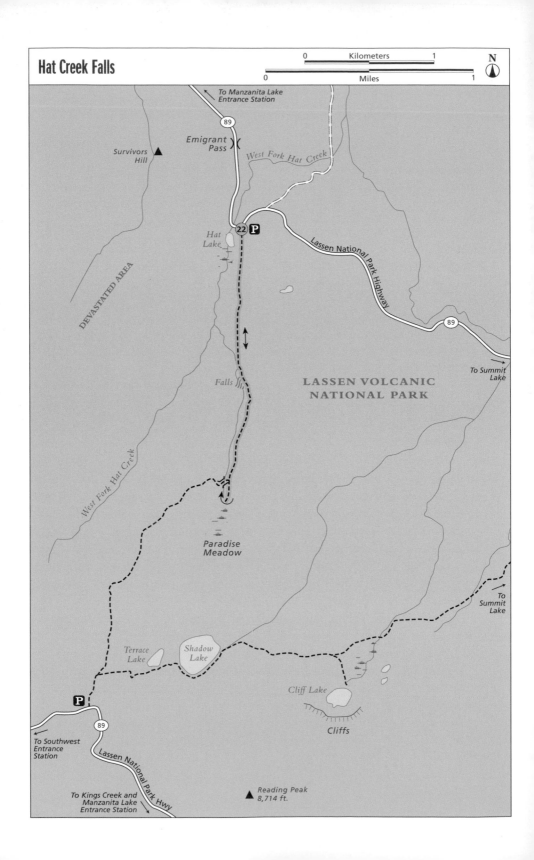

Hat Creek Falls

0 Kilometers 1
0 Miles 1

N

To Manzanita Lake
Entrance Station

89

Emigrant
Pass

West Fork Hat Creek

Survivors
Hill

Hat
Lake

22 P

Lassen National Park Highway

DEVASTATED AREA

89

Falls

LASSEN VOLCANIC
NATIONAL PARK

To Summit
Lake

West Fork Hat Creek

Paradise
Meadow

To
Summit
Lake

Terrace
Lake

Shadow
Lake

Cliff Lake

P

89

To Southwest
Entrance
Station

Lassen National Park Hwy

Cliffs

To Kings Creek and
Manzanita Lake
Entrance Station

Reading Peak
8,714 ft.

A small waterfall tumbles down a tributary of Hat Creek below Paradise Meadow.

Above the fall, thankfully, the angle of the climb becomes almost flat. Pass the trail leading up to Terrace Lake, staying left (straight) toward Paradise Meadow. Pass through a stand of firs and … the meadow opens before you, cupped in a spectacular bowl rimmed by volcanic cliffs. Paintbrush, clover, penstemon, lupine, and gentian add depth to the grasses that stretch across the bowl. The path trickles to an end; step carefully, for the ground is uneven beneath its green carpet. The stream loses its steam as it meanders through the grasses, becoming a thick-banked snake that can be straddled or waded through easily. At the head of the meadow, talus lines the base of the shadowy cliff that forms the southern horizon. Don't forget the bug juice! When you wish, return as you came.

Miles and Directions

0.0 Start at the Hat Creek trailhead.

1.0 Reach the cataracts, with the short falls not far above.

1.5 At the junction with the trail leading up to Terrace Lake, stay left (straight) on the path to Paradise Meadow.

1.6 Reach Paradise Meadow. Take a break, and then retrace your steps.

3.2 Arrive back at the trailhead.

23 Battle Creek Falls

A steep scramble drops to a half moon of short falls that drop into a small pool in South Fork Battle Creek.

Height: 16 feet
Beauty rating: ★★★
Distance: 0.2 mile out and back
Difficulty: Easy
Best season: Spring and summer
County: Tehama
Trailhead amenities: None. Battle Creek Campground, with restrooms, water, and camping facilities, is across CA 36. Mineral, with all amenities, is just east of the CA 36/Viola-Mineral Road junction.
Land status: Lassen National Forest
Maps: USGS Mineral CA
Trail contact: Lassen National Forest, Almanor Ranger District, 900 CA 36, PO Box 767, Chester, CA 96020; (530) 258-2141; www.fs .usda.gov/lassen/

Finding the trailhead: From Mineral head west on CA 36 for about 1.6 miles to the junction with the Viola-Mineral Road. Turn right onto the Viola-Mineral Road, and then immediately left onto FR 104A. Follow FR 104A for 0.7 mile to a parking pullout on the left. The road is negotiable by passenger cars, but go slowly, as it is pocked with potholes, drainage ditches, and speed bumps. Beyond the unmarked pullout the road passes through an open area and, after 0.2 mile, is barred by a gate. GPS: N40 21.290' / W121 38.293'

Viewing the Falls

Spilling over a bouldery ledge nearly two stories high, Battle Creek Falls fills a small pool in the South Fork Battle Creek near the Battle Creek Campground. The waterfall can be seen from the neighboring forest road: It flows year-round, splitting into several channels as water levels drop later in summer and autumn. The pool and creek are a cool destination for campers and locals on hot summer days.

South Fork Battle Creek splits into several falls above an inviting pool.

To reach the falls from the roadside parking area, follow the easiest of several steep use trails down the hillside a tenth of a mile or less to the creek. An abandoned powerhouse disintegrates on the near shore. Just upstream from the parking pullout, an angler's trail is marked with hand-painted yellow signs warning users to "pack it in and pack it out" and to clean their fish downstream.

24 Upper Deer Creek Falls

An inviting apron of volcanic rock surrounds Deer Creek's upper falls.

Height: 18 feet
Beauty rating: ★★★★
Distance: 0.1 mile out and back
Difficulty: Easy
Best season: Spring and summer
County: Tehama
Trailhead amenities: None. Potato Patch Campground, with restrooms, water, and camping facilities, is about 1.5 miles farther southeast on CA 36.

Land status: Lassen National Forest
Maps: USGS Onion Butte CA
Trail contact: Lassen National Forest, Almanor Ranger District, 900 CA 36, PO Box 767, Chester, CA 96020; (530) 258-2141; www.fs.usda.gov/lassen/

Finding the trailhead: From the junction of CA 36 and CA 32, about 14 miles west of Chester and about 16 miles east of Mineral, head southeast on CA 32. Follow the scenic highway for about 10.8 miles to a signed pullout on the east (left) side of the road. GPS: N40 12.107' / W121 30.837'

Viewing the Falls

Deer Creek's upper falls aren't more than a 5-minute walk from CA 32, but the cascade, the creek that pools above and below, and the surrounding spread of sun-warmed rock invite a long stay. The fall itself is a punchbowl: As described on the trailhead signboard, the creek is funneled into a narrow chute and then plunges into the deep pool below. Deer Creek is a year-round stream, so even with some of the flow diverted into the adjacent fish ladder, the falls are always noisy and vigorous.

The trail is short, leading down from the edge of the roadway for about 25 yards to a Y-junction. Go left onto the aprons of volcanic rock that surround the creek and fall; you can walk right up to the brink of the drop and look down into the bowl. Head right to an overlook with a picture-perfect view of the fall. Either stop, bordered by forest but open to the sun, with access to the creek, its fishing opportunities, and its swimming holes, is an excellent choice for a picnic lunch or an afternoon's rest. Retrace your steps to the parking area.

Deer Creek begins its punchbowl plunge. ▶

25 Lower Deer Creek Falls

A secluded trail leads down alongside Deer Creek to tiered falls funneled through a narrowing and boulder-strewn channel.

Height: A series of 10- to 30-foot drops
Beauty rating: ★★★★
Distance: 4.0 miles out and back
Difficulty: Moderate due only to length
Best season: Spring
County: Tehama
Trailhead amenities: None

Land status: Lassen National Forest
Maps: USGS Onion Butte CA
Trail contact: Lassen National Forest, Almanor Ranger District, 900 CA 36, PO Box 767, Chester, CA 96020; (530) 258-2141; www.fs.usda.gov/lassen/

Finding the trailhead: From Chester go 12.3 miles west on CA 36 to the junction with CA 32 (to Chico). Go left (south) onto CA 32 and go 12.2 miles to a metal truss bridge crossing Deer Creek. There is limited parking in a paved pullout with an information signboard alongside the highway on the east side. The trailhead is on the west side; there's a small sign near the northern bridge abutment. GPS: N40 10.411' / W121 33.319'

The Hike

Pick your day just right, and you may find yourself all alone on the out-of-the-way trail that follows Deer Creek downstream to its lower falls. Cupped in a rocky bend on the year-round stream, and accessible only by scrambling down a steep hillside, the falls present an elusive destination, though one that's been admired by many, as the memorial bench tucked in the woods above attests. The creek, its falls, and its steep-walled canyon offer solace and solitude in spades.

A short staircase leads up from the highway bridge spanning Deer Creek, passing an information signboard describing the salmon and steelhead that spawn in the stream. The creek, like many in Lassen country, is popular with anglers. Head down the dirt track into a mingled forest of oak woodland and riparian plants, manzanita tangling with maple. Moss, which puffs up and grows green when wet, coats the surfaces of the volcanic rocks that occasionally loom over the path. Road noise occasionally drifts down the canyon, but mostly what you'll hear is the creek rolling along its bed.

A series of side streams intersects the trail; these are mostly dry by late season but can require rock-hopping or wading after rains. A couple of the side streams flow year-round. The route is mostly shaded, and the rock formations, whether right alongside the trail or visible on the steep walls of the canyon, are intriguing.

Big Leaf Pool, with a fire pit and plenty of access to the creekside, is a little more than halfway along the route. Below the pool the creek widens and deepens, and then

Lower Deer Creek dives into a pool amid dark volcanic rock.

spills as a brief cataract into yet another deep, green pool. Beyond, the trail continues to roller-coaster through the woodland, never steep but mostly descending.

Eventually the path breaks out of the woods into a narrow curve of the canyon, with the start of the falls tumbling through slate-gray rocks below. The walking gets more serious at this point, with the singletrack climbing up into and through a gully before ducking back under the canopy. Views of the falls are plentiful along this final stretch, which leads to a bench commemorating the preservation of the stream and falls by the Western Rivers Conservancy in 2012. This is the turnaround point, though you can scramble down the steep hillside, flows permitting, to the streamside, where a pebbly beach may be exposed and you can get closer views of the falls and the neighboring fish ladder/tunnel. Just beware the poison oak.

After your explorations retrace your steps to the trailhead.

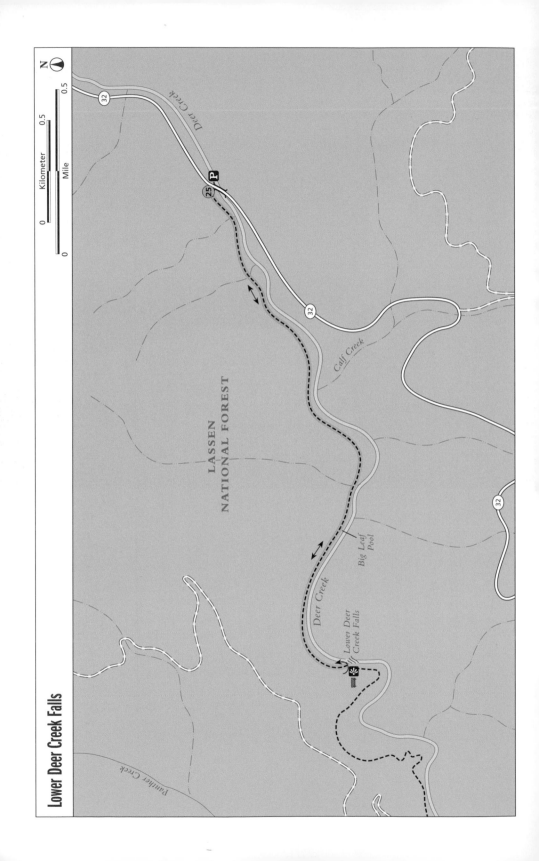

Lower Deer Creek Falls

Big Leaf Pool lies upstream of Lower Deer Creek Falls.

Miles and Directions

0.0 Start by crossing the highway to the bridge abutment. The trail and trailhead sign may be obscured by brush. Climb a short staircase to an information signboard and go left, into the woods.

0.3 Cross the fourth in a series of side streams.

0.5 Pass an alcove hollowed in a huge boulder on the right.

1.1 Cross a more substantial side stream.

1.3 Pass the fire pit and lovely stand of maples at Big Leaf Pool.

1.8 Reach an open section of trail that overlooks the start of the falls.

2.0 Reach the turnaround point at the commemorative bench overlooking the falls. Retrace your steps from here.

4.0 Arrive back at the trailhead.

Oroville

The forks of the Feather River, flowing down out of the northern Sierra Nevada into the Great Valley, are fed by tributaries that boast some of the prettiest waterfalls in the state. Chico and Oroville, neighbors on the flatlands, offer all the amenities, while just upstream to the east, in the foothills, things get considerably wilder. CA 70 links Oroville to Quincy via the North Fork Feather River, and the Oroville-Quincy Highway/CA 162 links the two towns via a scenic drive around Lake Oroville, the hub of recreation in the area.

Sunset in the North Table Mountain Ecological Reserve (hike 27).

26 Feather Falls

Fine trails lead down to a spectacular overlook of Feather Falls and the Middle Fork Feather River canyon.

Height: 640 feet
Beauty rating: ★★★★★
Distance: 8.8-mile lollipop and spur
Difficulty: Strenuous
Best season: Winter and spring
County: Plumas
Trailhead amenities: Restrooms, trash cans, campsites, and information signboard
Land status: Plumas National Forest

Maps: USGS Forbestown CA and Brush Creek CA; US Forest Service map and brochure available online at www.fs.usda.gov/Internet/FSE_DOCUMENTS/fsm9_034836.pdf
Trail contact: Plumas National Forest, Feather River Ranger District, 875 Mitchell Ave., Oroville, CA 95965; (530) 534-6500; www.fs.usda.gov/plumas/

Finding the trailhead: From CA 70 in Oroville, take the Oro-Quincy Highway/CA 162 exit and head west for 6.2 miles to Forbestown Road. Turn right onto Forbestown Road and go 6 miles to Lumpkin Road (there are signs at the junctions for Feather Falls). Turn left onto Lumpkin Road and go 10.7 miles to the signed Feather Falls Road/FR 21N35Y. Turn left and follow the paved access road for 1.6 miles to the large paved parking lot. GPS: N39 36.858' / W121 16.001'

The Hike

This is a great trail to a great waterfall. It's as simple and as perfect as that. The Feather Falls National Scenic Trail is straightforward, nicely maintained, and eminently pleasant, though it can be a chore in hot weather. It passes through a forest of mixed evergreens—oaks, pines, firs, and the occasional incense cedar and madrone—to an overlook on a rock promontory: Look one direction onto Feather Falls, a mighty horsetail plunging more than 600 feet down a vertical rock face, and then swing around and gaze in the other direction down the Middle Fork Feather River canyon, steep-walled, remote, and ringing with the thunder of the river and falls.

Two trails lead to the overlook. The Lower Trail, at 3.5 miles, is steeper and shorter; the Upper Trail, at 4.5 miles, is longer but perfectly graded, taking the edge off an elevation change of just more than 1,200 feet. This route makes a loop of both trails, with short sticks at both ends where the trails unite, but many hikers travel out and back on the Upper Trail, adding a gentle mile to the round-trip distance.

Begin by heading down the signed path to the junction. To make the loop, go left on the signed Lower Trail where the trail forks. Pass several benches as you begin the descent, as well as an interpretive side trail to a rock outcropping beneath an oak tree. The circular depressions in the rock are bedrock mortars used by the Maidu Indians to prepare acorns for consumption.

An overlook on a rock promontory offers stellar views of Feather Falls.

The steepening trail rounds a pair of switchbacks as it nears Frey Creek, crossing the creek via a bridge. A bench and interpretive sign are also alongside the chattering waterway. Less than a mile beyond the creek Bald Rock Dome comes into view, with an interpretive sign at an overlook explaining its significance for the Maidu.

Drop through a couple of ravines fed by seasonal streams and clotted with riparian vegetation, and then begin the climb to the trail junction. Your knees may have noticed the grade on the downhill; your lungs will notice it on this stretch.

At the bench at the junction of the Lower Trail, the Upper Trail, and the main trail to the overlook (unsigned in 2015), stay left on the ascending trail. The uphill pitch ends at a viewpoint looking down into the Middle Fork Feather River canyon, and a metal fence/rail protects the exposed side of the path. The footing is rough as you round the mountainside and descend to the overlook. At the switchback just above the overlook, the unsigned trail to the swimming holes upstream of the waterfall breaks right (use extreme caution if you head to the swimming holes, as there are

Feather Falls

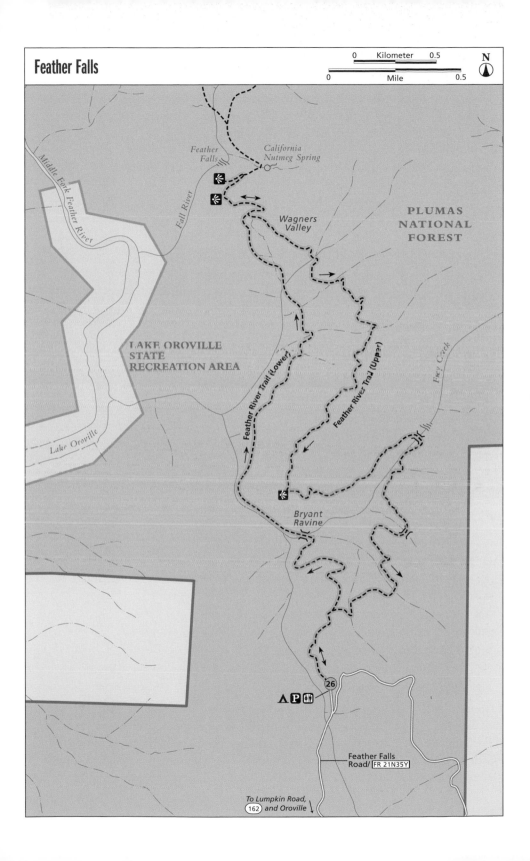

- Feather Falls
- California Nutmeg Spring
- Middle Fork Feather River
- Fall River
- Wagners Valley
- PLUMAS NATIONAL FOREST
- Fwy Creek
- LAKE OROVILLE STATE RECREATION AREA
- Lake Oroville
- Feather River Trail (Lower)
- Feather River Trail (Upper)
- Bryant Ravine
- 26
- Feather Falls Road/ FR 21N35Y
- To Lumpkin Road, 162 and Oroville

Kilometer 0 0.5

Mile 0 0.5

N

slippery rocks and other hazards). Stay left on the signed overlook trail and wind down to trail's end on the promontory.

Feather Falls, the sixth highest in the continental United States, is one of the main attractions in the 15,000-acre scenic area. The waterfall is actually on Fall River, which flows into the Middle Fork Feather River just downstream from the plunge, and within view of the overlook. The waterfall is Yosemite-impressive, sprawling across the reddish-blond rock face and perpetually powered by the river's flow. Take it in; then retrace your steps to the junction at the bench.

To close the loop—and take the easy way up—turn left at the junction onto the Upper Trail. The route climbs nearly imperceptibly at first, though moderately steeper pitches spice up the climb at intervals. The trail winds in and out of innumerable gullies, some with seasonal streams, most just curves in the mountainside. The crossing of Frey Creek is a highlight, with a 30-foot slide fall on the uphill side, an interpretive sign, and a bench for enjoying the scene. More curves and more bridges lie between the creek and the junction with the Lower Trail above. The junction is at 8.5 miles; retrace your steps from here to the trailhead.

Miles and Directions

0.0 Start by heading past the information signboard on the trail.

0.3 At the junction go left onto the Lower Trail.

0.5 Pass the side trail to the metates.

1.0 Round the first switchback.

1.3 Cross the bridge at Frey Creek.

1.7 Pass the Bald Rock Dome viewpoint.

2.6 Begin to climb.

3.3 The Upper and Lower Trails meet at a junction with a bench. Stay left and uphill on the merged trail.

3.7 At the switchback stay left on the signed trail to the overlook. The right path leads behind the falls to swimming holes.

3.8 Arrive at the overlook. Retrace your steps to the junction of the Upper and Lower Trails.

4.3 At the junction go left on the Upper Trail.

6.3 Pass another interpretive Bald Rock Dome overlook.

7.0 Reach Frey Creek, with a bridge, bench, interpretive sign, and slide waterfall.

7.5 Cross another bridge spanning a seasonal stream.

8.5 Close the loop at the junction with the Lower Trail. Stay left on the main path to the trailhead.

8.8 Arrive back at the trailhead.

Option: If you've got the time and the weather is warm, extend your walk by a half mile or so to swimming holes upstream of the waterfall along the Fall River. The trail departs to the right at the first switchback on the descent to the overlook, curls through a ravine to the top of the falls, and heads upriver to the swimming holes. Be sure to stay well upstream of the top of the falls, which are fenced off to prevent accidents.

27 North Table Mountain Waterfalls

Walk across the top of a table mountain to waterfalls that cut through broken basalt.

Height: 164 feet (Coal Canyon Falls)
Beauty rating: ★★★★
Distance: Variable
Difficulty: Moderate to strenuous, depending on route
Best season: Winter and early spring
County: Butte
Trailhead amenities: Information signboard. All routes are cross-country; please respect property boundaries. Dogs must be leashed.
Land status: North Table Mountain Ecological Reserve

Maps: USGS Oroville CA; Chico Hiking Association map at www.chicohiking.org/ Individual-Hike-Pages/Valley-and-Foothill/ Many-Waterfalls.htm
Trail contact: California Department of Fish and Wildlife; (916) 358-2869; www.wildlife.ca.gov/ regions/2/wildflower-tours. Please use the website as the office is staffed part-time only.
Other: Be sure to wear sturdy walking shoes or hiking boots. The basalt has a tendency to shred less hardy footwear, such as sneakers.

Finding the trailhead: From CA 70 in Oroville heading south, take the Nelson Avenue/Grand Avenue exit (exit 48). Go east on Nelson Avenue for 0.7 mile to Table Mountain Boulevard. Cross Table Mountain Boulevard onto Cherokee Road, and follow Cherokee Road northeast for 6.2 miles to the North Table Mountain Ecological Reserve parking area and trailhead on the left. From CA 70 heading north, take exit 48 and go east on Grand Avenue for about 1 mile. Turn left onto Table Mountain Boulvard and go about a tenth of a mile to Cherokee Road. Turn right onto Cherokee Road and proceed to the trailhead. GPS: N39 35.750' / W121 32.499'

Viewing the Falls

The basalt foundation of North Table Mountain Ecological Reserve gives rise to a remarkable landscape, one that boasts profuse springtime wildflower blooms, vernal pools supporting unique plant species, and seasonal waterfalls that tumble down broken-rock ravines. A number of waterfalls flow on the reserve property when conditions are right. But trails on the reserve are presently cross-country, at least until a planned accessible trail and directional signboards are in place.

Regardless of which waterfalls are flowing or accessible, a winter's walk on top of North Table Mountain is breathtaking. The Central Valley opens below, with the shadowy coast ranges defining the western horizon. To the south the rugged Sutter Buttes punch the sky. If fog or haze has settled onto the valley floor, a carpet of white streaks across the blues and greens and browns of the viewscape. The reserve is known for its wildflower blooms, which begin as early as February and typically peak in April, and feature foothills poppy, Indian paintbrush, bitterroot, meadowfoam, sky lupine, and monkeyflower, among others. Waterfalls may be the destination, but getting there is sublime.

As of 2015, no formal, marked trail leads to any of the falls, though hikers who've gone before have beaten paths across the rangeland to waterfalls shown on the Chico Hiking Association map. Avoid informal paths, as they may cross private land and should not be used. Reserve boundaries are shown on the map for reference.

The informal trails that presently exist on the reserve cross both grasslands and the dark, exposed, fractured basalt that forms North Table Mountain's foundation. This rough surface can be strenuous to traverse even when there are no hills to climb or descend. Though rainfall is the primary water source for all the falls on the property, water also pools in the fractured rock that forms the mountain's underpinning, providing an additional source.

This is also cattle country: Whether lowing in the distance or having left sign of their passage in the form of pies, cows are as much a part of the experience as the vistas. The bovines are gentle, but hikers should maintain a distance of at least 300 feet. Another resident of the preserve, the California newt, can be seen (but never touched or moved; see the website for regulations) in the winter and spring. Songbirds, raptors, and other wildlife are also reserve residents or visitors.

Options: Hikers can link up to 10 waterfalls, depending on rainfall, by traveling cross-country. But hikes of a variety of distances are possible. An out-and-back walk from the parking lot to an overlook of Phantom Falls in Basalt Canyon is about 3 miles round-trip. Visit http://chicohiking.org and check out the "Valley & Foothills Hikes" page for details.

◀ *The setting sun illuminates the stream filling a shadowy pool on the North Table Mountain Ecological Reserve.*

28 Chambers Creek Falls

An unrelenting climb leads high above the North Fork Feather River to a bridge spanning the falls on Chambers Creek.

Height: About 200 feet
Beauty rating: ★★★★
Distance: 4.0 miles out and back
Difficulty: Strenuous
Best season: Winter and spring
County: Plumas
Trailhead amenities: Information signboard

Land status: Plumas National Forest
Maps: USGS Storrie CA
Trail contact: Plumas National Forest, Mount Hough Ranger District, 39696 CA 70, Quincy, CA 95971; (530) 283-0555; www.fs.usda .gov/plumas/

Finding the trailhead: From Oroville follow CA 70 about 40 miles east toward Quincy. The signed trailhead is on the left (north) side of the highway about 4 miles beyond the Rock Creek powerhouses, 2.8 miles beyond Storrie, and 1.3 miles beyond a bridge that swings the highway to the north side of the North Fork Feather River. GPS: N39 57.010' / W121 18.124'

The Hike

The distance isn't great, but grade and exposure combine to make the hike to Chambers Creek Falls a lung- and leg-burner. The views are wonderful along the traversing lower reaches of the trail, ranging up and down the forested North Fork Feather River canyon. The upper mile of the trail passes through forest still recovering from the Storrie Fire, which burned more than 52,000 acres in the Lassen and Plumas National Forests in 2000.

You'll gain more than 1,600 feet climbing from the trailhead to the falls, so set a comfortable pace and settle in. The only flat spot you'll encounter before reaching the bridge at the falls is the creek crossing just 0.1 mile above the parking area. After that the incline is unbroken.

The Feather River has been repeatedly harnessed to generate electricity, as the series of powerhouses along CA 70 attest. For a short stretch along the lower reaches of the trail, the river's power is contained both in its bed and in high-voltage lines strung between massive towers near the trail, which crackle and hum loudly enough to be heard over river, wind, and traffic. Climbing above the transmission lines, the long, sloping traverse boasts an amazing spring wildflower display, rainfall and snowmelt permitting.

Several switchbacks lead up into the Chambers Creek drainage and into the recovering forest, where pines offer some shade. Ferns and wildflowers bloom in the understory in season. The trail still traverses relentlessly upward, but the footing is softer, cushioned by pine needles.

Pass a spring and curl through a ravine where, water permitting, a short cascade tumbles below the footpath. Climb around the shoulder of the mountain, and the

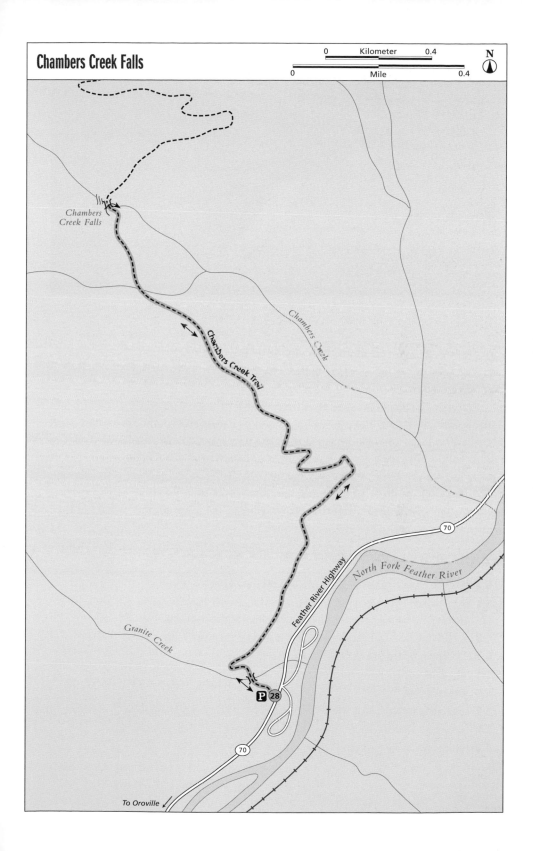

Chambers Creek Falls

Chambers
Creek Falls

Chambers Creek Trail

Chambers Creek

70

Feather River Highway

North Fork Feather River

Granite Creek

P 28

70

To Oroville

0   Kilometer   0.4
0   Mile   0.4

N

The bridge spanning Chambers Creek offers views of the falls both upstream and down.

roar of Chambers Creek and its waterfall come into earshot. A short descent leads to the bridge spanning the creek, which offers views both up onto the falls above and down onto the falls below.

Chambers Creek Falls consists of tiered drops in a steep ravine. Trees and brush make it difficult to view the waterfall in its entirety: You can spy an uppermost plume, perhaps 30 feet high, which drops out of sight and reappears below in another 30-foot plume, and then another about 15 feet high, and another about 20 feet … and below the bridge the creek is funneled down a 30-foot drop. On the far side of the bridge, a side trail drops onto a rock apron beside the lower spill, warming in the fleeting sun that grazes the bottom of the ravine in winter. Take a rest on the rocks, and then return as you came.

Miles and Directions

0.0 Start by climbing past the gate and heading up the rocky roadway.

0.1 An unsigned but obvious footpath breaks right. Leave the roadway for the trail, which crosses a creek via rock-hopping and a makeshift metal footbridge.

0.2 Regain the roadway, heading right and uphill under the power lines.

0.7 Round the first of several switchbacks.

1.1 Enter the woods.

1.6 Pass a spring.

1.7 Cross a seasonal stream; when there's water, a small fall lies below the trail.

2.0 Drop down onto the bridge spanning Chambers Creek Falls. Retrace your steps.

4.0 Arrive back at the trailhead.

Option: In the event the climb to the falls wasn't workout enough, the trail continues up onto Chambers Peak. The one-way distance to trail's end is 4.2 miles.

Graeagle and the Lakes District

The wonders of the northern Sierra Nevada, which are mellower and greener than the High Sierra to the south, include the sprawling Lakes District and the Sierra Buttes. Watersheds originating in these forested highlands feed the powerful Yuba and Feather Rivers, which in turn flow into the mighty Sacramento. Graeagle, a quaint resort community, is the biggest draw in this part of the high country, with historic Sierra City and Downieville downslope to the west along scenic CA 49.

Webber Falls (hike 33).

29 Little Jamison Falls

Hike through the remnants of a historic mine to a secluded waterfall and lake.

Height: About 45 feet
Beauty rating: ★★★★
Distance: 3.0 miles out and back
Difficulty: Moderate
Best season: Late spring (snow permitting) and early summer
County: Plumas
Trailhead amenities: Information signboard with map; picnic sites

Land status: Plumas National Forest
Maps: USGS Gold Lake CA; Plumas-Eureka State Park map available at the visitor center and online
Trail contact: Plumas-Eureka State Park, 310 Johnsville Rd., Blairsden, CA 96103; (530) 836-2380; www.parks.ca.gov. Plumas-Eureka State Park Association, PO Box 1148, Graeagle, CA 96103; www.plumas-eureka.org

Finding the trailhead: From Graeagle (located about 43 miles north of Truckee on CA 89), go left (west) on CR A14 for about 4.5 miles to a left turn onto the gravel road signed for the Jamison Creek/Mine day-use area. Travel the gravel road for 1.2 miles to the parking area near the mine buildings (stay left at the Camp Lisa turn). GPS: N39 44.532' / W120 42.085'

The Hike

History meets the mountain on the trail to Little Jamison Falls. An old service road links the remnants of a gold rush–era mining complex to a relatively remote wildland, climbing to a lovely waterfall and a peaceful lake in the shadow of Mount Washington.

The trail begins by winding through the remnants of the Jamison Mine complex, curling around a tin-walled shack and overlooking foundations and pits (leave no trace, and take no souvenirs). After a brief, easy, traversing ascent above the mine complex, the route becomes more challenging, climbing stone steps, some of them with substantial, thigh-building rises. The steps come in flights of three to six (or so) and negotiate a pair of switchbacks. The elevation gain isn't extreme, but the stairs may present a challenge both on the way up (for the lungs) and on the way down (for the knees).

The route breaks out of the woods near the 1-mile mark, with views opening up to the Jamison Creek valley. Eureka Peak, where gold was discovered back in the mid-1800s, rises across the valley to the north.

At the junction with the trail to Smith Lake, stay right on the signed trail to Grass Lake. The route flattens, crosses a seasonal stream, and passes a park boundary sign before reaching the signed junction with the spur trail to Little Jamison Falls. A short hop over open terrain drops to the falls overlook, where several evergreens shade a rock outcropping that makes a nice viewing platform. The falls cascade down a brushy cliff across the ravine, streaming down and out of sight into the Jamison Creek gorge.

Little Jamison Falls plunges down a cliff opposite an overlook.

From the falls it's a short, easy walk up to Grass Lake at 1.5 miles. Hike back to the falls trail junction and turn right, heading gently uphill through willow and aspen that have been sculpted by heavy snowfall. As its name implies, Grass Lake is surrounded by meadowland, with the long, gray-and-green slopes and ridges of Mount Washington forming the northern rampart of the valley cradling both the lake and the creek. This is the turnaround point; return as you came.

Miles and Directions

0.0 Start by passing the gate and map signboard on the signed Grass Lake Trail.

0.3 Reach the first staircase.

0.6 Round a pair of switchbacks.

0.9 At the junction with the trail to Smith Lake, stay right toward Grass Lake.

1.0 Pass the park boundary sign; enter the Plumas National Forest.

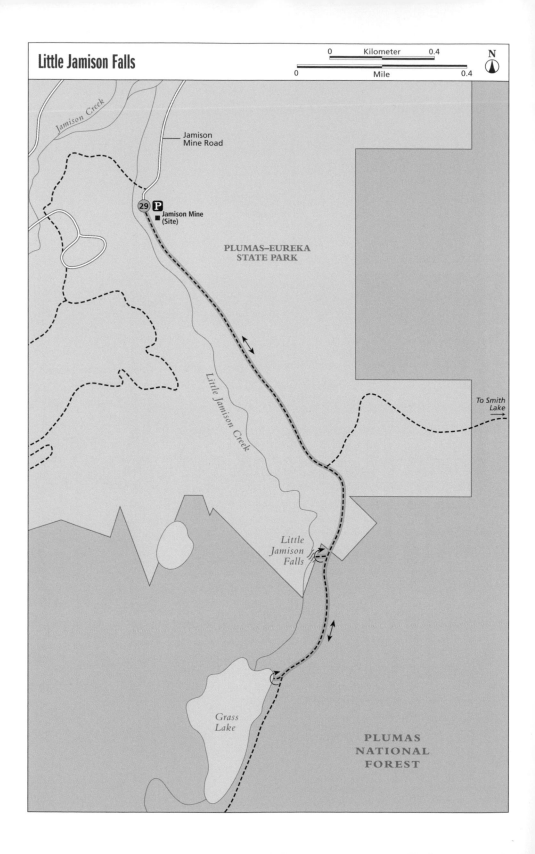

Little Jamison Falls

0 Kilometer 0.4
0 Mile 0.4

N

Jamison Creek

Jamison
Mine Road

29 P
■ Jamison Mine
(Site)

PLUMAS–EUREKA
STATE PARK

Little Jamison Creek

To Smith
Lake

Little
Jamison
Falls

Grass
Lake

PLUMAS
NATIONAL
FOREST

1.1 Turn right onto the signed Little Jamison Falls trail. The falls are about 50 yards ahead.

1.2 Return to the signed junction and turn right, continuing up to Grass Lake.

1.5 Reach the shores of Grass Lake. Retrace your steps.

3.0 Arrive back at the trailhead.

LEGACY IN THE NORTH SIERRA

Take the time to visit the core of Plumas-Eureka State Park, located about 0.25 mile past the day-use area turnoff. Hallmarks of California's gold rush are preserved in the park's museum and surrounding grounds, including an assay office, adit, blacksmith shop, and stamp mill. The site was a working mine for nearly a century, from the mid-1800s until World War II, and millions of dollars in gold was gleaned from the mountains in that time. Visitors can tour the preserved mine structures and the museum year-round (hours are limited outside the summer months); the park also hosts living history days, with docents reenacting life in an old-time mining town.

The site is also on the National Register of Historic Places, recognized as the site of the first ski competition in the Western Hemisphere. According to park literature, skiers in the 1860s hitched themselves to 12-foot-long Nordic boards and screamed downhill at speeds of up to 80 miles per hour; the mine tramways may have served as ski lifts.

Plumas-Eureka State Park preserves remnants of the Jamison Mine.

30 Fern Falls

This cascade is not a destination in and of itself, but the short hike down to Fern Falls is easy to check off while exploring other waterfalls in the Lakes Basin Recreation Area.

Height: About 35 feet (in short intervals)
Beauty rating: ★★★
Distance: 0.4 mile out and back
Difficulty: Easy
Best season: Late spring and early summer
County: Plumas
Trailhead amenities: None
Land status: Plumas National Forest

Maps: USGS Gold Lake CA; www.fs.usda.gov/ Internet/FSE_DOCUMENTS/fsm9_034853.pdf
Trail contact: Plumas National Forest, Beckwourth Ranger District, 23 Mohawk Rd., PO Box 7, Blairsden, CA 96103; (530) 836-2575; www.fs.usda.gov/recarea/plumas/recreation/ recarea/?recid=71116&actid=29

Finding the trailhead: From Graeagle follow CA 89 south for about 1 mile to a right turn onto the Gold Lake Highway/FR 24, signed for Gold Lake and the Lakes Basin Recreation Area. Travel 6 miles up the Gold Lake Highway to the large paved pullout on the right, with a sign for Fern Falls. GPS: N39 42.701' / W120 39.825'

The Hike

It has the "falls" moniker, but Fern Falls—at least the section accessible by the trail—is more of a cataract: a series of small drops on a stream not far off the Gold Lake Highway. The short walk to the cascade is easy and pleasant; the setting is pretty; and the stream, flow permitting, is inviting. Rock outcroppings along the trail offer fine perches from which to watch the water tumble, or to gaze down the Gray Eagle Creek valley, or to look up the wooded ridges toward Mount Elwell.

Reaching the cataracts is straightforward. From the parking area drop into the woods and cross the footbridge. The trail arcs right and downstream on the far side, leaving the woods for rockier, more open terrain. Follow the winding path down alongside the cataracts to where the path peters out at the rim of the Gray Eagle Creek drainage, where the views are best. The rock outcroppings beside the creek are particularly inviting when bathed in sunshine. Take in the views, and then retrace your steps to the trailhead.

Miles and Directions

0.0 Start by dropping down through the woods to cross the footbridge.
0.2 Reach the cataracts. Enjoy the vistas; then retrace your steps.
0.4 Arrive back at the trailhead.

The cascades at Fern Falls in the Lakes Basin.

31 Frazier Falls

An easy, paved path leads through groves of mixed conifers and rock gardens to stunning Frazier Falls.

Height: 178 feet
Beauty rating: ★★★★★
Distance: 1.0 mile out and back
Difficulty: Easy
Best season: Late spring and early summer
County: Plumas
Trailhead amenities: Restrooms and a handful of picnic sites

Land status: Plumas National Forest
Maps: USGS Gold Lake CA; www.fs.usda.gov/Internet/FSE_DOCUMENTS/fsm9_034853.pdf
Trail contact: Plumas National Forest, Beckwourth Ranger District, 23 Mohawk Rd., PO Box 7, Blairsden, CA 96103; (530) 836-2575; www.fs.usda.gov/recarea/plumas/recreation/recarea/?recid=71116&actid=29

Finding the trailhead: From Graeagle follow CA 89 south for about 1 mile to a right turn onto the Gold Lake Highway/FR 24, signed for Gold Lake and the Lakes Basin Recreation Area. Climb for 1.6 miles to the signed left turn onto Frazier Falls Road (CR 501). Follow narrow, winding, scenic Frazier Falls Road for 4 miles to the Frazier Falls picnic area. You can also reach the trailhead from the other end of the Frazier Falls Road, located 8.3 miles up the Gold Lake Highway opposite the access road to Gold Lake. GPS: N39 42.494' / W120 38.766'

The Hike

Frazier Creek drops about 2,000 feet from Gold Lake, high in the Lakes Basin Recreation Area, to the Feather River as it flows out of Graeagle, and about 200 feet of that drop is in the form of a dramatic waterfall. The trail leading to the Frazier Falls overlook gives no hint of the chasm ahead, or the cleft in the mountainside that the creek flies through as a flume of whitewater.

The stair-step backdrop to the falls is only apparent when the water flow is lower, in late season. But it's there, carved by the same glacial forces that sculpted the rest of this spectacular stretch of the northern Sierra.

The trail leading to the falls overlook is short and straightforward, with a number of benches lining the route. From the trailhead on scenic Frazier Creek Road, a paved path winds through fragrant evergreen forest and gardens of rolling granite and mountain manzanita to a bridge crossing Frazier Creek. A short distance beyond, the path curls northward and descends to a series of viewpoints protected with fences that overlook the falls. Interpretive signs describe the forces that sculpted the unexpected landscape. Take in the amazing views; then return as you came.

Not yet swollen by snowmelt, Frazier Falls displays its stair-step underpinning.

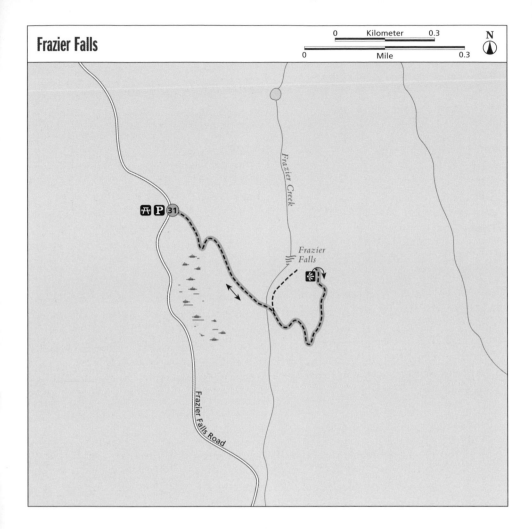

Miles and Directions

0.0 From the signed trailhead in the picnic area, follow the trail into the woods.

0.3 Cross the bridge spanning Frazier Creek.

0.5 Reach the falls overlooks. Retrace your steps.

1.0 Arrive back at the trailhead.

32 Hawley Falls

A series of pool-to-pool cascades tumble through a canyon upstream from Gray Eagle Lodge.

Height: 30 feet, with smaller cascades below
Beauty rating: ★★★
Distance: 2.5 miles out and back
Difficulty: Easy
Best season: Spring and early summer
County: Plumas/Sierra
Trailhead amenities: Restrooms and information signboards

Land status: Plumas National Forest
Maps: USGS Gold Lake CA. These falls are also known as Halsey Falls.
Trail contact: Plumas National Forest, Beckwourth Ranger District, 23 Mohawk Rd., PO Box 7, Blairsden, CA 96103; (530) 836-2575; www.fs.usda.gov/recarea/plumas/recreation/recarea/?recid=71116&actid=29

Finding the trailhead: From Graeagle follow CA 89 south for about 1 mile to a right turn onto the Gold Lake Highway/FR 24, signed for Gold Lake and the Lakes Basin Recreation Area. Follow the Gold Lake Highway for about 5 miles to the signed junction with the access road to Gray Eagle Lodge. Turn right onto the Gray Eagle Lodge Road and go 0.5 mile to the signed right turn onto the Gray Eagle Creek/Smith Lake trailhead access road. Go 0.1 mile on the gravel trailhead road to the signed Smith Lake and Long Lake trailheads, which are located behind the restroom. GPS: N39 43.553' / W120 39.828'

The Hike

Gray Eagle Lodge is a major draw in this part of the Lakes Basin Recreation Area, but you don't have to stay at the lodge to hike the easy trail that follows Gray Eagle Creek up to Hawley Falls (aka Halsey Falls). The trailhead on the lodge access road provides easy access to the forested route, which leads to a lovely set of cascades.

Confusion is possible at the trailhead, which serves several routes and is minimally signed, though new signage was planned as of 2015. Take the trail to the left, toward Long Lake; the signed Smith Lake Trail heads right, and the Gray Eagle Creek Trail is farther back down the trailhead road. A pair of junctions near the Gray Eagle Lodge may also be diverting. Stay right at these: At the first follow the singletrack up and around a little knob, and at the second proceed through a clearing.

Beyond the lodge intersections the path leads through open woodlands alongside the stream, climbing almost imperceptibly. The last junction is signed; take a left toward Hawley Falls, following the narrowing path into the rocky gorge that cradles the waterway.

The falls are preceded by cataracts, with the water tumbling over a series of short drops. Climb over rocks into the narrowing canyon, where the cataracts morph into a series of falls no more than 10 feet high, spilling from pool to pool and corralled by steep slabs on either side. A final scramble into the rock-walled gorge reveals Hawley

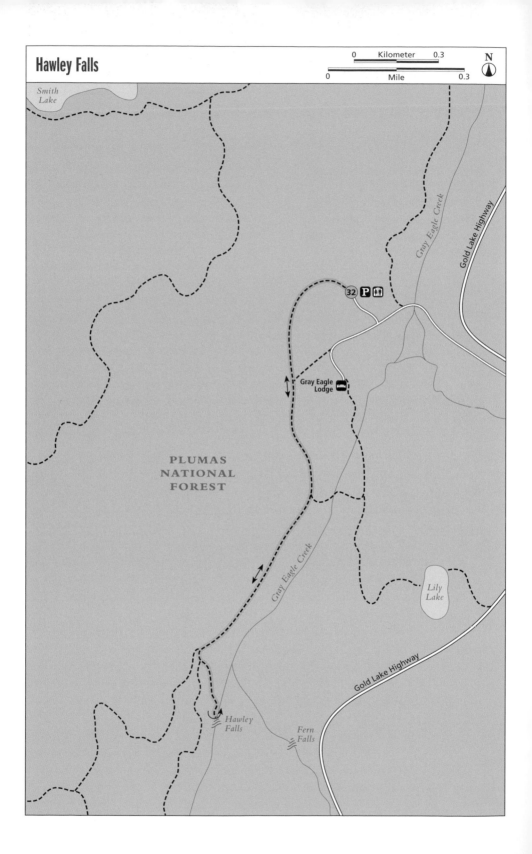

Hawley Falls

0   Kilometer   0.3

0   Mile   0.3

N

Smith Lake

Gray Eagle Creek

Gold Lake Highway

32 P

Gray Eagle
Lodge

PLUMAS
NATIONAL
FOREST

Gray Eagle Creek

Lily
Lake

Gold Lake Highway

*Hawley
Falls*

*Fern
Falls*

Hawley Falls tumbles down a narrow, forested canyon near Gray Eagle Lodge.

Falls, an impressive 30-foot cascade. Find a perch on a rock and enjoy the sights; then return as you came.

Miles and Directions

0.0 Start behind the restroom on the trail to Long Lake, headed left. The trail to the right leads to Smith Lake.

0.3 At the junction go right on the trail signed for Long Lake. The left trail leads to Gray Eagle Lodge.

0.6 At the junction stay right on the signed trail to Long Lake.

1.1 Rock-hop over a streamlet to a junction. Go left on the path signed for Hawley Falls.

1.3 Scramble into the rocky gorge to view the falls. Return as you came.

2.5 Arrive back at the trailhead.

33 Webber Falls

A hike and scramble lead to an out-of-the-way Sierra waterfall.

Height: About 75 feet in two tiers
Beauty rating: ★★★★
Distance: 0.5 mile out and back
Difficulty: Easy, but use extreme caution as soils at the edge of the river canyon are loose, eroded, and drop into a steep gorge. A fall could cause serious injury or death.
Best season: Spring
County: Sierra
Trailhead amenities: None. This trail is not recommended when it is wet or snowy, and not recommended for young children. The water for the falls comes out of Webber Lake, which has been acquired by a land trust but is not expected to be open to the public until 2017. Please do not trespass.
Land status: Tahoe National Forest
Maps: USGS Webber Peak CA
Trail contact: Tahoe National Forest, Sierraville Ranger District, 371 South Lincoln St. (CA 89), PO Box 95, Sierraville, CA 96126; (530) 994-3401; www.fs.usda.gov/main/tahoe/home

Finding the trailhead: From I-80 in Truckee follow CA 89 north, toward Sierraville and Graeagle, for about 14.5 miles to the signed junction for Jackson Meadows Road/Bear Valley Road. Turn left onto Jackson Meadows Road (also labeled FR 07) and then sharply left again to stay on FR 07, passing the parking lot for the OHV/snowmobile staging area. Follow the graded gravel forest road for 6.6 miles to the junction with the signed dirt road to Lake of the Woods, which breaks to the right. Remain on FR 07, traveling less than 0.1 mile past the Lake of the Woods turnoff to a small pullout on the left, with boulders blocking access to the unused forest road below. This is the trailhead. Park carefully alongside FR 07. GPS: N39 29.141' / W120 23.458'

The Hike

The Little Truckee River presents two faces as it rambles toward Stampede Reservoir. Below Webber Falls the stream meanders in great oxbows through Perazzo Meadows, watering wildflowers that flourish after the snow melts. The ridges on either side of the broad mountain valley are gentle and wooded. It's a friendly river in an inviting setting.

At the falls the Little Truckee puts on a fiercer face. The river bunches up in a narrowing canyon and then dives over a couple of tiers in a narrow gorge. The first plunge is shorter—maybe 25 feet—with broken basalt cliffs channeling the watercourse. The second plunge is about 50 feet high, tumbling into the rocky cradle of the gorge.

To reach the falls from the trailhead/pullout on FR 07, pass the boulders blocking vehicle access to the unused dirt road. Follow the road around a switchback into what looks like a parking area. Cross the clearing, walking south toward the edge of the canyon, an obvious goal visible through the trees. Use the sound of the waterfall as your guide. You'll see the falls as soon as you clear the woods. Pick one of the social

The Little Truckee River tumbles over Webber Falls.

trails that drops toward the river, and take care on the descent as the footing is loose and the slope steeply pitched. The path to the left leads to views of the longer plunge, while paths to the right overlook the shorter tier, which drops from a shallower pool into a deeper pool cupped in the split rocks and dotted with pockets eroded into the basalt by swirling water. Pull up a rock or patch of dirt on the slope or down by the river above the falls and enjoy. Retrace your steps to the trailhead.

Miles and Directions

0.0 Start by passing the boulders blocking vehicle access to the old forest road that leads down toward the falls.

0.1 Cross the clearing toward the canyon edge.

0.25 Descend the steep hillside paths to the falls. Return as you came.

0.5 Arrive back at the trailhead.

34 Big Springs Falls

These falls are an eye-catcher as you descend scenic CA 49 between Bassetts Station and Downieville.

Height: 30 feet
Beauty rating: ★★★
Best season: Late winter and spring
County: Sierra
Trailhead amenities: None
Land status: Private

Maps: USGS Haypress Valley CA; no map is needed
Trail contact: Tahoe National Forest, Yuba River Ranger District, 15924 CA 49, Camptonville, CA 95922; (530) 478-6253; www.fs.usda .gov/main/tahoe/home

Viewing the Falls

The massive pullout on the north side of CA 49 about 1.5 miles south of Bassetts Station and the Gold Lake Highway junction would be an eye-catcher in itself, but the

waterfall that sprawls across the mountainside is what pulls people off the highway. Big Springs Falls, with its dedication plaque and ease of access, is a magnet for pictures and for those seeking a break as they descend out of the High Sierra into the foothills. The source is in the private Big Springs Gardens. GPS: N39 35.791' / W120 36.638'

Big Springs Falls cascades alongside a pullout on CA 49.

35 Loves Falls

An easy, traversing hike leads to a thunderous fall on the North Yuba River.

Height: A series of 10- to 25-foot cascades
Beauty rating: ★★★★
Distance: 0.9 mile out and back
Difficulty: Easy
Best season: Spring and early summer
County: Sierra
Trailhead amenities: None
Land status: Tahoe National Forest

Maps: USGS Haypress Valley CA; no map is needed.
Trail contact: Tahoe National Forest, Truckee Ranger District, 10811 Stockrest Springs Rd., Truckee, CA 96161; (530) 587-3558; www.fs.usda.gov/recarea/tahoe/null/recarea/?recid=80793&actid=50

Finding the trailhead: From Sierra City follow CA 49 1 mile east to the signed Pacific Crest Trail trailhead. Parking for about five cars is on the left (north) side of the highway. GPS: N39 34.602' / W120 36.762'

The Hike

Looking both upstream and downstream from the bridge at Loves Falls, the North Yuba River is big and furious. When flush with snowmelt it explodes through the boulders hemming in the canyon bottom, and even when summer mellows the flows, the cataracts still flash and enliven.

Reaching the falls entails hiking a friendly stretch of the famous Pacific Crest Trail (PCT), which rides the ridges from the Mexican border to Canada. The trail traverses the north side of the North Yuba River canyon, passing through stands of mixed evergreen forest. The route is vaguely upside down, but the inclines are so gentle, except for the final drop to the bridge spanning the Yuba, that neither legs nor lungs should be inordinately taxed.

The route begins by crossing CA 49. Pick up the signed PCT on the south side of the road and turn left, heading upstream. Signs for Loves Falls and Milton Creek keep you on track as you drop into the Yuba canyon, paralleling the highway. Pass a set of tanks on the right, and then roller-coaster along the canyonside through the woods. A flume runs between the trail and the river for a stretch.

A short descent drops onto the narrow metal bridge spanning the river at the falls. The river is a tempest both coming and going, with cascades varying in height from 10 feet to 25 feet on either side of the bridge. The noise drowns out the highway and the voices of companions. And the setting is spectacular, with close, steep canyon walls and monstrous boulders cluttering the riverbed. There's really no place other than the bridge to safely enjoy the falls, though a use trail does skitter down the canyon wall to the riverside. Take it all in; then return as you came.

Looking upstream from the bridge spanning the North Yuba River at Loves Falls.

Miles and Directions

0.0   Start by crossing CA 49. Pick up the signed Pacific Crest Trail on the south side of the highway and go left (east).

0.1   Pass a cluster of tanks and a Pacific Crest Trail sign.

0.4   Round a bend in the trail. Loves Falls comes into view. Drop onto the bridge spanning the North Yuba River and check out the cataracts; then retrace your steps.

0.9   Arrive back at the trailhead.

Lake Tahoe

The blue gem of the Sierra Nevada, Lake Tahoe is a hikers' wonderland. Trails range from short, easy treks along streams and through meadows to challenging, long-distance treks among the stony peaks of Desolation Wilderness and across the high points on the lake's rim. Major towns around the lakeshore include Tahoe City and South Lake Tahoe. The bulk of these hikes are on the South Shore, near Emerald Bay, with a few lying outside the basin to the south, including a great hike near the historic hamlet of Markleeville.

Emerald Bay and southern Lake Tahoe (hike 37).

36 Shirley Canyon Cascades

A series of cascades on Squaw Creek is an easy walk upstream from the base of the Squaw Valley ski resort.

Height: 15 feet, with smaller falls above and below
Beauty rating: ★★★
Distance: 1.5 miles out and back
Difficulty: Easy
Best season: Late spring and early summer
County: Placer
Trailhead amenities: An information signboard. All amenities are available in the Squaw Valley Resort Base Village.
Land status: Tahoe National Forest

Maps: USGS Tahoe City CA, and Granite Chief CA; Lake Tahoe Basin Management Unit map; National Geographic 803 Lake Tahoe Basin trail map
Trail contact: Squaw Valley Resort, 1960 Squaw Valley Rd., PO Box 2007, Olympic Valley, CA 96146; (800) 403-0206 or (530) 452-4331; www.squawalpine.com. US Forest Service, Lake Tahoe Basin Management Unit, Forest Supervisor's Office, 35 College Dr., South Lake Tahoe, CA 96150; (530) 543-2600; www.fs.usda.gov/ltbmu/

Finding the trailhead: From the intersection of CA 89 and CA 28 in Tahoe City, follow CA 89 northwest (toward Truckee) for 5 miles. Turn left (west) onto Squaw Valley Road and go 2.5 miles, past the huge village parking lot, to Squaw Peak Road. Turn right onto Squaw Peak Road and follow it for 0.4 mile to its junction with Squaw Peak Way. The signed trailhead is at the junction. Limited parking is available alongside both Squaw Peak Road and Way. GPS: N39 11.910' / W120 14.480'

The Hike

Squaw Creek, which rocks and rolls in a meltwater rush in late spring and early summer, fuels small waterfalls and cascades that mist travelers on the trail that runs alongside. The falls and cascades are within easy walking distance of the Squaw Valley ski resort, which can be as busy in summer as it is when the slopes are slick with snow.

The waterfalls are ephemeral, though Squaw Creek, originating in the Shirley Lake basin above, flows throughout the year. But, as with hikes to many seasonal falls, the journey can prove as gratifying as the destination. And after the hike you can immerse yourself in the activities offered at the Squaw Valley resort, where the aerial tram runs daily, offering access to High Camp's pool, skating rink, restaurant and bar, and the hiking trails that skim the high ridges overlooking the Truckee River valley and the Tahoe Basin.

The trail up Shirley Canyon is rustic almost from the start: no wide treadways or boardwalks to keep you on track. Instead, the rocky singletrack climbs alongside the creek, sometimes flowing with meltwater itself.

Waterfalls leave watermarks: White stains delineate the seasonal cascades along Squaw Creek, which go dry in the summer season.

Begin by passing behind the large information signboard, which shows a map of the route. The trail is obvious at first but grows indistinct as it meanders up into the steep-walled canyon. Watch for brown trail signs and blue blazes painted on rocks, which show the way, and stay left of the creek. The path steadily ascends, but the real challenge is in picking the most logical and obvious way forward.

Pass a trail marker, and then reach the first cascade/waterfall at 0.3 mile. This is the biggest plunge, with the water tumbling over a 15-foot rock lip into a jumble of granite boulders. But there is more above: Continue uphill to a second tumble, this one shorter and muddled by boulders, but still frothy. To reach the second set of cascades, pass another trail marker and then bear left through the woods on a nice, straightforward stretch of trail along the left side of the creek. Where paths diverge at about 0.75 mile, stay left and then cross a granite slab (follow the blue blazes) to the second cascade view. The trail continues upward and onward, but this is the turnaround for those satisfied with a waterfall walk.

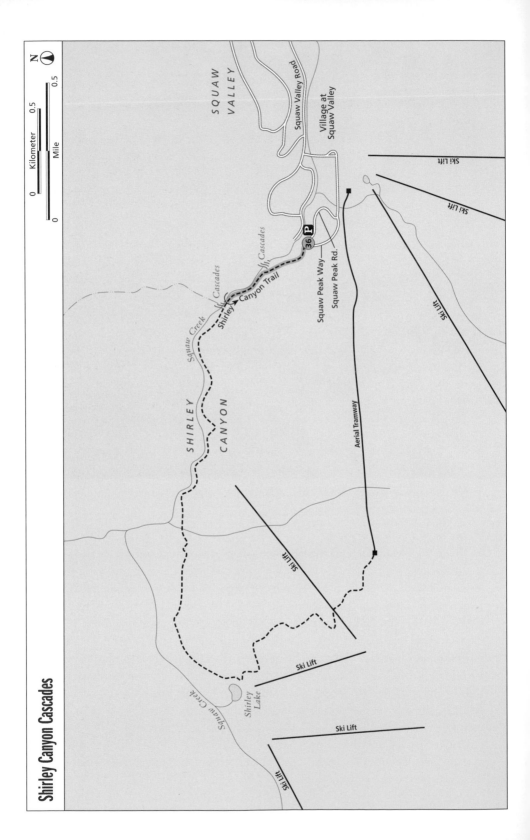

Shirley Canyon Cascades

Miles and Directions

0.0 Start at the Shirley Canyon trailhead, passing behind the signboard and heading up the trail. Where the trail becomes indistinct, blue blazes mark the route.

0.2 Pass a trail marker.

0.3 Reach the waterfall. You can turn around here or continue to a second series of cascades.

0.5 Pass a second trail marker, cross a side stream, and then stay left on a straightforward path through the woods.

0.75 Where the paths diverge, stay left, cross a granite slab following blue blazes, and reach the second cascade view. Check it out, and then return as you came.

1.5 Arrive back at the trailhead.

Option: For hardier hikers the trail continues upward to Shirley Lake and then to High Camp and a spectacular (and free) tram ride from the top of the ski resort to the base. To complete the one-way hike to the tram from the second cascade, continue uphill, following the blue blazes where the trail grows faint. Steep pitches are interspersed with relatively flat sections, leading up to a trail junction at 1.3 miles from the trailhead where signs point the way to Shirley Lake. About 2.0 miles from the trailhead, you'll encounter the crux of the hike: a steep granite headwall. Climb the imposing slab on its left side, again following blue blazes and the occasional rock cairn. Top out and proceed through woodland to Shirley Lake and the Solitude basin (with a ski lift), which is 3.25 miles from the trailhead.

The trail to High Camp climbs a rocky slope out of the basin (follow the Solitude/High Camp trail markers) and then winds up the barren slopes to the broad roadway that links back to High Camp and the aerial tram. The views from on high are panoramic, with Lake Tahoe winking blue among the ridges. Total mileage to High Camp from the trailhead is just more than 4 miles.

37 Eagle Falls

The falls on Eagle Creek are part of a watercourse that links Lake Tahoe's lovely Emerald Bay with the Desolation Wilderness above.

Height: About 40 feet
Beauty rating: ★★★★
Distance: 0.6 mile out and back
Difficulty: Easy
Best season: Late spring and summer
County: El Dorado
Trailhead amenities: Parking, restrooms, picnic sites, trash cans, and an information signboard and wilderness permit site. The parking lots at Eagle Falls and neighboring Vikingsholm are congested during the high season. Additional parking is available along the highway. Please be courteous and safe in selecting a parking space. A free, day-use wilderness permit is required to hike in Desolation Wilderness and is available at the trailhead. A parking fee is charged.

Land status: Tahoe National Forest; Lake Tahoe Basin Management Unit
Maps: USGS Emerald Bay CA; a map on the signboard at the trailhead; Lake Tahoe Basin Management Unit Map; National Geographic 803 Lake Tahoe Basin trail map; Tom Harrison Recreation Map of Lake Tahoe
Trail contact: US Forest Service, Lake Tahoe Basin Management Unit, Forest Supervisor's Office, 35 College Dr., South Lake Tahoe, CA 96150; (530) 543-2600; www.fs.usda .gov/ltbmu/

Finding the trailhead: From the intersection of US 50 and CA 89 in South Lake Tahoe, head north on CA 89 for 10.3 miles to the signed Eagle Falls parking area on the left (south). From Tahoe City follow CA 89 south for 18 miles, past the parking area for Vikingsholm, to the Eagle Falls parking lot on the right. GPS: N38 57.118' / W120 06.811'

The Hike

The cascade on Eagle Creek is a waypoint for most hikers as they climb to Eagle Lake. The upper falls, reached via the Eagle Lake Trail, is an easy destination, and the setting couldn't be more spectacular. From the bridge spanning the creek below the upper falls, look east toward aptly named Emerald Bay and the vast blue expanse of Lake Tahoe beyond. In every other direction the silver granite walls of Desolation Wilderness peaks tower overhead. The main plunge of Eagle Falls is on the east side of CA 89 and is not accessible by formal trail, though it's visible from the road.

To reach the cascades, pass the information signboard and begin walking up the stone staircase. (If you plan to continue past the falls into the Desolation Wilderness, you must fill out a wilderness permit at the trailhead.) Stay on the signed Eagle Lake Trail where it connects with the shorter Eagle Loop. The path climbs gently at first, allowing you to enjoy views of the cascades and the pinnacles and great gray domes of the Desolation Wilderness.

Eagle Falls; Cascade Falls

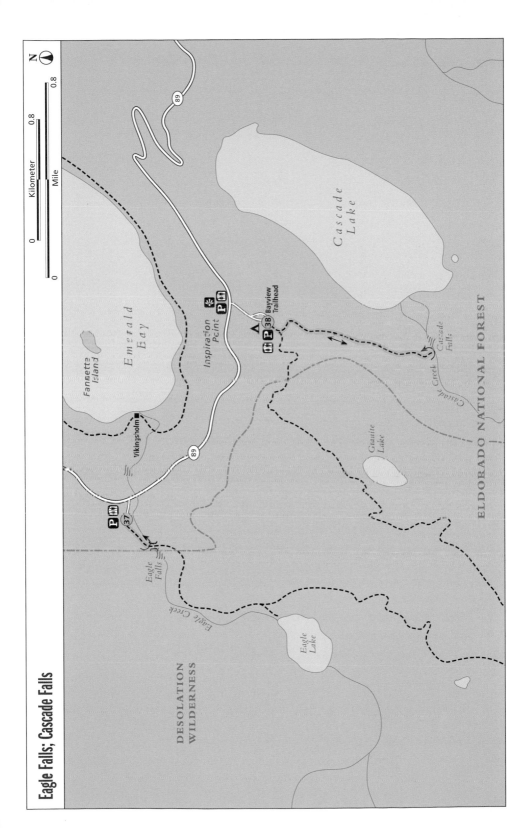

Lower Eagle Falls descends toward Emerald Bay.

Nearing the cascade, a twisting stone stairway leads up and then down to a vista point and the sturdy bridge spanning the cataract. Check out the fall, which roars with snowmelt early in the season and becomes more inviting as summer's heat mellows the flow, and then return as you came.

Miles and Directions

0.0 Start by climbing steps to the junction of the Eagle Lake Trail and the Eagle Loop. Stay left (southwest) on the Eagle Lake Trail.

0.2 Climb granite steps past the second Eagle Loop trail junction and stay left, heading down the stone steps.

0.3 Reach the bridge below the falls. Retrace your steps.

0.6 Arrive back at the trailhead.

Option: Eagle Lake is a short but steep climb beyond the fall, and a divine destination. Cupped in a stark Desolation Wilderness cirque—steep, silver and gray, and formidable—the lake is about the easiest alpine destination on Tahoe's South Shore. The trail leading up to the lake is varied and moderately challenging but quite short, making it well within reach of any hiker seeking an alpine experience without excess effort. From the bridge below the falls, climb another set of stairs, cross a granite slab, and traverse above the stream canyon. Stay right at the junction with the trail to Velma Lakes, dropping to the shores of Eagle Lake. The out-and-back distance is 2.0 miles.

38 Cascade Falls

Follow a rocky path to the raucous creek that feeds Cascade Falls. The falls themselves can only be viewed from a distance, but a seat on the granite terrace at the apex presents great views of Cascade Lake and Lake Tahoe.

See map on page 127.
Height: About 200 feet
Beauty rating: ★★★★
Distance: 2.0 miles out and back
Difficulty: Moderate due to climbs and descents over rocky terrain
Best season: Late spring and summer
County: El Dorado
Trailhead amenities: Restrooms, trash cans, water, and information signboards are available in the Bayview campground.

Land status: Tahoe National Forest; Lake Tahoe Basin Management Unit
Maps: USGS Emerald Bay CA; Lake Tahoe Basin Management Unit Map; National Geographic 803 Lake Tahoe Basin trail map; Tom Harrison Recreation Map of Lake Tahoe
Trail contact: US Forest Service, Lake Tahoe Basin Management Unit, Forest Supervisor's Office, 35 College Dr., South Lake Tahoe, CA 96150; (530) 543-2600; www.fs.usda.gov/ltbmu/

Finding the trailhead: From the intersection of US 50 and CA 89 in South Lake Tahoe, head north on CA 89 for 9.4 miles to a left (south) turn into the Bayview Campground. From Tahoe City follow CA 89 south for 18.9 miles, past the parking areas for Vikingsholm and Eagle Falls, to a right turn into the campground. Follow the campground road 0.3 mile to limited parking at the signed trailhead. Direct access to the trailhead may be difficult in high season; be prepared to park outside the campground or in safe pullouts along the highway. GPS: N38 56.607' / W120 06.000'

The Hike

Cascade Creek spills out of the Desolation Wilderness, fueling Cascade Falls and filling secluded Cascade Lake. Both the falls and the dark, still lake are off-limits to hikers, with the falls rendered inaccessible by steep granite cliffs and the lake by private property.

But above the misting cascades, hikers can cool their heels in pools and riffles on Cascade Creek, which courses over and among smooth granite slabs before taking the plunge. A seat at trail's end on a platform of sunbaked stone affords great vistas beyond the Cascade Lake basin to Lake Tahoe.

To begin, walk behind the information kiosk and turn left (south) onto Cascade Trail. The trail bends around two stubby trail posts in the mixed evergreen forest and then climbs a short, stone stairway to overlook the falls, Cascade Lake, and Lake Tahoe. At about the 0.5-mile mark, begin a rocky downward traverse above the northwest end of Cascade Lake. Pick your way down to and then along the base of a granite cliff; watch your step on the uneven trail surface. You can catch glimpses of the falls tumbling toward the lake from the traverse, but make sure you stop before you look.

A seat on the sunbaked slabs atop Cascade Falls offers great views down onto Emerald Bay and Lake Tahoe.

Cross a relatively narrow ledge, and then climb granite steps and broken rock to the broad sunny slabs that cradle the creek. A lovely granite bowl opens upstream, stretching back into Desolation Wilderness. A maze of trails has been worked onto the landscape over the years, some marked by "ducks" (stacks of rocks also called cairns) and others delineated by lines of rocks. Look left and downhill for a wooden trail marker that points the way to the falls overlook. Stay low (left and north) to get closer to the falls, but don't get too close, as you don't want to take a tumble near the cliff face. Stay high (right and south) to reach stretches of the creek that permit water play and toe dipping.

The whole terrace opens on wonderful views across the southern Tahoe Basin. Take in the sights, and then return as you came.

Miles and Directions

0.0 Start behind the information signboard, turning left (south) at the sign on the trail to Cascade Falls.

0.5 Head up the stone steps to views of Cascade Lake and its falls.

0.7 Traverse via slabs and steps at the base of a granite wall.

0.8 The trail levels as you approach the creek, and the granite cirque opens uphill to the south.

1.0 Reach the creek above the falls. Enjoy the sun and views, and then return as you came.

2.0 Arrive back at the trailhead.

39 Glen Alpine Falls and Modjeska Falls

Two waterfalls, roaring with snowmelt in late spring and early summer, enliven the cobblestone road/trail that climbs to ruins of the historic Glen Alpine Springs Resort.

Height: 75 feet (Glen Alpine); 50 feet (Modjeska)
Beauty rating: ★★★★
Distance: 2.2 miles out and back
Difficulty: Easy
Best season: Early summer
County: El Dorado
Trailhead amenities: Restrooms, trash cans, and an information signboard and wilderness permit station. Parking is limited at the Glen Alpine trailhead. More parking is available in pullouts along the access road. Fallen Leaf Lake Road is one lane and busy in summer.

Travel slowly and be courteous by stopping in wide spots to let oncoming traffic pass safely.
Land status: Tahoe National Forest; Lake Tahoe Basin Management Unit
Maps: USGS Emerald Bay CA; Lake Tahoe Basin Management Unit Map; National Geographic 803 Lake Tahoe Basin trail map; Tom Harrison Recreation Map of Lake Tahoe
Trail contact: US Forest Service, Lake Tahoe Basin Management Unit, Forest Supervisor's Office, 35 College Dr., South Lake Tahoe, CA 96150; (530) 543-2600; www.fs.usda .gov/ltbmu/

Finding the trailhead: From the intersection of US 50 and CA 89 in South Lake Tahoe, take CA 89 north for 3 miles to Fallen Leaf Lake Road. Turn left (west) on Fallen Leaf Lake Road and follow it for 5 miles, past the lodge and marina, to a fork. Go left (west) on FR 1216, following the sign for Lily Lake. The trailhead parking area is 0.6 mile ahead, across the bridge. The trailhead is at the northwest end of the parking lot, marked by a green metal gate. A free wilderness permit is required and is available at the trailhead. GPS: N38 52.627' / W120 04.836'

The Hike

Glen Alpine Creek drops over two falls in the final leg of its descent from the Desolation Wilderness to Fallen Leaf Lake, and depending on the quantity of snowmelt and the timing of your visit, the falls can be furious. But the hiking is not: The route follows a wide, moderately graded, gravel-and-cobblestone road that offers access to private cabins, the remnants of the Glen Alpine Springs Resort, and the Wilderness. This route takes you to the resort, as it's not that far above the second fall (Modjeska) and adds yet another attraction to a fine day hike.

The trail is relatively straightforward. At the outset the treadway is paved in ankle-twisting cobbles, but the grade is not steep. In early season or during heavy snow years, however, the track may be half submerged in flowing snowmelt, foretelling the abundance of water in the roadside falls. Gates and trail signs keep you on route at forks in the road, though the signs are an inconspicuous brown and mounted above eye level on tree trunks. Parcels of private land line the trail, with rugged driveways leading to small cabins.

Glen Alpine Falls is the first along the route. It's broad and impressive when brimming, hiding the broken cliff behind in a curtain of white. Modjeska Falls, reportedly named for an actress who frequented the Glen Alpine Springs Resort, tumbles not far above, but, being smaller and narrower, doesn't garner the awe that its neighbor does. Beyond the falls, ramble past a few more private cabins through a lovely mixed evergreen forest with a lush understory of wild berries and flowers.

Just beyond the old barn, a trail sign directs you to the right and into the remains of the Glen Alpine Springs Resort, established by 1878. This is the turnaround: Take a break and check out the remnants of what was once a thriving enterprise, including the soda spring, which still burbles and pops. Interpretive signs describe the history of the resort, which operated into the 1960s, and a map directs you to the different structures that were part of the complex.

The remnants of Glen Alpine Springs Resort, including the soda spring, lie upstream from the two trailside waterfalls.

Nathan Gilmore, prospector and future cofounder of the Sierra Club, established the resort, Lake Tahoe's first upscale getaway; other Gilmore land holdings in the area would eventually become part of the Desolation Wilderness, designated in 1969. The threat of development led to Glen Alpine's designation as a Federal Historic District in the 1970s.

Miles and Directions

0.0 Start by passing the green gate and heading up the gravel-and-cobblestone roadway.

0.3 Cross a stream (dry in late season) and pass a gate and trail sign.

0.4 Reach Glen Alpine Falls, on the left side of the roadway. At the junction with a private access road, stay right, following the "Trails" sign.

0.5 Reach Modjeska Falls, also on the left side of the roadway. At the next junction stay left, again following the "Trails" sign.

1.1 Pass the old barn and enter the Glen Alpine Springs Resort. Explore the site, and then return as you came.

2.2 Arrive back at the trailhead.

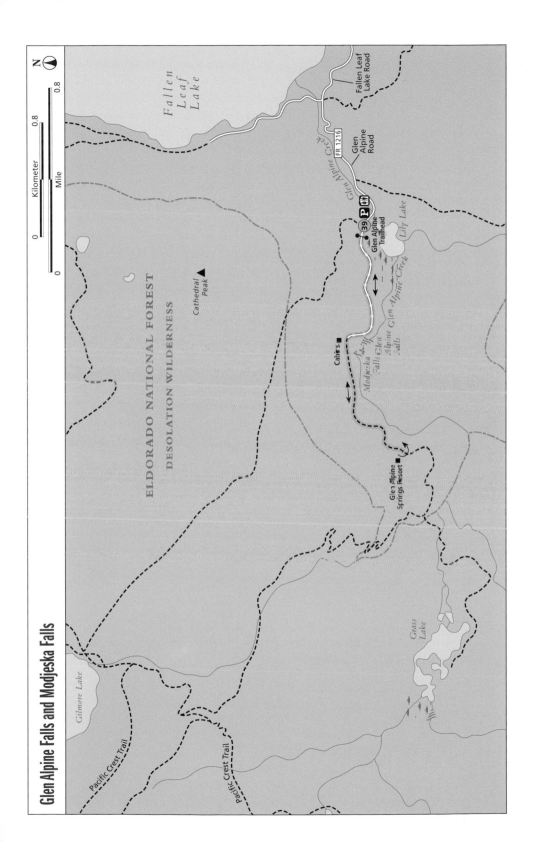

Glen Alpine Falls and Modjeska Falls

Fallen Leaf Lake

Fallen Leaf Lake Road

Glen Alpine Creek

FR 1216 Glen Alpine Road

Glen Alpine Trailhead

Lily Lake

ELDORADO NATIONAL FOREST

DESOLATION WILDERNESS

Cathedral Peak

Cabins

Modjeska Falls Glen

Glen Alpine Falls

Alpine Creek

Glen Alpine Springs Resort

Grass Lake

Gilmore Lake

Pacific Crest Trail

Pacific Crest Trail

N

Kilometer

Mile

0   0.8

0   0.8

Option: To reach a seasonal fall at Grass Lake, continue into the Desolation Wilderness, which begins at a granite staircase at the far end of the Glen Alpine Springs Resort. The route is lovely, traversing alternating groves of ponderosa pine and open granite shelves with views across the valley onto the Keith Dome ridgeline. A trail fork lies just beyond the Desolation Wilderness sign at 1.5 miles; go left (west) to Grass Lake. Three creek crossings follow, of varying difficulty depending on water flow and your tolerance for crossing logs and rock-hopping. Beyond the last creek crossing, series of short granite-and-timber staircases lead up the short ramparts of granite below the lake. Travel a final stretch through a brushy gully to reach Grass Lake at 2.4 miles. Contained by low, rolling expanses of granite and clusters of fir, pine, and brush, a spectacular waterfall spills off a red rock cliff to the west in season; beyond and above the lake and falls, the walls of the glacial basin rise skyward. The total round-trip distance is 5 miles.

40 Horsetail Falls

No proper trail leads to the giant spill of whitewater that pours from the heights of the Desolation Wilderness above Twin Bridges, but the path along Pyramid Creek offers great views of the waterfall, as well as an up-close visit to a lovely cataract.

Height: 791 feet
Beauty rating: ★★★★
Distance: 2.5-mile lollipop and spur
Difficulty: Moderate due to route finding
Best season: Late spring and early summer
County: El Dorado
Trailhead amenities: Restrooms, trash cans, water, an information signboard with map, and picnic tables. A fee is charged to park, and

visitors planning to enter the Desolation Wilderness must fill out a free wilderness permit.
Land status: Eldorado National Forest
Maps: USGS Echo Lake CA
Trail contact: Eldorado National Forest, Forest Supervisor's Office, 100 Forni Rd., Placerville, CA 95667; (530) 622-5061; www.fs.usda .gov/main/eldorado/home

Finding the trailhead: From the Y-junction of US 50 and CA 89 in South Lake Tahoe, head west on US 50 for 15.3 miles, over Echo Summit, to the Pyramid Creek Trail parking area on the right. GPS: N38 48.098' / W120 07.420'

The Hike

Though visible from US 50 as you descend a switchback from Echo Summit to Twin Bridges—in fact, a traffic stopper in peak season—Horsetail Falls is relatively remote. No established trail leads directly to the base or to the summit, which is high in the Desolation Wilderness. But the trail along Pyramid Creek offers great views of the waterfall, and the creek rocks with excitement when flush with meltwater.

Pyramid Creek, Horsetail Falls, and the cascades run year-round, fed by outflows from alpine lakes high in the wilderness, including Avalanche Lake, Pitt Lake, Ropi Lake, and Lake of the Woods. Only the top few tiers of the falls can be seen from the trail; cross-country travel (and the appropriate advanced route-finding skill set) is required to reach those heights. But granite slopes and terraces below the falls present classic Sierran hiking terrain, spiced by the fact that the trail can be difficult to follow in places. Artfully constructed rock cairns litter the slabs above the lower cataract, linking lengths of crushed stone treadway. The intent is to keep hikers on track, but the route the cairns demark is meandering. No worries: Keep the creek on your right, head upvalley (north) toward the falls, and you won't get lost.

Begin in the woods, hiking past a modest platform of granite overlooking a small splash of whitewater, and then climb to a marked trail junction at the base of a steep granite slab. Noise from the highway follows you up the trail, but once you ascend the slab and walk farther north toward the woods, all but the loudest engine sounds fade

A rock cairn marks the Pyramid Creek Trail; Horsetail Falls plummets from the cliff top in the distance.

away. Trend to the right as you climb the slab, angling toward the creek, to intersect the trail on top.

Follow the neat path of crushed stone threading through the slabs to a trail marker. You can see the top tiers of Horsetail Falls as you navigate this flat section. Pass a wilderness boundary sign a tenth of a mile beyond and continue toward the woods, where a wilderness permit sign is posted on a tree next to Pyramid Creek. You won't find a wilderness permit station here, however—only the end of the trail proper, petering out on the banks of Pyramid Creek. This is the turnaround point, though if you are prepared to go cross-country and water levels permit, you can ford the creek and carry on. Otherwise, retrace your steps to the Pyramid Creek Trail junction and turn left, heading down along the creek corridor.

Cairns dot the slabs above the creek drainage, leading down to the Pyramid Creek cataract. An excellent destination in and of itself, the cataract races down a low-angle slab, jumping or cascading depending on the flow. It can be enjoyed from perches on the neighboring granite shelves. From the cataract head down to the right, following the easiest route to the trail junction at the base of the slab. From the junction retrace your steps to the trailhead.

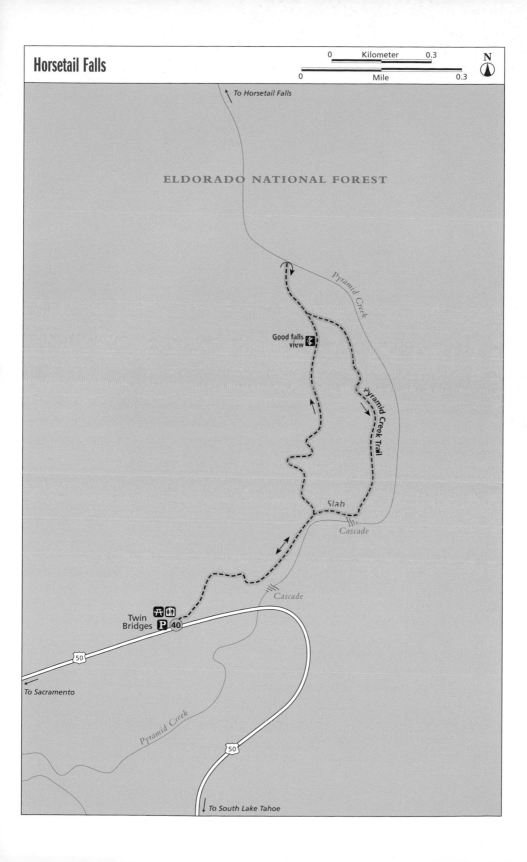

Horsetail Falls

0 Kilometer 0.3
0 Mile 0.3

N

To Horsetail Falls

ELDORADO NATIONAL FOREST

Pyramid Creek

Good falls view

Pyramid Creek Trail

Slab

Cascade

Cascade

Twin Bridges
P 40

50

To Sacramento

Pyramid Creek

50

To South Lake Tahoe

Pyramid Creek cascades down a slab at trailside.

Miles and Directions

0.0 Start at the trail sign behind the restroom.

0.2 Pass a slab overlooking a small cascade on the creek.

0.5 Reach the base of a steep granite slab. Stay left toward the wilderness boundary, and then angle right and pick your way up the slab. The Pyramid Creek Trail (the return route) breaks to the far right.

1.1 At the signed trail junction, stay left (straight). The right-hand path along Pyramid Creek is the return route.

1.2 Pass a wilderness boundary sign.

1.3 Arrive at Pyramid Creek, the end of the formal trail and the turnaround point. Retrace your steps from here to the Pyramid Creek Trail junction.

1.5 At the Pyramid Creek Trail junction, go left.

2.0 Reach the cataract. Continue down the granite to the first junction at the base of the steep slab. Retrace your steps from here.

2.5 Arrive back at the trailhead.

41 Bassi Falls

A short hike leads to the welcoming expanse of sunny slabs that spreads below the stair-step drop of Bassi Falls.

Height: About 110 feet
Beauty rating: ★★★★
Distance: 1.2 miles out and back
Difficulty: Easy
Best season: Spring and early summer
County: El Dorado
Trailhead amenities: None

Land status: Eldorado National Forest
Maps: USGS Loon Lake CA
Trail contact: Eldorado National Forest, Forest Supervisor's Office, 100 Forni Rd., Placerville, CA 95667; (530) 622-5061; www.fs.usda .gov/main/eldorado/home

Finding the trailhead: From Placerville drive about 21 miles east on US 50 to the Ice House Road turnoff, which is right before a bridge sweeping over the South Fork American River. Turn left onto Ice House Road and drive 16.1 miles, across the Silver Creek bridge, to the junction with the access road to Big Silver Group Camp on the left and Bassi Road on the right. Turn right onto Bassi Road. Go 0.2 mile to a left turn onto Upper Bassi Road/FR 12N32A, which is signed "Bassi Falls Access." This road is best navigated with a high-clearance vehicle, though passenger cars can make it to the trailhead, which is 1.5 miles up the dirt track. If the road is too slick or bumpy to drive, you can walk the dirt track to the trailhead. GPS: trailhead, N38 53.658' / W120 20.386'; Upper Bassi Road access, N38 52.960' / W120 21.520'

The Hike

Located on the Bassi Fork of Big Silver Creek, Bassi Falls spills into a channel on a rolling terrace of granite open to the sun and sky. The surrounding ridges are shaded with ponderosa pines and incense cedar, which also hide the reservoirs—Ice House and Union Valley—that draw visitors to this remote locale on the western slope of the Sierra Nevada. A scattering of cedar and pine also finds purchase on the rocky borders of the waterfall, which arcs down a broken cliff face before disappearing into the boulders at its base.

The hike is mostly upside down and relatively easy, rolling first through a park-like woodland of evergreens and scattered alder. Where the woods end and the slabs begin, the roar of the falls overtakes the whisper of wind in the treetops. Stay left on the slabs, following the sound and the cairns that mark the way. A dike of paler granite runs down toward the creek, evoking a massive, almost ruler-straight concrete foundation.

The top of the falls is visible from the upper slabs, and lost to view as you near the base. Depending on the time of year, water may puddle in depressions on the slabs or

Broad slabs spread below Bassi Falls and alongside the mellowing creek.

flow briskly through depressions seeking to rejoin the creek. But mostly the slabs are open and sun-warmed, inviting exploration and relaxation.

Return as you came. It's mostly uphill, but the hardest part may be route-finding across the slabs. Follow the cairns, and when in doubt, look right.

Miles and Directions

0.0   Begin by climbing a few steps from the parking area onto the trail and into the woods.

0.3   The woods open onto the granite slabs.

0.6   Reach the base of the falls near the Big Silver Creek channel. Check it all out; then retrace your steps.

1.2   Arrive back at the trailhead.

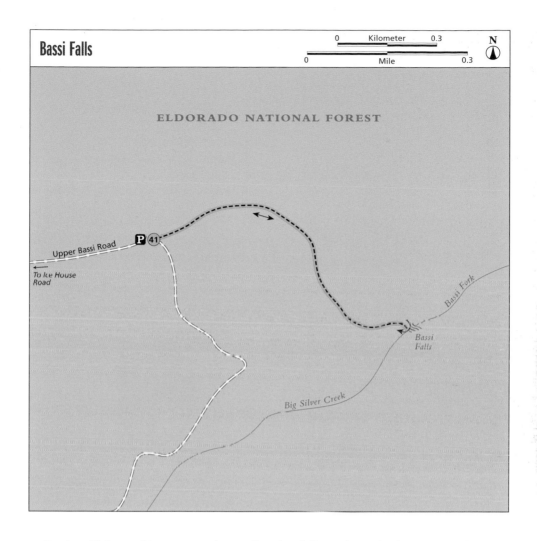

Bassi Falls

ELDORADO NATIONAL FOREST

Upper Bassi Road

To Ice House Road

Bassi Fork

Bassi Falls

Big Silver Creek

Option: If the parking area at the trailhead is full, or if you don't want to take on the bumpy dirt access road in a passenger vehicle, you can walk from additional parking areas located near the start of the Bassi Falls access road. A hike on the road, mostly in the woods and gently ascending to the trailhead, will add about 3 miles round-trip.

42 Bridal Veil Falls

This roadside cascade flows year-round. No need to hike; just pull off US 50 as you're climbing from Placerville to South Lake Tahoe and enjoy.

Height: 80 feet
Beauty rating: ★★★
Distance: None from the roadside pullout; 0.8 mile out and back from the Bridal Veil picnic area
Difficulty: Easy
Best season: Spring and early summer
County: El Dorado

Trailhead amenities: None
Land status: Eldorado National Forest
Maps: USGS Riverton CA
Trail contact: Eldorado National Forest, Forest Supervisor's Office, 100 Forni Rd., Placerville, CA 95667; (530) 622-5061; www.fs.usda .gov/main/eldorado/home

Finding the trailhead: From Placerville drive east on US 50 for about 18 miles to the roadside pullout fronting Bridal Veil Falls. The Bridal Veil picnic area is located 0.4 mile east. GPS: Bridal Veil pullout, N38 45.949' / W120 29.424'; Bridal Veil picnic area, N38 45.912' / W120 28.928'

Viewing the Falls

Bridal Veil Falls marks where Esmeralda Creek spills down a vertical rock face onto the verge of historic US 50 and then under four lanes of highway to join the South Fork American River. Eastbound traffic moves swiftly along this stretch, so there's a chance you might not be able to stop fast enough on the approach. No worries if that happens, as you can turn around or park at the Bridal Veil picnic area 0.4 mile farther on and either drive or walk back up the highway to view the falls. If you are traveling westbound, a sign marks the spot, and another pullout is located about 100 yards beyond the falls themselves.

Bridal Veil is easy to check off before or after visits to its nearest neighbors, Bassi Falls and Horsetail Falls. Falling a bit more than 80 feet over the steep canyon wall, the falls are a burst of white and wet in the otherwise deep green of the river canyon, and a nice stop along the historic highway, which originated as part of an emigrant trail during the California gold rush and also served as part of the Pony Express route.

The water at Bridal Veil Falls, sapped by drought, slips down the cliff alongside US 50. ▶

43 Hot Springs Creek Falls

An easy walk through the woods ends with a mildly challenging scramble to waterfall overlooks. Not to be missed: the park's hot springs pool and its unbeatable views.

Height: 50 feet
Beauty rating: ★★★★
Distance: 3.5 miles out and back
Difficulty: Easy
Best season: Late spring and summer
County: Alpine
Trailhead amenities: Parking is available only at the trailhead, but restrooms, information, water, trash cans, and camping facilities can be found at Grover Hot Springs State Park.

Land status: Grover Hot Springs State Park; Toiyabe National Forest
Maps: USGS Markleeville CA; park map available online or in park brochure
Trail contact: Grover Hot Springs State Park at the end of Hot Springs Road, PO Box 188, Markleeville, CA 96120; (530) 694-2248 (park office), (530) 694-2249 (hot springs pool); www.parks.ca.gov; groverhotspringsinfo @parks.ca.gov

Finding the trailhead: From the Y-junction of CA 89 and US 50 in South Lake Tahoe, follow US 50 west for 4.5 miles to the junction with CA 89 in Meyers. Turn left onto CA 89 and drive 10.9 miles to where CA 89 and CA 88 meet. Turn left onto CA 89/88 and drive 5.7 miles to Woodford. Turn right onto CA 89 and continue 6.3 miles to Markleeville. Turn right onto Hot Springs Road, following the signs, and continue to Grover Hot Springs State Park. Pay the fee. Parking is available in the day-use area near the campground entrance station; this is best for off-season access. In season follow the campground road to its end in the trailhead parking area. GPS: entrance station parking, N38 41.722' / W119 50.227'

The Hike

This out-of-the-way hike leads through quintessential Sierran woodland bordering a classic mountain meadow to a waterfall that flows year-round. Grover Hot Springs may not be a destination on the bucket lists of most hikers, but it should be.

The park has a relatively typical western mountain history. First came the Washoe, who hunted and gathered in the lovely alpine valley in the summer months. Historians believe explorer John Frémont traveled through the valley on a passage through the Sierra Nevada. Then came the emigrant homesteaders, including John Hawkins, who, according to park literature, used the hot springs water to fortify a bath on his ranch, and later Alvin Grover, who built the hot springs pool as well as a hotel in the nearby high country village of Markleeville.

The water that feeds the hot springs—snowmelt filtered down through fractures to a hot spot and then regurgitated at a scalding 148°F—seeps from the slopes above the pools and burbles from a font on the edge of the meadow. The water, fortified with sodium and a plethora of other minerals, but mostly lacking sulfur (responsible for the off-putting rotten-egg smell of many hot springs), is tempered and funneled

Mineral-infused hot spring water pools adjacent to the broad meadow at Grover Hot Springs.

into a soaking pool maintained at between 102° and 104°F. Aaahhh. A lap pool heated by hot springs water via a heat exchanger is also available.

The route, for the most part, is wide enough for hikers to walk two abreast, a walk-and-talk path that's flat, meandering, and offers views through a lacing of ponderosa pines onto the wide Hot Springs meadow to the left. Several trail junctions, all well marked, offer landmarks and options, but the main route heads straight into the narrowing canyon where the waterfall flows.

At the 1-mile mark, alongside Hot Springs Creek, take a left onto the narrower Waterfall Trail, which rolls through gullies as it heads upstream. Rocky ridges abut the sky on three sides. The well-defined trail ends in a jumble of rocks and slabs below the falls, becoming a web of footpaths that leads up and through boulders to the falls

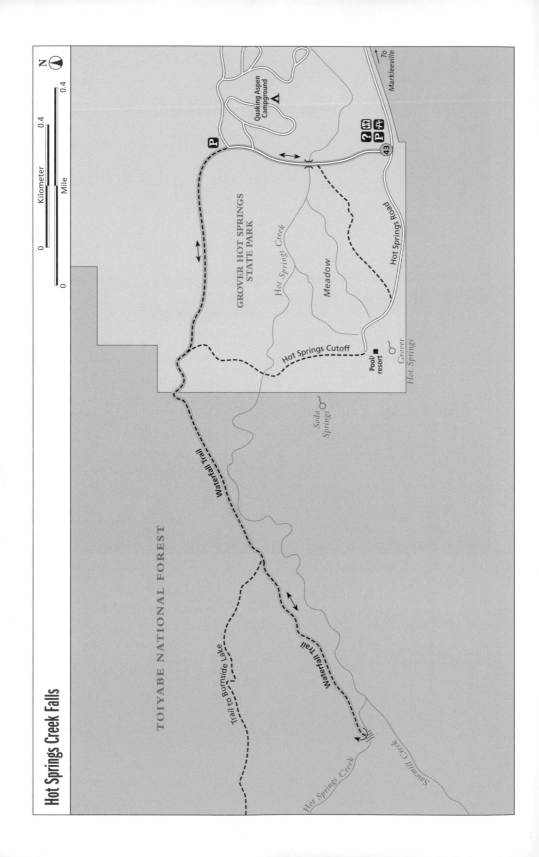

Hot Springs Creek Falls

N

Kilometer
0   0.4

Mile
0   0.4

TOIYABE NATIONAL FOREST

Trail to Burnside Lake

Waterfall Trail

Waterfall Trail

Hot Springs Creek

Summit Creek

Soda Springs

Grover Hot Springs

Pool/ resort

Hot Springs Cutoff

GROVER HOT SPRINGS STATE PARK

Hot Springs Creek

Meadow

Hot Springs Road

P

Quaking Aspen Campground

?

P

43

To Markleeville

themselves. It's a minor route-finding challenge and, depending on how you proceed, may demand some hands-on scrambling. But all routes lead to the falls, which in high water spill down a rock face more than 100 feet across, and in low water (or drought) trickle down the stair steps in slender splashes. Platforms on the rocks and below the trees offer great vantage points. Retrace your steps to the trailhead.

Miles and Directions

0.0 Start on the wide, obvious path heading left from the trailhead parking area.

0.25 At the first trail Y, stay left, following the Waterfall Trail.

0.4 Pass a trail marker and cross a side stream.

0.5 At the signed trail junction, stay straight (left) on the signed trail to Burnside Lake. The left turn is the Hot Springs Cutoff.

0.9 The trail swings alongside Hot Springs Creek.

1.0 At the signed junction with the Waterfall Trail, go left. A right turn leads to Burnside Lake.

1.5 Start the scramble up and around rock faces to reach the falls overlook.

1.75 Reach the falls. When you've had your fill, retrace your steps.

3.5 Arrive back at the trailhead.

Option: Honestly, I'd say this is more mandatory than an option. Granted, the hot springs pools may be crowded in high season, but the setting couldn't be more lovely, and a good soak after a good hike—well, let's just call that bliss. The hike isn't so long that you can't tote a suit and towel in your pack, and branching off from the waterfall route to the hot springs pool leads across a meadow that glows with color: green in spring, white in winter, golden in fall. To reach the pools from the Waterfall Trail (on the return), head right on the Hot Springs Cutoff. Cross the bridge over the creek at the midpoint and then climb gently to the pool parking area. A fee is charged, but it's well worth the price. Return to the trailhead via Hot Springs Road. Total mileage for this lollipop is about 3.7 miles.

It may slow to a trickle at season's end, but Hot Springs Creek Falls runs year-round.

Auburn and Gold Country

Calidornia's modern history began in the foothills of the Sierra Nevada in 1848, with the discovery of gold west of Sacramento. Nearly every waterfall trail in this region has a gold rush history, whether it follows a former flume or connects two former mining boomtowns. Auburn anchors the area, with significant satellites in Nevada City, Grass Valley, and Colfax. The main east-west thoroughfares are I-80 and US 50, with CA 49 and CA 20 serving as significant (and scenic) secondary roads.

The trail to Bear River Falls leads through a foothills woodland bright with color in autumn (hike 48).

44 Shingle Falls

A pleasant loop through rolling woodlands in the foothills east of Marysville ends at a waterfall and swimming hole on Dry Creek.

Height: 70 feet
Beauty rating: ★★★★
Distance: 5.2-mile lollipop
Difficulty: Moderate due to distance and a few steep sections of trail
Best season: Spring and summer
County: Nevada
Trailhead amenities: None
Land status: Spenceville Wildlife Area
Special considerations: Hunting is allowed in the Spenceville Wildlife Area from Sept 1 to Jan 31, and during spring turkey season. During the first 9 days of the spring turkey season, the wildlife area is closed to all individual and group uses except those with a permit from the California Department of Fish and Game. The spring turkey season opens on the last Saturday in March. If hiking in hunting season, be sure to wear bright colors, such as blaze orange.
Maps: USGS Camp Far West CA, and Wolf CA; online at www.wildlife.ca.gov/Lands/Places-to-Visit/Spenceville-WA
Trail contact: Spenceville Wildlife Area, California Department of Fish and Game, 945 Oro Dam Blvd. West, Oroville, CA 95965; (530) 538 2236; www.wildlife.ca.gov/Lands/Places-to-Visit/Spenceville-WA

Finding the trailhead: From Sacramento head north on I-5 to CA 99. Continue north on CA 99 for about 12 miles to CA 70. Make a slight right onto northbound CA 70 toward Marysville. Travel another 22 miles to the Feather River Road exit off CA 70. Go right (east) on Feather River Road to the first intersection and then right again onto North Beale Road (no obvious street signs at these junctions). Travel 0.2 mile to a signalized arterial and go left to continue on North Beale Road. Go another 0.8 mile on North Beale to Hammonton-Smartville Road. Go left on Hammonton-Smartville Road, staying right at the signalized Y-intersection with Simpson Lane, which leads to downtown Marysville. Drive for about 15 miles to the intersection with Chuck Yeager Road. Go right on Chuck Yeager Road for about 4 miles to Waldo Road (no sign). Go left on Waldo Road, a graded dirt road, for nearly 2 miles, across the single-lane bridge, to Waldo Junction and the signed intersection with Spenceville Road. Go left on Spenceville Road, traveling about 2.3 miles to the parking area on the left, past the camping area and near the road's end. The trailhead is at the yellow gate at the old stone bridge; a small sign identifies the Fairy Falls (aka Shingle Falls) Trail. GPS: N39 06.824' / W121 16.245'

The Hike

I've gone with calling this Shingle Falls, deferring to the US Geological Survey, but the waterfall is identified as Fairy Falls on trail signs and as Beale Falls or Dry Creek Falls in some printed and online guides. Being "also known as" may create some confusion, but no matter the name, the falls are a stunning destination, a stair-step spill into a punchbowl that runs year-round, though fullest in spring when swollen with snowmelt or after rainstorms. The second drop is the longest, a 50-foot plunge into

Shingle Falls finishes by plunging into a punchbowl.

a dark pool. The inkwell gives the impression of bottomlessness, which makes it as mysterious as the falls are invigorating.

A linkage of well-maintained wildlife area service roads, perfect in width and grade for family outings, and an engaging, well-signed singletrack lead to the falls. A web of social paths connects the main trail to the overlook at the top of the falls and to the creek below the spill, where a swimming hole awaits. These smaller trails may be challenging in steepness and footing, especially for little ones, but standing at the overlook and watching the whitewater dive into the inkwell is ample reward for your effort.

The trail begins at the site of the Spenceville mine, crossing the stone bridge over Dry Creek, and then heads right at the fence line on the dirt roadway, crossing two smaller bridges. Follow the road up into the hills, avoiding a pair of side trails that diverge in the first 0.5 mile. Beyond these the route is straightforward and marked with signs for Fairy Falls, leaving little chance to stray.

After a long, gentle climb, with scattered oaks offering dollops of shade, the trail hooks sharply right at a white gate (a "Fairy Falls" sign points the way, though signs are often vandalized and may be missing). Pass a second white gate and then climb through a sloping meadowland, with views stretching down into the Dry Creek drainage and north across more rolling pastureland into the foothills.

A cattle guard spans the road at the hilltop. You have a choice here: You can follow either the trail to the right or the road beyond the cattle guard to the left. Both meet within sight at the edge of the woods. At the second signed trail junction, you have another choice: The described route heads up on singletrack into the oaks and returns via the roadway to the right. The road is signed for Upper Falls and the trail for Fairy Falls, but the falls are one and the same. The signed trail climbing into the woodland is described here, but following the road out and back is the easiest option.

The singletrack is mildly challenging, with occasional downed trees forcing hikers onto social trails that bypass the obstacles. It dips through several drainages and then traverses a grassy hillside before hitching up with the dirt roadway. Go left on the road, which runs alongside Dry Creek, now rollicking in its rock-bottomed bed through a riparian corridor thick with brambles, poison oak, and maples that fire yellow and orange in late fall.

After passing a streamside clearing, the roadway hitches uphill. A use trail breaks right just before a gate, offering access to a large swimming hole fed by two short falls, each no higher than 3 feet.

A web of steep and winding use trails climbs the hillside between the swimming hole and Shingle Falls proper. The paths merge onto a narrow track running alongside the rickety chain-link fence that separates hikers from the 100-foot drop into

A RECLAMATION SUCCESS STORY

For more than 50 years, copper and other mineral resources were removed from the Spenceville mine. After the mine became part of the Spenceville Wildlife Area, the California Department of Fish and Game (DFG) and the California Department of Conservation (DOC) worked to reclaim the land so that its residual toxicity would not pose significant danger to the fish populations in Dry Creek or threaten the well-being of other critters in the area, including humans. The result is what you see today: Essentially nothing remains of the mine except stone bridges that aid stream crossings at the Shingle Falls trailhead, a chain-link fence, and low-key signage noting areas that are closed. The mitigation was so successful that the DOC earned the Governor's Environmental and Economic Leadership Award for its work.

As with other wildlife areas under the purview of the DFG, hunting and fishing are permitted in the area, as is grazing. The terrain is ideal for both. Rolling hills support a healthy blue oak–gray pine woodland, home to deer and other game. Open meadows provide ample forage for cattle. The grasslands are mostly cropped close, but where they aren't (and even after they've been grazed), wildflowers bloom in profusion. Encompassing almost 12,000 acres, the wildlife area offers plenty of space for all users to enjoy.

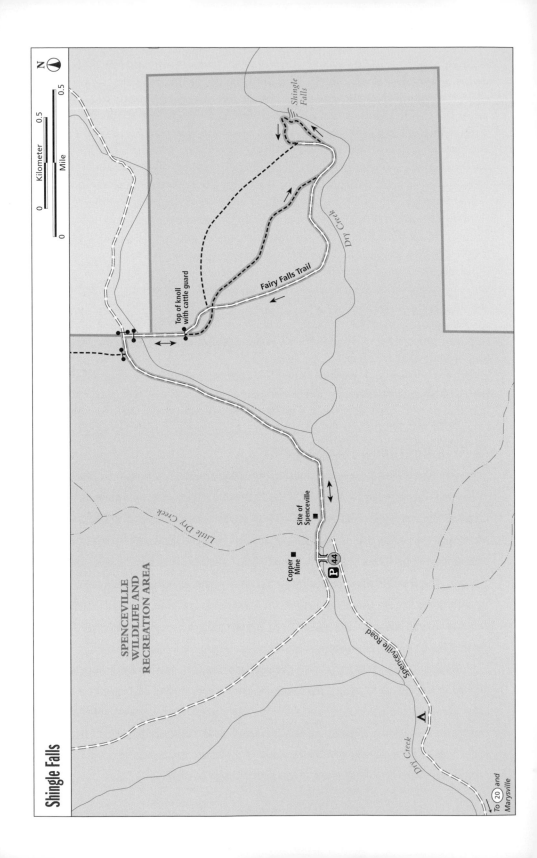

Shingle Falls

Shingle Falls

SPENCEVILLE WILDLIFE AND RECREATION AREA

Little Dry Creek

Copper Mine

Site of Spenceville

Top of knoll with cattle guard

Fairy Falls Trail

Dry Creek

Spenceville Road

Dry Creek

To 20 and Marysville

N

0   0.5
Kilometer

0   0.5
Mile

the steep-walled chasm below the falls. The fence looks like it could be pushed over with a gentle shove; take care to stay on the safe side. Though a long jump into the chocolate waters of the inkwell may look inviting to an adventurous soul, it's better to approach from below and simply observe from above.

To vary the return, stick to the road on the way back to the trailhead. Stay left where the trail meets the narrow Fairy Falls path and make a gentle climb back to the upper trail junction and then to the cattle guard on the hilltop. From there retrace your steps to the trailhead.

Miles and Directions

0.0 Start by crossing the stone bridge with the yellow gate. On the far side of the bridge, turn right and follow the dirt roadway over two smaller bridges.

0.1 Pass a singletrack trail behind a gate on the left. Stay right on the gravel road.

0.5 At the unsigned junction stay left on the roadway. The right-hand path drops into a blackberry hedge; this route connects with the road below the falls, an option for a more adventurous hiker.

1.2 At the first white gate, a "Fairy Falls" trail sign directs you right. Pass a second white gate and head up through the meadowland.

1.5 Reach a cattle guard and go right on the trail. You can also follow the roadway down to the next trail junction.

1.7 At the five-way junction, a trail sign indicates that Fairy Falls is 1 mile ahead via a single-track path and that Upper Falls is 0.9 mile distant via the roadway. Take the signed Fairy Falls trail.

2.2 The trail ends on the dirt road. Go left on the broad track.

2.4 Take the well worn use trail that breaks right, toward the creek, just before a twisted open gate. This leads down to the swimming hole.

2.6 Wander up via social trails to the falls overlook. Check out the falls and punchbowl. To return, retrace your steps to the junction with the Fairy Falls singletrack. Stay left on the gravel roadway, which winds through woodland up to the cattle guard on the hilltop. From here retrace your steps to the trailhead.

5.2 Arrive back at the trailhead.

45 Rush Creek Falls

A fabulous, accessible trail winds along the mountainside above the South Yuba River to a wooden flume/bridge overlooking Rush Creek Falls.

Height: About 100 feet
Beauty rating: ★★★★★
Distance: 2.2 miles out and back
Difficulty: Easy
Best season: Year-round
County: Nevada
Trailhead amenities: Restrooms, trash cans, and an information signboard
Land status: South Yuba River State Park

Special considerations: Take care on the wooden bridges and walkways when conditions are wet or frosty, as they can be slippery.
Maps: USGS Nevada City CA; map in park brochure available online
Trail contact: South Yuba River State Park, 17660 Pleasant Valley Rd., Penn Valley, CA 95946; (530) 432-2546; www.parks.ca.gov

Finding the trailhead: From CA 20 in Nevada City, take the CA 49 exit. Go north on CA 49 for 7 miles, dropping into the South Yuba River drainage. The parking area is a pullout on the right side of the highway, signed for the Independence Trail. If you reach the bridge spanning the river, you've gone too far. GPS: N39 17.493' / W121 05.842'

The Hike

Hundreds of miles of flumes—wooden or earthen channels built in the late 1800s and early 1900s to move water from rivers and streams to mining and logging camps—wind across mountainsides in the Sierra Nevada. The declines of the channels were typically gentle so that flows could be controlled, and paths ran alongside so that miners and loggers could maintain the flumes and, in the case of those built to help transport lumber, clear logjams. Long fallen into disuse, these relics serve as crumbling reminders of California's gold rush boom times.

Or, they serve as delightful foundations for recreational trails.

Such is the case with the stretch of the Independence Trail between CA 49 and Rush Creek Falls. This former mining ditch, which funneled water out of the South Yuba River for use in hydraulic mining operations, has been transformed into a first-class trail by any standard, but is even more impressive for the fact that it is accessible, outfitted with ramps, benches, and railings all thoughtfully constructed not only for ease of use but also so that they blend seamlessly into the surrounding oak woodland.

The trail begins at the uphill end of the mossy stone retaining wall in the parking pullout. It passes under the highway through a low-ceilinged tunnel and then winds along the mountainside above the South Yuba. The route is two-tiered, with a wider

A flume arcs across the top of Rush Creek Falls. ▶

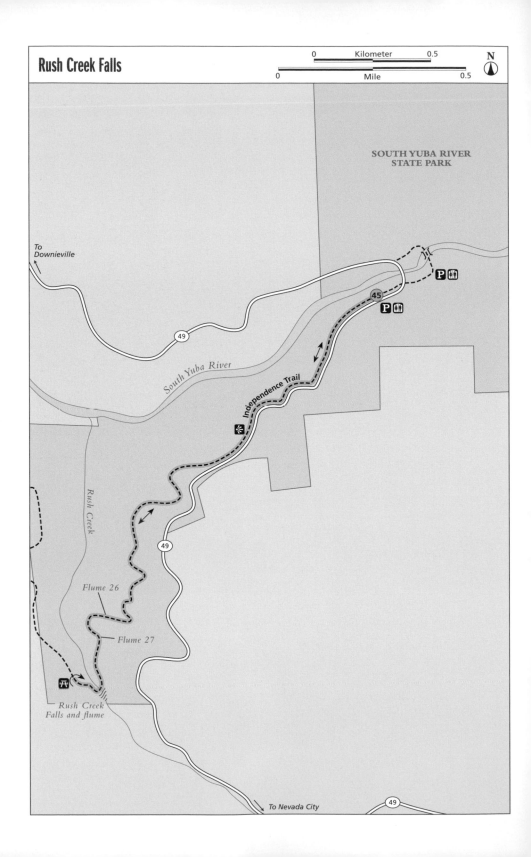

Rush Creek Falls

0 Kilometer 0.5
0 Mile 0.5

N

SOUTH YUBA RIVER
STATE PARK

To
Downieville

49

South Yuba River

Independence Trail

45

P 👫

P 👫

Rush Creek

49

Flume 26

Flume 27

🅿

Rush Creek
Falls and flume

To Nevada City

49

path below (in the bed of the ditch) and a narrower path riding the low berm on the canyon side; the two are connected on occasion by footpaths and short wooden staircases. Footbridges and ramps ease passage when needed, and a number of overlooks and benches have been installed—though the views are generally overgrown, screened by the dense foliage of the oak woodland, but better when the leaves are off the deciduous trees in late fall, winter, and early spring.

After crossing a couple of numbered wooden flumes that hint at what's to come, you'll reach the main attraction: a flume curling through the Rush Creek drainage, suspended on the hillside by a string of wooden support beams, with the waterfall flowing underneath. On the west side of the creek, a switchbacking ramp leads down to picnic sites on the banks at the head of the waterfall. *Note:* If the ramp to the picnic sites is too slick to navigate, you can continue another 0.1 mile to a trailside picnic site.

The fall is best viewed from the far side of the flume. The water cascades in tiers for more than 100 feet before being lost to sight in the overgrown gorge below. Views open north and west from the flume, finally unobscured by the oak canopy, onto the wooded ridges of the western slope and down toward the South Yuba.

Return as you came.

Miles and Directions

0.0 Start by the restroom at the uphill end of the retaining wall. Go right on the Independence Trail, passing through the tunnel under the highway. The stairs on the right beyond the tunnel lead back up to the highway; stay left on the obvious, two-tiered track.

0.2 Pass the junction with the Jones Bar Trail, which departs to the right. Stay left on the Independence Trail.

0.4 Pass the covered overlook dedicated in memory of Thomas Orzalli.

0.5 Pass the Diamond Head outhouse. A picnic site lies just beyond.

0.7 Pass a bench dedicated to Tera, "the best dog ever."

0.9 Cross Flume 26.

1.0 Cross Flume 27.

1.1 Reach the curving flume that overlooks Rush Creek Falls. Cross to the far side for the best views. This is the turnaround point. Retrace your steps.

2.2 Arrive back at the trailhead.

Options: Continue down CA 49 for 0.5 mile to the South Yuba River bridge. A large parking area/trailhead is on the south side of the bridge, outfitted with restrooms, trash cans, and information signboards (GPS: N39 17.854' / W121 05.333'). A short walk down to the river leads to the South Yuba's historic rainbow arch bridge, built in the 1920s. The lovely structure now serves as a pedestrian bridge; the vehicular bridge just downstream, built in 1993, mimics the design. Picnic sites are available, as is the Hoyt's Crossing Trail, which climbs upstream on the north side of the river. But the highlight is the river: Stand on the bridge and watch the South Yuba crash through the huge boulders in its bed, green and white and furiously playful.

46 Spring Creek Falls

A rustic path leads along a secluded stretch of the South Yuba River to these year-round falls.

Height: About 15 feet
Beauty rating: ★★★
Distance: 2.0 miles out and back
Difficulty: Easy
Best season: Spring
County: Nevada
Trailhead amenities: Restrooms and information signboards

Land status: South Yuba River State Park
Maps: USGS North Bloomfield CA; map in park brochure available online
Trail contact: South Yuba River State Park, 17660 Pleasant Valley Rd., Penn Valley, CA 95946; (530) 432-2546; www.parks.ca.gov

Finding the trailhead: From Nevada City follow CA 20 east to the junction with CA 49. Head north on CA 49 for 0.3 mile to North Bloomfield Road. Go right onto North Bloomfield Road; at the T-junction go right, staying on North Bloomfield Road (following the sign for South Yuba River State Park). Stay on winding North Bloomfield Road for 7.3 miles, driving to the bottom of the river canyon at Edwards Crossing. Parking is on the south side of the river and bridge. GPS: N39 19.794' / W120 59.052'

The Hike

The path to the confluence of Spring Creek and the South Yuba River is as rough-and-tumble as the river that flows next to it. It's generally easy, but the uneven footing, the narrowness, and the exposure demand concentration and nimbleness. It's just plain fun.

The waterfall itself is a short spill from the mouth of the Spring Creek drainage into the South Yuba. The friendliness of the falls, and the pool it splashes into, depends on how much water is flowing: If the flows are high, it's best to sit on the rocky sidelines and watch, but if the flows are low, you can pick your way through the boulders down to the river and pool. Scrambling up alongside Spring Creek is also inviting, with the creek cascading through boulders in drops several feet high into smaller pools, all shaded by oaks and madrones.

The route is straightforward, heading upstream along the north side of the river from the rustic Edwards Crossing bridge. The path is overhung with buckeyes at first, naked for most of the winter, bearing fragrant flowers in spring, and sporting seeds like Christmas ornaments in autumn. Anglers' trails break left, down toward the riverbank. To reach the falls, stay straight on the obvious, if narrow and rough, traversing path. At times you may find yourself proceeding hands-on across portions of the route that have washed out.

Buckeye nuts dangle from bare branches, framing the Edwards Crossing bridge over the South Yuba River.

At the confluence of the South Yuba and Spring Creek, the formal trail splits into social paths, one leading left to a huge, gnarly old madrone and then splintering into river- and waterfall-bound routes. The right route leads up into the canyon, skittering along the steep east-side slope before disappearing into the brush.

After you've enjoyed the falls and cataracts on both the South Yuba and Spring Creek, return as you came.

Miles and Directions

0.0 Start by crossing the scenic bridge. The trail is on the north side on the left, heading down steps to the dirt path that traces the north side of the river.

1.0 Reach the confluence of the South Yuba River and Spring Creek at trail's end. The waterfall is to the left, spilling into the river. Retrace your steps.

2.0 Arrive back at the trailhead.

47 Little Humbug Creek Falls

The Malakoff Diggins offers provocative insight into the damage wrought by hydraulic mining in the Sierra Nevada, while the falls on Little Humbug Creek display the power of natural hydraulics.

Height: About 150 feet
Beauty rating: ★★★★★
Distance: 3.2 miles out and back
Difficulty: Moderate
Best season: Late spring and early summer
County: Nevada
Trailhead amenities: None. A museum, restrooms, water, trash cans, and picnic facilities are located farther down the park road in North Bloomfield.

Land status: Malakoff Diggins State Historic Park
Maps: USGS North Bloomfield CA; park map available at the museum/visitor center and online
Trail contact: Malakoff Diggins State Historic Park, 23579 N. Bloomfield Rd., Nevada City, CA 95959; (530) 265-2740; www.parks.ca.gov. Malakoff Diggins Park Association, 23579 N. Bloomfield Rd., Nevada City, CA 95959; malakoffdigginsstatepark.org

Finding the trailhead: There are a number of ways to reach the park from Nevada City. The Malakoff Diggins Park Association suggests following CA 49 north from its junction with CA 20, toward Downieville, for 10.5 miles. Turn right onto Tyler-Foote Crossing Road, marked with a Malakoff Diggins State Historic Park sign. Follow the paved road for 15 miles; the name will change to Cruzon Grade and then to Backbone. When the double yellow line ends, turn right onto Derbec Road and proceed about 1 mile to North Bloomfield Road. Turn right onto North Bloomfield Road and drive 1.5 miles, past the Chute Hill Campground, to historic North Bloomfield and park headquarters. The Humbug Creek trailhead is located about 1.5 miles farther along North Bloomfield Road.

Alternatively, you can get to the Humbug Creek trail using graded gravel roads. From the junction of CA 20 and CA 49, head north on CA 49 for 0.3 mile to North Bloomfield Road. Go right onto North Bloomfield Road; at the T-junction go right, staying on North Bloomfield Road (following the sign for South Yuba River State Park). Stay on North Bloomfield Road for 8.1 winding miles, driving to the bottom of the river canyon at Edwards Crossing, proceeding across the bridge, and then climbing to a junction. Stay right on North Bloomfield Road, and continue on the good gravel surface to a second signed junction. Stay right on North Bloomfield Road, following the sign for Malakoff Diggins State Historic Park. Continue for 2.5 miles to the signed park boundary; the signed Humbug Creek parking area is 3.3 miles from the last junction. This route may be closed in winter due to snow. GPS: N39 21.920' / W120 55.409'

The Hike

Malakoff Diggins State Historic Park lies well off the beaten path, but is well worth the travel time. It preserves a swath of gorgeous foothills country, a secluded waterfall, and the remnants of some remarkable gold rush history.

The centerpiece of the park is the diggings. The cliffs of the mining pit, the legacy of a massive hydraulic mining operation that thrived in the late 1800s, are a colorful

Runoff from the diggings uphill color the water that pools at Little Humbug Creek Falls

exclamation point in the midst of the heavy greens of the surrounding pines and firs, orange fading to peach fading to cream from top to bottom. A path leads through the pit, which is slowly being reclaimed by evergreens. Other paths explore historic North Bloomfield, the company town that grew up around the mining operation.

Little Humbug Creek Falls, reached via a long downhill run through shady ravines, is a hydraulic exclamation point of an entirely different kind. Here the relentless passage of water over time has created a natural feature. Its power reinforced annually by snowmelt, Humbug Creek begins its fall by plunging from pool to pool and then is shot as if from a flume down a relatively low-angled cliff. The force of the water has sculpted the rock face and etched a thin channel that partially hides the flow; a platform about midway down the steep hillside next to the fall offers a safe viewpoint, with cables protecting the steep, rocky path above and below.

The Humbug Trail begins by crossing a tributary of Humbug Creek via a footbridge and then curling down alongside the stream through a dark, dense woodland of spindly second-growth pines. The needle-coated, moderately graded trail passes several mining pits as it drops, one bleeding an unnaturally vivid orange runoff.

Negotiate several steep descents (and ascents) through ravines, crossing the feeder streams by rock-hopping or wading. A Humbug Trail sign marks where the route merges with an unused roadway; continue downhill on the walk-and-talk track. At the base of the decline, pass a big pit on the left, cross a streamlet, and pass the "Hiking Only" trail sign. The trail becomes a winding singletrack beyond, rounding

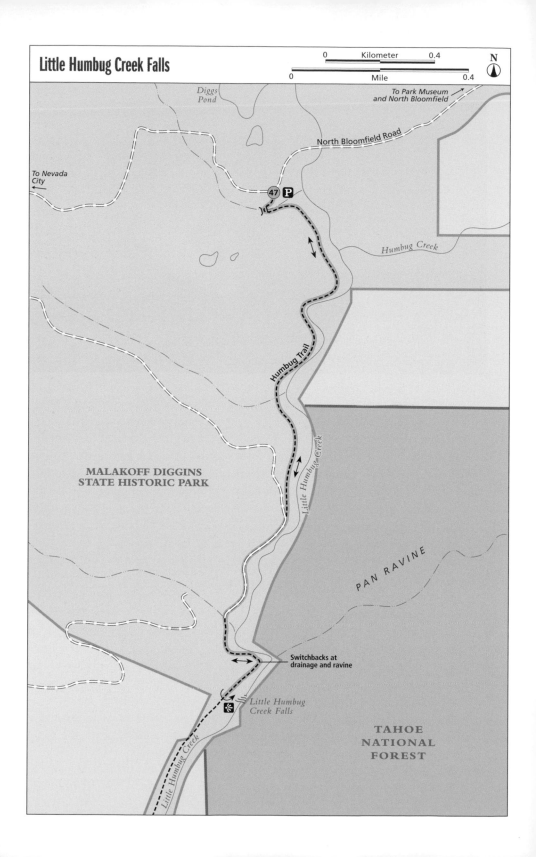

Little Humbug Creek Falls

0   Kilometer   0.4
0   Mile   0.4

N

Diggs Pond

To Park Museum and North Bloomfield →

North Bloomfield Road

To Nevada City →

47 P

Humbug Creek

Humbug Trail

MALAKOFF DIGGINS STATE HISTORIC PARK

Little Humbug Creek

PAN RAVINE

Switchbacks at drainage and ravine

Little Humbug Creek Falls

TAHOE NATIONAL FOREST

Little Humbug Creek

THE LEGACY OF HYDRAULIC MINING

In the mid-1800s, after gold was discovered in the foothills surrounding Nevada City, miners flooded into the region, some building a camp/town called Humbug (later North Bloomfield). When the placer gold played out, enterprising argonauts turned to more radical methods, carving a pit and cliff into the mountainside using a powerful but destructive new mining technique: hydraulics. They trained water cannons on the mountainside, blasting the gold out and making a nice profit in the process.

But hydraulic mining had a huge environmental downside, creating massive tailings piles and thousands of cubic feet of debris, some of which continued downstream, into the Humbug Creek drainage, then down into the South Yuba River, then into the Sacramento River, and on into San Francisco Bay. Accumulations of silt hampered navigation in the bay and surrounding rivers and led to the flooding of towns in the lowlands. After Marysville was devastated by a flood in 1875, a lawsuit was filed against the North Bloomfield Gravel Mining Company, which operated at Malakoff Diggins. Judge Lorenzo Sawyer handed down an injunction against hydraulic mining in that case, essentially rendering the practice unprofitable. The Sawyer legislation led to the shuttering of operations of the North Bloomfield Gravel Mining Company. In its wake the massive mining operation has left a provocative and strangely beautiful landscape.

switchbacks and descending steeply over rocky terrain to the waterfall and its overlook. Check out the fall, with its slots and pools, and then return as you came.

Miles and Directions

0.0 Start by dropping down across a bridge spanning a tributary of Humbug Creek. The trail curves downstream.

0.4 Pass an old pit filled with water stained an unnatural shade of orange.

0.7 Roller-coaster through a ravine, crossing a streamlet in the bottom.

1.0 Pass a Humbug Trail sign and meet up with an unused roadway coming in from the right. Continue left, heading downhill on the roadway.

1.2 At the base of the hill, cross a streamlet and pass a "Hiking Only" trail sign.

1.4 A cataract spills out of a side canyon; the trail curls sharply around a switchback, narrows, and steepens.

1.6 Reach Little Humbug Creek Falls. Descend the steep, sometimes slick trail to the platform that serves as an overlook. Retrace your steps.

3.2 Arrive back at the trailhead.

Option: The Humbug Trail continues down to the South Yuba River Trail. The round-trip distance for this strenuous upside-down hike is 5.4 miles.

48 Bear River Falls

A short walk along the interpretive Sierra Discovery Trail leads to a pretty waterfall and provides a lesson in emigrant history.

Height: 15 feet
Beauty rating: ★★★
Distance: 1.1-mile lollipop
Difficulty: Easy
Best season: Late spring and summer
County: Placer
Trailhead amenities: Restrooms, information signboards, trash cans, and picnic sites. Leashed dogs are permitted.
Land status: PG&E Bear Valley Recreation Area
Special considerations: The Bear River is part of PG&E's hydroelectric power generation system. Be aware of your surroundings. Hydro operations can change water depth, flow speeds, and temperatures. Know a path to higher ground. Obey all signage. Signs are posted for your safety.
Maps: USGS Blue Canyon CA; trail map on information signboards at the trailhead
Trail contact: PG&E Bear Valley Recreation Area; (530) 389-2236. Tahoe National Forest, Nevada City Ranger District, 631 Coyote St., Nevada City, CA 95959; (530) 265-4531; www.fs.usda.gov/tahoe/

Finding the trailhead: From I-80 at Emigrant Gap, take the CA 20 exit toward Nevada City. From the junction at the interstate, drive west on CA 20 for 3.5 miles to Bowman Lake Road. Turn right onto Bowman Lake Road and drive 0.4 mile to the Sierra Discovery Trail parking lot and trailhead on the left. GPS: N39 18.544' / W120 39.942'

The Hike

Hold out your left hand, palm up, fingers spread. Now picture this: Mount Shasta is at the tip of your thumb. Lassen Peak is at the tip of your index finger. The Sutter Buttes are on your palm. And the major rivers draining the watersheds of the Sierra Nevada into the mighty Sacramento—the Pit, the Feather, the Yuba, the American—flow down the gaps, watering the Great Valley at California's heart.

Talk about falling water …

This image is but one that is described on the interpretive displays at the beginning of the Sierra Discovery Trail. In addition to the hydrology lesson on your fingertips, you can also learn about the Native peoples who hunted and foraged in the High Sierra, the emigrants who made their way through the dangerous mountain gaps (they lowered their wagons 700 feet into the Bear River valley!), the wildlife and plant life that thrives in the woods and meadows, and the hydroelectric power generated by the water that flows out of the high country.

There's a waterfall too. It's not terribly big, but the setting is peaceful and the falls are easy to access via the partially paved interpretive trail that loops through a pocket of woodland alongside the Bear River.

Autumn colors highlight the falls on Bear River on the Sierra Discovery Trail.

The route is easy to follow. Pick up the path leading left from the information pavilion and head toward the river. A boardwalk spans an expanse of meadow that boasts a wildflower display in season and blushes golden-brown in fall. At the one and only junction, stay left to follow the loop in a clockwise direction. Spur trails leave the main path at various intervals, leading to the overlooks of the river and its falls, which are tucked in a shallow ravine, half hidden from view by the trees and brush that flourish alongside the waterway. Watch for petite water ouzels, which frequent the falls. From the falls the path continues through the woods, with interpretive signs offering further insight into the ecology of the area. The only climb along the route, which is short and moderate, is mitigated by switchbacks. The loop portion of the lollipop closes at the bridge spanning the Bear River; from here retrace your steps to the trailhead.

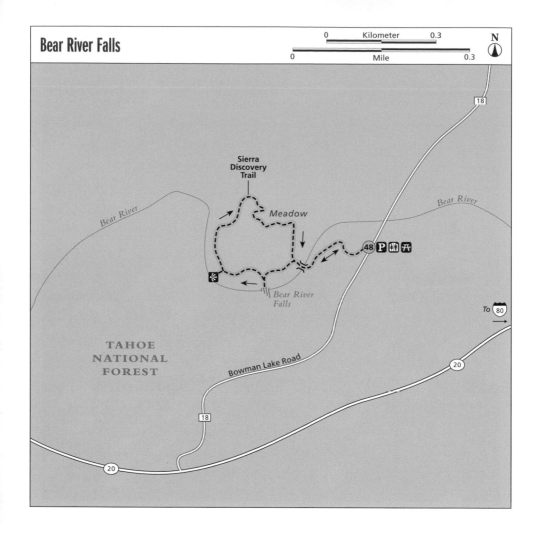

Miles and Directions

0.0 From the interpretive kiosk at the trailhead, go left on the paved path (the right path leads to the picnic area). Cross the boardwalk through the meadow.

0.2 Cross the bridge over the Bear River. At the junction on the far side, begin the loop by heading left, traveling clockwise.

0.3 At the junction go left to the riverside to view the falls. Return to the trail and go left to continue the loop.

0.4 A spur on the left leads a river overlook. A second spur to another overlook follows shortly.

0.6 A small meadow borders the trail on the left. Switchbacks lead up a moderate grade, and a pair of switchbacks lead back down to the riverside.

0.9 Close the loop at the bridge. Retrace your steps.

1.1 Arrive back at the trailhead.

49 Stevens Trail Falls

A walk in the footsteps of the forty-niners leads to a long cascade and a great overlook of the North Fork American River.

Height: About 300 feet
Beauty rating: ★★★★
Distance: 3.0 miles out and back
Difficulty: Moderate
Best season: Spring and early summer
County: Placer
Trailhead amenities: Restrooms, trash cans, and information signboards

Land status: Bureau of Land Management
Maps: USGS Colfax CA
Trail contact: Bureau of Land Management, Mother Lode Field Office, 5152 Hillsdale Circle, El Dorado Hills, CA 95762; (916) 941-3101; www.blm.gov/ca/st/en/fo/folsom/stevens trail.html

Finding the trailhead: From I-80 westbound in Colfax, take exit 135 for Colfax/Grass Valley. Go left at the stop sign onto North Canyon Road. Follow North Canyon Road, which parallels the interstate, for 0.5 mile to the signed trailhead and parking area on the left. If the lot is full, park carefully along North Canyon Road. GPS: N39 06.330' / W120 56.824'

The Hike

The Stevens Trail dates back to the California gold rush, built and managed as a toll road by a pair of enterprising miners, one with the surname of Stevens. The trail linked Colfax with the boomtown of Iowa Hill and was well traveled in the late 1800s. When the boom went bust, the trail fell out of service—and essentially out of sight. It began its renaissance in the late 1960s, when a Boy Scout from Sacramento rediscovered it. It is on the National Register of Historic Places.

The route sees a lot of traffic these days, with hikers, mountain bikers, and equestrians seeking rich vistas, fresh air, and exercise. The upside-down trek to the falls—and to the North Fork American River, if that's the goal—begins in a wash of highway noise; the interstate runs close by. But the noise fades as the path traverses down a slope forested in oaks, slipping across a few seasonal streams that feed a more substantial stream on the right.

At the base of the first descent, rock-hop across a small stream in the bed of the ravine and then bear right on the dirt road (a trail sign with an arrow points the way). The roadway leads up into a saddle, where several unsigned dirt roadways meet. Head down and left on the singletrack that slips back into the oaks; an inconspicuous trail sign points the way.

A final descent under a canopy of oaks leads to the waterfall, which flows in tiers down the brushy cleft of Robbers Ravine. You can walk to its base or beat a path through brush and poison oak up alongside, but arguably the best place to experience

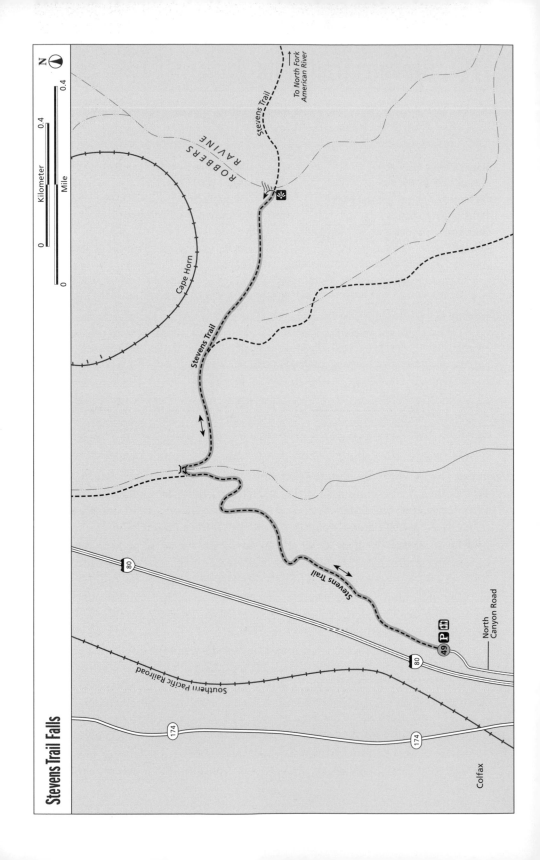

Stevens Trail Falls

N

Kilometer
0   0.4   0.4

Mile
0   0.4

Cape Horn

ROBBERS RAVINE

Stevens Trail

Stevens Trail
To North Fork
American River

Stevens Trail

80

80

49 P

Stevens Trail

North
Canyon Road

174

174

Southern Pacific Railroad

Colfax

The falls on Stevens Trail are best viewed from an overlook opposite Robbers Ravine.

the fall in all (or most) of its glory is from the substantial rock outcropping passed on the descent. A use trail leads out onto the fractured rock of the outcropping's summit. Look north to check out the entirety of the waterfall, which begins hundreds of feet above what can be seen from the approach. Then look south and down the wooded North Fork American River canyon, hundreds of feet below, as a silver thread winds through folds of green. Return as you came.

Miles and Directions

0.0 Start by taking the signed trail down through an open area. The path soon passes into oak woodland, with the trees and a hillside screening the sounds of the nearby freeway.

0.8 Reach a substantial creek crossing in the bed of a ravine. Cross either on rocks or on a narrow plank. On the far side a trail sign with an arrow points to the right, down a wide dirt road.

1.0 At the saddle stay left for a short distance on the roadway; then go left again on the signed trail.

1.3 At the Y-junction stay left on the signed hikers' trail. The route to the right is for cyclists.

1.5 Round a bend, and the falls come into view. Descend to the base, and then retrace your steps to a substantial rock outcropping, which offers the best waterfall views as well as views down into the North Fork American River canyon. Retrace your steps.

3.0 Arrive back at the trailhead.

Option: If time and leg power permit, you can continue downhill to the confluence of the North Fork and Steep Ravine, and the end of the Stevens Trail. Keep in mind that it's all uphill on the return trip. The round-trip distance is 9 miles, and the elevation change is about 1,200 feet. Highlights include views of Cape Horn, a radical turn in the historic Central Pacific rail line, and the remnants of gold rush–era mines, as well as the river itself.

50 Codfish Falls

The trail to Codfish Falls skims through a secluded portion of the North Fork American River canyon to a pretty cascade tucked away in a narrow gorge.

Height: About 25 feet
Beauty rating: ★★★★
Distance: 3.2 miles out and back
Difficulty: Moderate
Best season: Late spring and early summer. The falls dry up in the hot summer sun, and winter rain and snow may render the trail inhospitable.
County: Placer
Trailhead amenities: None. Bring drinking water.
Land status: Auburn State Recreation Area

Special considerations: The trailhead is reached via a steep, winding road. The final 2.4 miles of the road is unpaved, and a high-clearance vehicle is recommended.
Maps: USGS Colfax CA and Greenwood CA; Auburn State Recreation Area brochure available at recreation headquarters on CA 49 and online at www.parks.ca.gov
Trail contact: Auburn State Recreation Area, 501 El Dorado St., Auburn, CA 95603-4949; (530) 885-4527; www.parks.ca.gov

Finding the trailhead: Follow I-80 east from Auburn to the town of Weimar in the Sierra foothills (about 11 miles). Take the Weimar Cross Road exit. Turn right (west, then southwest) on Ponderosa Way. Follow Ponderosa Way to a gate at the end of the pavement at 3.2 miles; then drive down the steep dirt road into the canyon. The road leads another 2.4 miles to the bridge over the North Fork American River (5.6 miles total). Park along the wide stretch of road just northeast of the bridge. The trail is beyond the metal guardrails at the bridge's north abutment. GPS: N39 00.028' / W120 56.391'

The Hike

The trail leading to secluded Codfish Falls, in a side canyon carved by Codfish Creek, begins by following the North Fork American River. In late spring and early summer—the prime waterfall viewing times—the river swells with snowmelt, frothy and imposing. When the fury dies down and the summer sun begins to bake the foothills, the route skirts pools that invite side trips to sandbars and rocky beaches along the riverbank. That's when the year-round falls, which tumble down a jumble of dark rocks, fade to thin streams, watering a pocket of verdant mosses, oaks, and grasses in an otherwise parched environment.

Ponderosa Way, which dives into the American River canyon from Weimar, offers a huge hint at how out-of-bounds this stretch of trail in the Auburn State Recreation Area is. The dirt road falls steeply into the gorge, requiring a driver's full concentration. The narrow trail departs from the north abutment of the sturdy but rustic metal-truss Ponderosa Way bridge, which spans the North Fork at the bottom of the canyon. In summer a beach spreads below the trailhead, offering access to the cooling waters of the river—the first of several such opportunities to take a break and dip your toes, if the weather and water flow permit.

The dirt path traces the riverbank for about a mile before curving north into the Codfish Creek canyon. River canyon views dominate that mile, a classic tableau of water and rock walls. The trail is uneven in places, and sometimes exposed, but is relatively easy to negotiate. Markers along the way are keyed to an interpretive guide that may be stocked in the box near the trailhead ... and maybe not. Just to be sure, you can download and print a copy from the website at www.parc-auburn.org/codfish_creek.pdf. Compiled by a local high school student as a senior project, the guide describes the plant and animal life you'll see along the trail. Straddling the interface between the oak woodlands that dominate at lower elevations and evergreen forests that flourish higher up, the mixed forest on the canyon floor includes live and black oaks, red-barked mountain manzanita, bay laurels, redbuds (gorgeous in spring), the occasional madrone, and ponderosa pines. Pause at the golden-barked

Codfish Falls shrinks to a trickle in late season.

pines to sniff their vanilla scent—hugging a tree has never smelled so sweet.

Pass an outhouse as you curve away from the river and into the Codfish Creek canyon. The falls themselves are about 25 feet high, and whether vigorous with winter rain and snowmelt or thinning to a trickle in the summer season, they provide enough moisture to support a healthy coat of moss for the dark rocks on either side, and a cool destination for a hike at any time of year.

After your visit retrace your steps to the trailhead.

Miles and Directions

0.0 Start on the north side of the Ponderosa Way bridge, climbing over the guardrail onto the singletrack trail.

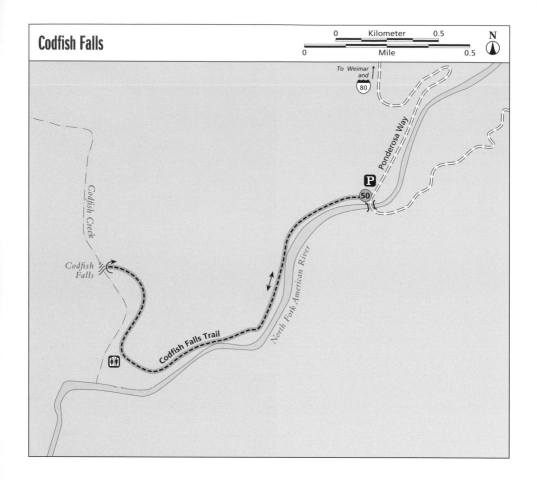

Codfish Falls

0.2 Pass a Codfish Falls/Discovery Trail sign and the box that may hold interpretive guides.

0.4 Flat sheets of shale pave a patch of trail.

0.6 The trail rides about 30 feet above the river, separated from the water by a relatively steep, rocky slope.

0.8 The trail narrows in a gully.

1.0 A narrow social trail breaks left (southeast) to the river. Stay straight on the obvious Codfish Falls Trail.

1.1 The trail curls northwest, away from the river.

1.2 Pass a little outhouse. The trail splits just beyond, with a couple of social tracks leading left (southeast), back toward the river. Stay right (northwest), heading up the side canyon toward the falls.

1.4 Cross a seasonal stream, dry in the late season. The trail gently climbs through the mixed evergreen forest.

1.6 Reach Codfish Falls. Enjoy the cool and the green; then return as you came.

3.2 Arrive back at the trailhead.

51 Devils Falls

The most accessible waterfall in the Auburn State Recreation Area tumbles into Shirttail Creek near its confluence with the North Fork American River.

Height: 150 feet
Beauty rating: ★★★
Distance: 1.0 mile out and back
Difficulty: Easy
Best season: Spring and early summer
County: Placer

Trailhead amenities: Portable toilets, trash cans, and fee station. A fee is charged.
Land status: Auburn State Recreation Area
Maps: USGS Colfax CA
Trail contact: Auburn State Recreation Area, 501 El Dorado St., Auburn, CA 95603-4949; (530) 885-4527; www.parks.ca.gov

Finding the trailhead: From westbound I-80 in Colfax, take the Canyon Way exit. Go right onto Canyon Way and drive 0.7 mile to the Yankee Jim Road intersection. Turn left onto Yankee Jim Road and go 4.5 miles to the bottom of the canyon. A rustic bridge spans the North Fork American River; a small parking area is on the north side of the bridge, with additional parking available in turnouts alongside the roadway on either side of the bridge. Yankee Jim Road is unpaved, narrow, and winding, but easily negotiated in a passenger car. GPS: N39 02.411' / W120 54.180'

The Hike

The bridge at the base of Yankee Jim Road in the scenic North Fork American River canyon is the jumping-off point for two waterfall hikes, as well as a popular stop for river buffs and anglers and a take-out point for kayakers. It can be crowded on warm spring and summer days.

You can drive to Devils Falls, but I recommend walking across the bridge and up the gravel road to check it out. Not only is there no parking alongside the roadway at the falls, making it difficult to spend time at the base, but hiking up the gently ascending road also allows you to enjoy the cataracts on Shirttail Creek in the steep ravine to the north. The walking is best in early spring and fall; the road can be busy during the summer months.

Devils Falls is an easy half-mile hike up the roadway on the right-hand side. The entirety of the cascade can't be seen from the track, but the 70 or so feet that are visible are impressive when the water falls in full force, fanning out across a mossy rock face, filling a shallow pool in the verge, and then emptying into a culvert that feeds into Shirttail Creek below. In dry season the falls are a seeping trickle down on the mossy cliff. Check it out, and then retrace your steps.

Devils Falls flows under Yankee Jim Road and into Shirttail Creek.

Miles and Directions

0.0 Start by crossing the bridge and continuing up Yankee Jim Road.

0.5 Reach the falls on the right side of the roadway. Return as you came.

1.0 Arrive back at the trailhead.

Option: Indian Creek Falls lies upstream along the North Fork American River from the Yankee Jim bridge. Unfortunately, reaching it involves crossing Shirttail Creek at its confluence with the American River—a jumble of boulders and channels that can be impassable during spring, when meltwater swells all watercourses in the foothills and when the Indian Creek Falls would be at its fullest. Take on the challenge as water levels permit, and be prepared to turn around if the crossing is unsafe. To reach the ford, cross the Yankee Jim bridge and head left at the trash containers, dropping onto the staircase that leads down through an oak glen to the riverside. Follow the river upstream to the creek and … well, good luck.

52 Calcutta Falls

These falls flow year-round but are ethereal, enlivening a walk through history on a rail-trail in the Sierra foothills.

Height: About 50 feet
Beauty rating: ★★★
Distance: 4.2 miles out and back
Difficulty: Easy
Best season: Late winter and spring
County: Placer
Trailhead amenities: Limited roadside parking; trash cans. Restrooms and information signboards are at the Stagecoach trailhead on the west side of the Old Foresthill Bridge, about 0.5 mile north of the CA 49 trailhead for the Riverview/Mountain Quarries Railroad Trail.

Land status: Auburn State Recreation Area
Maps: USGS Auburn CA; Auburn State Recreation Area brochure available at recreation headquarters on CA 49 and online at www.parks.ca.gov. The interpretive guide put together by the Auburn State Recreation Area Canyon Keepers is also a helpful resource. Keyed to posts along the trail, it provides information about the natural and human history of the route.
Trail contact: Auburn State Recreation Area, 501 El Dorado St., Auburn, CA 95603-4949; (530) 885 4527; www.parks.ca.gov

Finding the trailhead. From I-80 in Auburn take the CA 49 exit. Take CA 49 south through Auburn (toward Placerville), following the signs for 0.5 mile through the downtown area to where the highway plunges down into the American River canyon. CA 49 meets Old Foresthill Road at the base of the hill at 2.5 miles. Turn right (southeast), cross the bridge, and park alongside the road. The trailhead is at the gate immediately on the southeast side of the bridge. GPS: N38 54.894' / W121 2.404'

The Hike

The Mountain Quarries Railroad Trail rolls across the historic No Hands Bridge below the confluence of the Middle and North Forks of the American River, and then follows the river downstream through a lovely stretch of canyon. Before trail's end Calcutta Falls spills down a splintered cliff at trailside.

The falls aren't the only attraction along this stretch of rail-trail, which occupies the bed of a historic rail line that linked a limestone quarry on the Middle Fork American River with the town of Auburn and Southern Pacific tracks that continued down into Sacramento. The No Hands Bridge is so named, according to local trail guides, because for many years it didn't have guardrails (now it does). Once the longest bridge of its kind in the world, the scenic bridge, also known as the Mountain Quarries Bridge, survived the collapse of the Hell Hole Dam in 1964, as well as subsequent floods, and now provides hikers with a tangible encounter with history.

Enjoyably straightforward, the trail deviates from the original rail line only where trestles have been removed. Their concrete abutments, overgrown with shrubs and

The trail to Calcutta Falls follows an old railroad grade across No Hands Bridge.

inscribed with the dates they were poured—1915, 1921—overlook the gullies that the trestles spanned. The railroad, unable to negotiate the sharp curves in the river canyon, used trestles to straighten the line. Swinging through folds in the terrain poses no hardship to those on foot.

Railroads, even in the mountains, had to follow gentle grades, and the Mountain Quarries line was no exception. You'll encounter only one steep set of pitches along the route, where the trail dips into a gully washed by the small waterfall sometimes called the Black Hole of Calcutta. The year-round cascade offers a dark, cooling respite along the track. It's not very tall, but the dark rock of the cliff behind is striking, and finding flowing water (other than the river) in a landscape that is often parched by early summer is refreshing.

You can turn around at the falls, but the rest of the line makes for a pleasant walk. Continue along the flat, pleasant trail, enjoying great views down to the river.

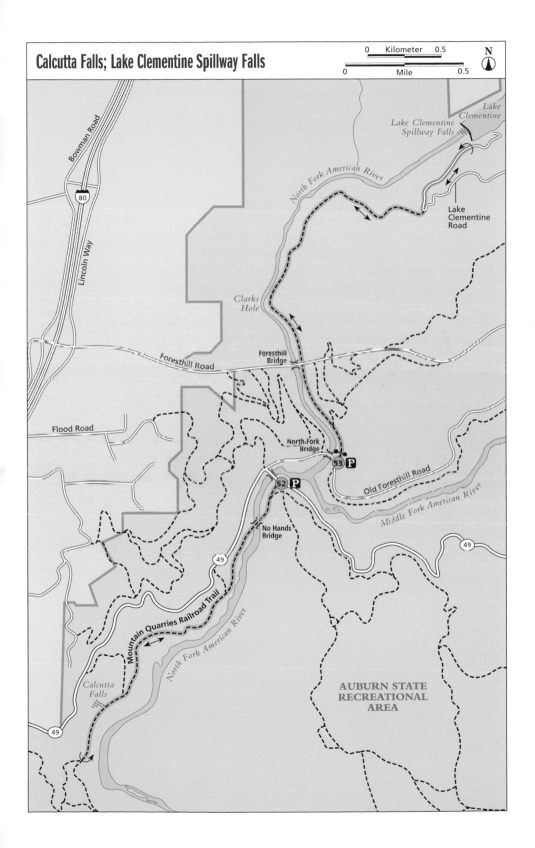

Calcutta Falls; Lake Clementine Spillway Falls

The exposed section of trail at the base of Eagle Rock, a steep, flaking monolith with debris spilling downslope, is particularly striking. Side trails lead both uphill and down to the riverside, but stay straight and flat and you'll never lose your way.

If there's a downside to this route, it's only that road noise from nearby CA 49 echoes in the canyon. The scenic and historic attributes of the route mitigate this potential distraction. The trail is also a portion of the Western States Trail, a 100–mile-long venue for endurance races for runners and equestrians.

Miles and Directions

0.0 Start by passing the gate at the trailhead.

0.2 Pass the junction with the Pointed Rocks Trail (which leads up toward Cool) on the left (south). Go right (west) across the No Hands (Mountain Quarries) Bridge.

0.3 Reach marker 3 on the west side of the No Hands Bridge and continue on the obvious rail-trail. An interpretive sign at the end of the bridge offers information about its historic significance.

0.6 Pass a Western States Trail sign and a pair of side trails. Remain on the obvious rail-trail.

0.8 Reach the first trestle abutment. The trail departs from the railroad grade, narrows to singletrack, and scoops through a gully.

1.0 Pass a trestle foundation dated 1915.

1.1 Reach Calcutta Falls, negotiating a steep up-and-down around the falls. You can turn around here or continue on the railroad grade, where you'll pass another Western States Trail marker.

1.3 Pass another trestle abutment.

1.4 At the unmarked trail intersection, stay left (straight/west) on the obvious railroad grade.

1.7 Skirt Eagle Rock, a giant, flaking rock face.

2.1 Pass a mile marker and another Western States Trail marker at the end of the railroad grade. This is the turnaround point. Retrace your steps.

4.2 Arrive back at the trailhead.

53 Lake Clementine Spillway Falls

There'll be some quibbling, but if a waterfall is defined as falling water, this fine spill out of Lake Clementine, reached via an easy out-and-back hike along the North Fork American River, definitely qualifies.

See map on page 177.
Height: 155 feet
Beauty rating: ★★★★
Distance: 4.6 miles out and back
Difficulty: Moderate
Best season: Year-round
County: Placer
Trailhead amenities: Restrooms, information boards, and additional parking are at the Stagecoach trailhead on the west side of the North Fork Bridge.
Land status: Auburn State Recreation Area

Maps: USGS Auburn CA; Auburn State Recreation Area brochure available at recreation headquarters on CA 49 and online at www .parks.ca.gov. The interpretive guide put together by the Auburn State Recreation Area Canyon Keepers is also a helpful resource. Keyed to posts along the trail, it provides information about the natural and human history of the route.
Trail contact: Auburn State Recreation Area, 501 El Dorado St., Auburn, CA 95603-4949; (530) 885-4527; www.parks.ca.gov

Finding the trailhead: From I-80 in Auburn take the CA 49/Placerville exit. Follow CA 49 through downtown Auburn (signs point the way) for about 0.5 mile to where the highway dives into the American River canyon. Proceed another 2.5 miles to the floor of the canyon and the junction of CA 49 and Old Foresthill Road. Continue for about 0.5 mile on Old Foresthill Road to the trailhead on the left, on the east side of the North Fork Bridge. Parking is alongside the roadway just beyond the bridge. The trail begins behind Gate 139, signed for Lake Clementine. GPS: N38 54.978' / W121 2.129'

The Hike

Not every dam spillway looks like a waterfall. Sometimes the water shoots from a tunnel; sometimes it is sluiced down one side of the dam face or the other. In the case of Lake Clementine, however, the spillway can only be described as a fall—a block or sheet waterfall, in fact, in the tradition of Niagara Falls ... albeit not nearly as spectacular. But from a perch overlooking the dam, with the lake pooling behind and the American River flowing away down its steep-walled canyon, the 155-foot wall of water is a worthy destination.

The route begins at the confluence of the North and Middle Forks of the American River, in the bottom of a spectacular canyon long slated for submersion beneath a huge and controversial reservoir. But the proposed Auburn Dam, besieged by seismic, environmental, and economic concerns since construction began in the mid-1960s, was brought to an apparently permanent halt in late 2008 when water rights held by the US Bureau of Reclamation were revoked. If completed, the dam would have

The spillway at Lake Clementine forms a wall of falling water.

impounded the river behind a 690-foot wall, and the popular trails that explore the North and Middle Forks would have been drowned. Now (hopefully) they can be enjoyed in perpetuity.

The trail to Lake Clementine showcases the lovely natural setting of the canyon, but man-made structures along the route also demand attention. The green lattice arches and massive concrete support columns of the Foresthill Bridge frame the trail's outset, the boom and clank of cars passing overhead echoing into the canyon. The high-flying bridge, reportedly the tallest in California, was built to span the reservoir that never materialized; the water would have reached as high as 22 feet below the deck once the lake was filled. More information on this bridge, and others along the route, is provided in an interpretive guide produced by the Auburn State Recreation Area Canyon Keepers.

Below the structure the wide dirt road to Lake Clementine follows the river's curves, with anglers' trails dropping off to the left to the rocky banks. The foundations of smaller historic bridges jut from forested hillsides, which are also scarred by minor slides and small fires. Islands and rocky shoals in the midst of the river harbor stands of willow that blush yellow in fall.

A little less than a mile upstream from the confluence, the river widens and deepens into Clarks Hole, a popular swimming spot formed by an "underwater dam" built by placer miners more than 100 years ago. This is a popular destination in and of itself, and makes a great turnaround spot for those seeking a shorter hike.

Beyond Clarks Hole the trail begins an easy, steady climb through a mixed evergreen forest, heavy on the oaks and light on the pines. It eventually reaches the paved Lake Clementine Road; a short trek down the pavement and along a singletrack trail leads to an up-close and personal view of the waterfall spillway of the North Fork Dam, with Lake Clementine pooling behind. The dam overlook is a perfect place to snack, rest, and watch small boats ply the smooth waters of a reservoir that actually came to be.

From the dam retrace your steps to the trailhead.

Miles and Directions

0.0 Start by passing the gate at the signed trailhead.

0.1 Stay left (riverside) at the unmarked trail fork.

0.2 Pass interpretive marker 7 at the concrete bridge abutment.

0.5 The trail narrows to singletrack as it passes beneath the massive support tower of the Foresthill Bridge.

0.8 Reach Clarks Hole. Social trails drop left to the riverside for the length of the pond-smooth pool.

1.0 The abutment for a historic (now defunct) covered bridge juts from the opposite bank. The trail begins to climb.

1.2 Pass a social trail leading down to the riverside. The trail continues to climb through oaks and scrub, with limited views opening of water spilling over North Fork Dam and Lake Clementine.

1.8 Arrive at the end of the dirt road/trail at a gate. Go left (north, then northeast) on the paved roadway.

2.2 A singletrack path leads left (north) toward the dam/spillway overlook.

2.3 Reach the overlook, take in the falling water views, and then retrace your steps to the trailhead.

4.6 Arrive back at the trailhead.

54 Hidden Falls

A loop hike through Hidden Falls Regional Park, just west of Sacramento, leads to the headline falls and also to an overlook of the Seven Pools.

Height: About 30 feet

Beauty rating: ★★★★★

Distance: 5.2-mile double loop

Difficulty: Moderate

Best season: Fall, winter, and spring (can get hot in the summer)

County: Placer

Trailhead amenities: Parking for both cars and equestrian trailers, restrooms, trash cans, picnic sites, and information signboard with park map. The park underwent significant improvements that were completed in 2013, expanding from 220 acres to 1,200 acres and opening 30 miles of trails, including a route to a second viewpoint overlooking falls in the Coon Creek drainage.

Land status: Hidden Falls Regional Park

Maps: USGS Gold Hill CA; online at www .placer.ca.gov/departments/facility/parks/ parks-content/parks/hidden-falls. Maps are also posted at numbered trail junctions, along with mileages.

Trail contact: Placer County Facilities Services, 11476 C Ave., Auburn, CA 95603; (530) 886-4900; www.placer.ca.gov/departments/ facility/parks/parks-content/parks/ hidden-falls

Finding the trailhead: From Sacramento head east on I-80 for about 25 miles to the exit for CA 49 to Grass Valley and Placerville in Auburn. Go north on CA 49 toward Grass Valley. Drive 2.5 miles to the junction with Atwood Road and turn right onto Atwood. Follow Atwood Road for about 1.7 miles to where it becomes Mount Vernon Road; then follow Mount Vernon Road another 0.5 mile (2.2 miles total) to a T-junction with Joeger Road. Go left, continuing on Mount Vernon Road for another 2 miles to the intersection with Mears Road on the right. Turn right on Mears Road and drive 0.5 mile to Mears Place. Turn right on Mears Place and go 0.2 mile to the signed park entrance. GPS: N38 57.516' / W121 09.830'

The Hike

Hidden Falls spills over a cliff in the ominously named Deadman Canyon. Don't let the canyon's moniker intimidate you. The trails leading to the falls and the nearby Seven Pools are far from frightening, and a gem of an overlook deck offers visitors a safe platform from which to enjoy the waterfall. The platform is a gathering place for park visitors and their dogs: Acquaintances are made, lunches are shared, and dogs are allowed to meet and greet each other and their humans.

The Seven Pools, by contrast, are reclusive. It would take a feat of bushwhacking through tick- and snake-infested brush to reach them from the rocky overlook perched high above on the Seven Pools Vista Trail. The cascade spills through the steep-walled Coon Creek canyon, overflowing from pool to pool in short bursts of whitewater.

The trails that link these two highlights cruise through canyons, alongside creeks, and traverse slopes shaded by a variety of oaks, bay laurels, manzanita, and the

A large observation deck overlooks Hidden Falls.

occasional digger pine, with bracken fern, blackberry, toyon, poison oak, and wild-flowers enlivening the understory.

The route begins by dropping away from the parking area on the Poppy Trail, a well-maintained path broad enough to allow hikers—or horses—traveling in opposite directions to pass without having to step off the track. The trail drops into Deadman Canyon via a few switchbacks and then runs alongside the creek down to a convergence of trails at a bridge spanning the waterway. The route is obvious, though use trails break right toward the creek.

From the bridge pick up the Falls Overlook Trail, which follows the creek downstream. A signed hikers-only trail breaks left from the overlook trail, dropping down a short flight of stone steps. Stay right where a social path leads down to the creek through purple-flowering vinca, which competes with blackberry as ground cover in a grove of spindly oaks.

Views of the creek below, flowing through rock-lined pools that form perfect swimming holes, open as the trail switchbacks. Pass a stone staircase on the right that leads down to the swimming holes before reaching the wooden deck overlooking the falls. The deck offers a great vantage of the stepped spill, which remains vigorous year-round but is most spectacular (and loudest) in spring when the creek is flush with meltwater from the Sierra Nevada.

From the platform you can retrace your steps to the trailhead for an easy 3-mile out-and-back hike. To continue the double loop, head back to the start of the hikers-only trail and turn left, climbing up to a shaded picnic site. Continue uphill on North Legacy Trail (Turkey Ridge Road), a gravel access road that climbs to the crest of the ridge.

Just before topping out, take the Quail Run Trail, which breaks to the left. Quail Run meets up with the Seven Pools Loop, which in turn drops around switchbacks into the Coon Creek canyon, passing through thickets of manzanita, poison oak, and scrub oak.

Down near the creek the route parallels the stream for a distance, passing a junction with the Turtle Pond Trail (an option back to the trailhead), and then begins to climb away from the waterway. As you ascend, the trail is bordered by toyon; in the fall its bright red fruits glow in the sunlight. Below, the creek tightens into cataracts.

When you arrive at the next trail junction, take the signed Seven Pools Vista Trail. This leads up to a rock outcropping that offers a bird's-eye view of the Seven Pools, spilling through the rocky, brush-choked canyon. The pools are all but inaccessible, with nary even a social trail ferreting down through the tangle of brush and rocks.

From the overlook the vista trail climbs back onto the ridge separating the Deadman and Coon Creek drainages. Pick up the Blue Oak Trail and descend via sweeping traverses and a switchback into Deadman Canyon. The Blue Oak Trail ends at the bridge and the junction with the Turtle Pond, Poppy, North Legacy, and Falls Overlook Trails. Climb the broad South Legacy Trail—actually a road, wide enough for horses to travel side by side and still leave plenty of room for a hiker to pass. Look for bracken fern and wild grape on the hillside above and below the roadway as you climb; this gives way to grassland at the end of the route. Pass the junctions with the paved Hidden Gate Trail and the Poppy Trail, and then arrive back at the trailhead.

Miles and Directions

0.0 Start by passing the restrooms and information signs. Where the South Legacy Trail, paved Hidden Gate Trail, and singletrack Poppy Trail meet, take the Poppy Trail to the right.

0.1 At the second trail junction (with a map board), stay right on the Poppy Trail.

0.6 After the third switchback the trail follows Deadman Creek downstream.

0.8 The Poppy Trail ends at Whiskey Diggins Bridge. Cross the bridge to the trail junction and go left on the signed trail to the Falls Overlook Trail (Hidden Falls Access Trail).

1.3 Reach the junction with the hikers-only trail down to the falls. Go left on the signed Falls Trail, staying right where a social trail breaks left toward the creek.

1.5 Arrive at the observation deck overlooking Hidden Falls. Enjoy the views and visit the swimming holes; then retrace your steps to the beginning of the hikers-only trail.

1.7 At the junction of the Hidden Falls access route and the hikers-only path, turn left and climb to a shaded picnic area. Go left on the North Legacy Trail (Turkey Ridge Road), a gravel road.

1.9 Stay right on the North Legacy Trail where an unsigned road breaks to the left.

2.1 Pass through a cattle gate (close it behind you) and climb to a trail junction just below the ridgetop. Go left on the singletrack.

2.2 Arrive at the signed junction on the Quail Run Trail. Go left on Quail Run, which loops back toward the cattle gate and then arcs sharply right into the woods.

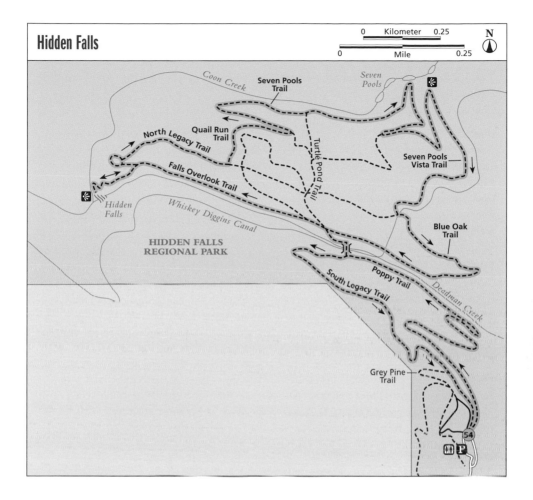

0   Kilometer   0.25

0   Mile   0.25

N

Coon Creek

Seven Pools Trail

Seven Pools

Quail Run Trail

North Legacy Trail

Turtle Pond Trail

Seven Pools Vista Trail

Falls Overlook Trail

Hidden Falls

Whiskey Diggins Canal

Blue Oak Trail

HIDDEN FALLS REGIONAL PARK

Poppy Trail

South Legacy Trail

Deadman Creek

Grey Pine Trail

54

2.4   At the signed junction (with a trail map board; this is junction 14), go left on the Seven Pools Loop.

2.9   At the signed junction with the Turtle Pond Trail, stay straight on the Seven Pools Loop.

3.1   Round a switchback with a trail sign and then cross a little bridge over a seasonal stream.

3.3   At the signed trail intersection, go left on the Seven Pools Vista Trail.

3.5   Arrive at the rock outcropping that serves as the Seven Pools overlook. Check out the views; then continue up the Seven Pools Vista Trail.

3.8   The Seven Pools Vista Trail ends on the Turkey Ridge Trail. Cross the road to the Blue Oak Trail and descend via the Blue Oak down into Deadman Canyon.

4.4   Reach the bridge and the junction with the North Legacy and Falls Overlook Trails (passed earlier). Go left, across the bridge, and then right on the broad South Legacy Trail.

5.0   The Grey Pine Trail merges with the track. Beyond, pass a trail map board and a junction with the Poppy Trail.

5.2   Arrive back at the trailhead.

55 Grouse Falls

Tucked in a remote ravine in the Sierra foothills, a short hike leads to an aerie view of Grouse Falls.

Height: About 500 feet
Beauty rating: ★★★★
Distance: 1.0 mile out and back
Difficulty: Easy
Best season: Late spring and early summer
County: Placer
Trailhead amenities: Information signboard

Land status: Tahoe National Forest
Maps: USGS Granite Creek CA
Trail contact: US Forest Service, American River Ranger District, 22830 Foresthill Rd., Foresthill, CA 95631; (530) 367-2224; www.fs.usda.gov/recarea/tahoe/home

Finding the trailhead: From westbound I-80 in Auburn, take the Auburn Ravine Road exit and head right (west) 1 block to the junction with Foresthill Road. Follow Foresthill Road for 12.5 miles to the junction with Mosquito Ridge Road in Foresthill. Turn right onto Mosquito Ridge Road and wind 19.2 miles to the junction with Peavine Road/FR 33. Turn left onto Peavine Road, a good gravel road, and go 4.6 miles to the junction with the forest road (FR 33) signed for the Grouse Falls overlook. There is parking for about five cars at this junction. Turn left onto the rougher gravel road and go 0.5 mile to the signed trailhead, with parking for about ten cars. While the rougher dirt road that leads to the trailhead proper can be traveled in a passenger car, conditions might warrant a high-clearance vehicle. GPS: junction of Peavine Road and FR 33 to the Grouse Falls overlook, N39 05.057' / W120 37.244'; Grouse Falls overlook trailhead, N39 05.265' / W120 37.262'

The Hike

The real adventure of getting to Grouse Falls is not the trail, but the drive. Both Foresthill Road and Mosquito Ridge Road traverse some of the most rugged, spectacular terrain on the west side of the Sierra Nevada, plunging into and out of forested canyons almost as pristine as when miners scoured the foothills looking for gold. On a winter's day, with the sun at a low angle and mist rising from the depths of the hollows, the views are stop-the-car fabulous.

And Grouse Falls, plunging more than 500 feet into an inaccessible ravine deep in the wild, is no slouch either. The falls themselves would require a herculean scramble to reach, but a short, easy, upside-down ramble through a woodland of pine, fir, and incense cedar leads to an overlook perched on the edge of the Grouse Creek ravine. The falls are across the void, a streak of white down a golden cliff in a green wilderness that could, and has, swallowed explorers, gold seekers, and tormented firefighters. The falls are split and tiered, fanning out as they descend and dropping out of sight into the creek drainage. Be humbled, and then return as you came.

Remote Grouse Falls spills into an inaccessible canyon in the Sierra foothills.

Miles and Directions

0.0 Start by descending from the trailhead into the woods.

0.5 Reach the overlook platform. Retrace your steps.

1.0 Arrive back at the trailhead.

56 Jenkinson Lake Falls

A pleasant hike along the shoreline of a foothills reservoir leads to a short but pretty fall and pool.

Height: 25 feet
Beauty rating: ★★★
Distance: 4.2 miles out and back
Difficulty: Easy
Best season: Late spring and early summer
County: El Dorado
Trailhead amenities: Large paved parking area, restrooms, picnic sites, trash cans, and boat launch
Land status: Sly Park Recreation Area, owned and operated by El Dorado Irrigation District
Maps: USGS Sly Park CA; online at www.eid .org/recreation/park-maps; available at the park entrance station

Other: Jenkinson Lake is the El Dorado Irrigation District's primary drinking water reservoir. While the state of California doesn't allow wading, swimming, or boating in reservoirs used for drinking water, Jenkinson Lake has a legislative exemption from that regulation. A condition of the exemption is that no domestic animals (pets) are allowed in the lake or its tributaries. Failure to abide by these conditions would result in the loss of the legislative exemption; please don't allow your pets in the water.
Trail contact: Sly Park Recreation Area/Jenkinson Lake (El Dorado Irrigation District), 4771 Sly Park Rd., Pollock Pines, CA 95726; (530) 295-6824; www.eid.org/recreation/contact

Finding the trailhead: From Sacramento head east on US 50 for about 50 miles, traveling through Placerville, to Pollock Pines. Take the Sly Park Road exit and go right (south) on Sly Park Road. Drive 4.2 miles to the Sly Park Recreation Area entrance on the left. GPS: N38 43.857' / W120 32.589'

The Hike

The waterfall on Park Creek, which feeds into sprawling Jenkinson Lake, is the primary draw of this route but just one of many pleasant diversions along the long trail that loops around the reservoir. The north shore of the lake, where about half of the route is located, is dotted with campgrounds and boat launches and picnic areas—a little flashy and a load of fun. The south shore—the waterfall is on this side—is more rugged and remote, very pretty, and just as much fun.

You can pick up the lakeside trail almost anywhere along the north shore of Jenkinson Lake. The challenge on busy summer days will be finding a place to park and get on the route. However, if you visit the park midweek, you may have the waterfall to yourself. Regardless of where you start, you'll travel on well-maintained footpaths, a few sections of gravel road, perhaps a stretch of campground road, and a sliver of boardwalk in the mix.

Beginning at the Stonebraker boat launch and picnic area, toward the northeast corner of the reservoir, descend a flight of steps to the Chimney-Sierra Trail, which

The pool below the falls on Park Creek is inviting on a hot summer day.

is unsigned but obvious. Head left (east) on the singletrack, enjoying great lake views. Here, and for most of the route, you'll pass plenty of places where you can drop off the trail to the lakeshore for a rest, a snack, or a swim.

The Chimney-Sierra Trail empties onto the paved lake service road at the Chimney campground. The campground is aptly named: There are two stone chimneys on the beach, one still upright and the other little more than a heap of broken rock. Follow the paved road east to Hazel Meadow and drop onto a boardwalk lined with interpretive signs describing the flora and fauna of the restored wetland surrounding one of Jenkinson Lake's inlet streams. The viewing platform affords great views down the length of the lake to one of its dams. Interpretive signs describe the importance of water conservation, the different species of bats in the park, and the annual lady-bug migration in spring, when the bright red, lucky bugs swarm on the trunks of the evergreens that line the meadow. Hazel Creek camp is behind the meadow, with picnic areas and restrooms.

The trail surface reverts to dirt singletrack on the signed South Shore Trail at the bridge over Hazel Creek. The path forks repeatedly as it follows the shoreline, with horses directed onto one path and hikers and bikers onto another (and sometimes bikers onto a separate trail of their own). Follow the signs, and don't worry if you make a "wrong turn"; the trails always merge again.

At about the 2-mile mark, the path leads into the Park Creek drainage, where a bridge spans the creek. There is no sign here, but the side trail to the Park Creek

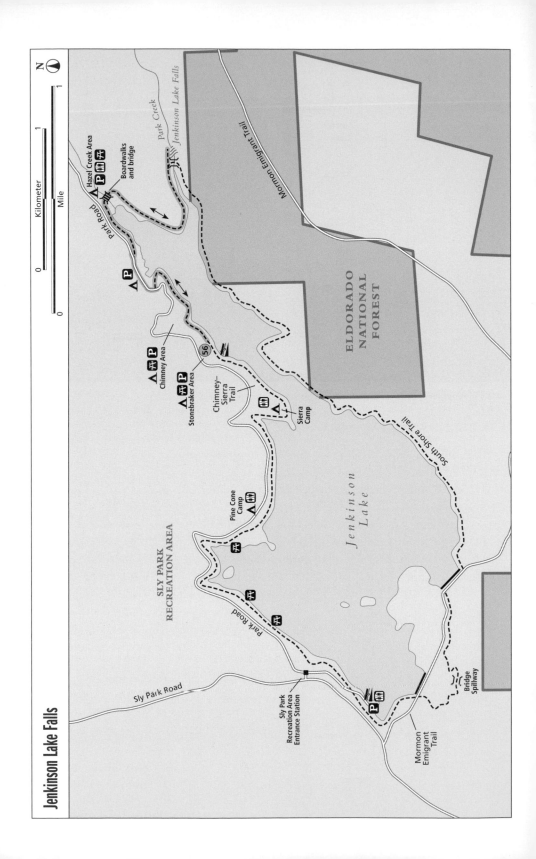

Jenkinson Lake Falls

SLY PARK
RECREATION AREA

ELDORADO
NATIONAL
FOREST

Jenkinson
Lake

Jenkinson Lake Falls

Park Creek

Park Road

Hazel Creek Area

Boardwalks
and bridge

Chimney Area

Stonebraker Area

Chimney–
Sierra Trail

56

Sierra
Camp

Pine Cone
Camp

South Shore Trail

Morrmon Emigrant Trail

Park Road

Sly Park Road

Sly Park
Recreation Area
Entrance Station

Mormon
Emigrant
Trail

Bridge
Spillway

N

Kilometer
Mile
0   1
0   1

waterfall is obvious, leading straight back along the waterway (around a fallen log) for less than 0.1 mile to the falls. The whitewater spill of about 25 feet lands in a clear pool, where you can wet your feet (or more), depending on the season. The pool is surrounded by a smooth rock outcropping, which is perfect for sunning and picnicking. Dark woods crowd the slopes surrounding the fall, lending a fairy-tale ambience to the spot. Enjoy; then return as you came.

Miles and Directions

0.0 Start by dropping from the Stonebraker parking area via a staircase to the unsigned Chimney-Sierra Trail. Go left on the dirt footpath.

0.25 Cross a little bridge in a wooded drainage.

0.6 Arrive at the paved road at the Chimney campground. Go right on the road, following trail signs painted on the pavement.

1.1 Reach Hazel Meadow and the Hazel Creek campground. Cross the boardwalk and the bridge over Hazel Creek, now on the signed South Shore Trail.

1.3 The trail splits. Stay right on the signed hiking trail (cyclists and equestrians are directed onto the left path). Social trails break right to the lakeshore; if you stay to the left, you'll stay on the loop trail.

1.75 The horse/bike and hiking trails merge. Stay right on the main path.

2.0 Arrive at the bridge over Park Creek. Go straight on the path around the fallen log to reach the waterfall.

2.1 Reach the waterfall. Retrace your steps.

4.2 Arrive back at the trailhead.

Option: The South Shore Trail is just one leg of a long, pleasant hike that circumnavigates the entire reservoir. From Park Creek a roller-coaster ramble continues through mixed evergreen forest, tracing the lakeshore with good views through the trees. As you near the first dam, the trail widens. Following a brief ascent, a descent drops you to the paved Mormon Emigrant Trail (not a trail, but a two-lane roadway). Go right, across the dam, to the signed trail on the far side. The well-signed trail parallels the road for a stretch and then crosses it again and switchbacks down to the spillway below the second dam. Follow the steep horse trail back up to the roadway and cross again to regain the lakeside path, now back on the north side of the lake. Be sure to take in the views from the boat launch parking area: Looking east across Jenkinson Lake, the Sierra crest, sometimes snowbound, is visible.

Beyond the boat launch the wide path passes through a stately evergreen forest, where the trees line up like columns on either side. The last few miles of the loop pass through the developed sections of the recreation area, with campgrounds and picnic areas lining the route. Occasionally the trail follows a stretch of paved campground road; sometimes it cruises through drainages and across bridges and boardwalks that span seasonal streams. The final leg, back on the Chimney-Sierra Trail, echoes the wild feel of the south shore. The loop is 8.9 miles total.

Mendocino

T he rugged Mendocino coastline is dotted with towns that evoke lazy weekends at bed-and-breakfast inns and savory meals of fresh seafood. One of these waterfalls spills from bluffs into the Pacific, and the other two are located in the coastal ranges to the east. Fort Bragg, Mendocino, and Point Arena are strung along scenic CA 1 like pearls on a strand.

The sun sets over the Stornetta Public Lands (hike 59).

57 Chamberlain Falls

A cleverly rerouted trail descends to a waterfall and pool in a steep, forested ravine.

Height: About 40 feet
Beauty rating: ★★★
Distance: 0.6 mile out and back
Difficulty: Easy
Best season: Winter and spring
County: Mendocino
Trailhead amenities: None
Land status: Jackson Demonstration State Forest

Maps: USGS Comptche CA, and Northspur CA; Jackson Demonstration State Forest map online at calfire.ca.gov/resource_mgt/downloads/JDSF_base_map.pdf
Trail contact: California Department of Forestry and Fire Protection, Jackson Demonstration State Forest, 802 N. Main, Fort Bragg, CA 95437; (707) 964-5674; calfire.ca.gov/resource_mgt/resource_mgt_state forests_jackson.php

Finding the trailhead: From Fort Bragg follow CA 20 east for 17 miles to the Chamberlain Creek Conservation Camp. Cross the highway bridge over Chamberlain Creek at highway marker 17.3 and turn immediately left onto FR 200 (not obviously signed, but a map and road marker are located just off the highway; the road is also signed for Camp Mendocino, a private Boy Scout camp). Follow FR 200 for 1.1 miles to the junction where Main Chamberlain and West Chamberlain Roads (aka FR 200) diverge. Go left on FR 200, a maintained dirt and gravel road, again signed for Camp Mendocino. Follow the good but winding road for 3.2 miles to a wide spot. A simple fence line framing a staircase marks the trailhead. Park alongside the roadway; there is room for four or five cars. GPS: N39 24.050' / W123 34.598'

The Hike

Secluded but easy to reach, Chamberlain Falls has the feel of a secret hideaway. Located in a dense stand of old-growth redwoods at the head of a steep ravine, with limited parking and no amenities, its appeal is its remoteness.

The waterfall is in the Jackson Demonstration State Forest, a one-of-a-kind forest managed by the California Department of Forestry and Fire Protection. Beginning in the 1860s, logging removed most of the old-growth redwoods and firs. The demonstration forest, established in 1949, manages the forest with sustainable timber harvests, and promotes research, restoration, and recreation. The forest offers vistas of redwoods, firs, and hardwoods, rustic camping, routes for equestrians and mountain bikers, and several interpretive trails, as well as the path leading down to Chamberlain Falls.

The route is short but engaging, and family friendly, provided children are supervised. Begin by descending a couple of flights of wooden stairs. The footpath then traverses down the steep, forested slope to a jumble of deadfall—huge evergreen trunks that obliterate the way forward. The route veers around these obstacles via

Chamberlain Falls drops into a shadowy hollow in the coastal mountains east of Fort Bragg.

quick switchbacks, hops over a step carved into one of the fallen trees, and then drops to the base of the falls.

The waterfall jumps about 25 feet off a dark cliff into a small pool in the thick shade of a stand of redwoods—the Eric Swanson Memorial Grove, according to a bronze plaque affixed to an adjacent boulder. Poolside rocks and flat patches of forest floor offer rough perches for waterfall viewing. West Chamberlain Creek below the falls is placid, an inviting place for children to explore. Return as you came.

Miles and Directions

0.0 Start by descending two flights of wooden stairs to a footpath.

0.3 Reach the base of Chamberlain Falls. Retrace your steps.

0.6 Arrive back at the trailhead.

Option: From the waterfall, you can continue upstream for about 1.5 miles to meet FR 200. The total for this loop is a little more than 3.0 miles.

58 Russian Gulch Falls

Cruise inland from the sea, through a fern canyon, into a wooded gulch that hosts a perennial waterfall.

Height: 40 feet
Beauty rating: ★★★★
Distance: 5.6 miles out and back
Difficulty: Moderate due only to distance
Best season: Winter, spring, and early summer
County: Mendocino
Trailhead amenities: Restrooms, water, trash cans, picnic facilities, and campsites. A fee is charged.

Land status: Russian Gulch State Park
Maps: USGS Mendocino CA; park map available at the entrance station and online
Trail contact: Russian Gulch, Mendocino Headlands, and Van Damme State Parks, 12301 North CA 1, Mendocino, CA 95460; (707) 937-5804; www.parks.ca.gov

Finding the trailhead: From Fort Bragg head south on CA 1 for about 8 miles to the signed entrance to Russian Gulch State Park. Go right into the park, pass the entrance station, and then follow the park road down and under the scenic highway bridge to the day-use parking area at the rec hall and campground. If the gate is open, you can continue through the campground to the parking area at the gated trailhead proper. Parking can be full on busy weekends, so your starting point for the hike may vary. GPS (parking at the camp entrance): N39 19.829' / W123 48.122'

The Hike

Despite its proximity to the Pacific Ocean, there's not much sign of the sea on the trail through Fern Canyon and up to Russian Gulch Falls. The water in the gulch is all fresh, filtering out of gullies and ravines into the main stream, and the sound that fills the bottomland is not that of pounding surf but of falling water.

The route to the falls follows a flat, mostly paved multiuse trail that traces the north side of the stream. Willows and oaks line the waterway, with redwoods and pines on the ridges, and an understory of ferns creeps up the canyon walls in places, forming alleys of verdant green. The path is easily shared by all users and invites walking and talking, making it a family favorite.

The route begins at the entrance to the campground (though if the gate is open and parking is available, you may shave 1.0 mile off the round-trip distance by starting at the Fern Canyon trailhead proper). Follow the road through the sites, then through the parking area, to the gate at the beginning of Fern Canyon. A long, easy walk lies ahead, punctuated by streamlets filtering down and under the path, fern-clad rock outcroppings, and trees that drip with lace lichen and sport bursts of fern and moss on their trunks.

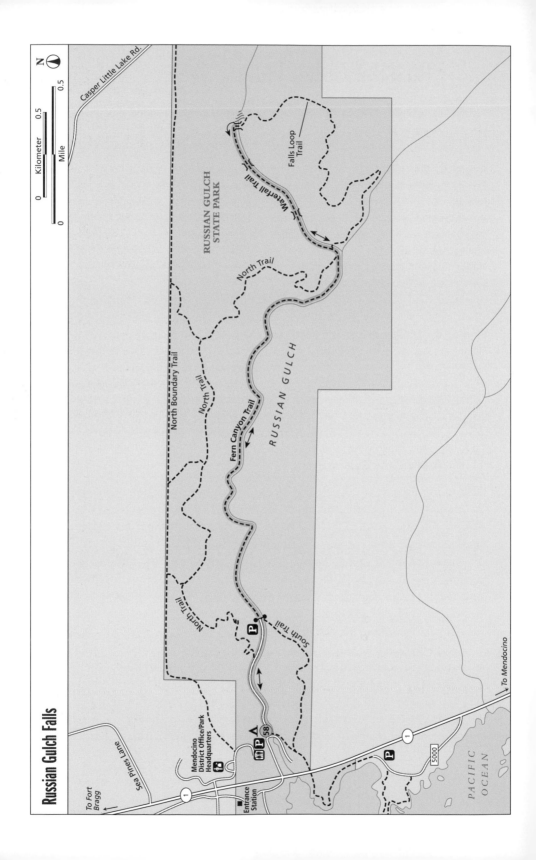

Russian Gulch Falls

RUSSIAN GULCH STATE PARK

Casper Little Lake Rd.

North Boundary Trail

North Trail

North Trail

North Trail

Fern Canyon Trail

South Trail

Waterfall Trail

Falls Loop Trail

RUSSIAN GULCH

Sea Pines Lane

To Fort Bragg

Mendocino District Office/Park Headquarters

Entrance Station

58

5000

To Mendocino

PACIFIC OCEAN

N

0   0.5   Kilometer
0   0.5   Mile

Cyclists must ditch their bikes where the pavement ends, a little more than 2 miles into the gulch. North Trail and the Falls Loop Trail intersect here, but the most direct path to the falls climbs straight ahead up a narrow dirt track. The going is more difficult, with the trail climbing steps and crossing wooden footbridges as it traverses above the steepening waterway. A final descent drops you onto the bridge below the falls, which sprawl over a rock face that bulges like the belly of a Buddha. Redwoods tower overhead, and ferns cluster on the steep slopes.

The bridge is a perfect overview, but possibly clotted with other hikers. Wide patches on the trails above the falls also provide nice vantage points. Return as you came.

Ferns, moss, and redwoods crowd the trail to Russian Gulch Falls.

Miles and Directions

0.0   Start by walking up the campground road toward the trailhead proper.

0.5   Meet the Fern Canyon Trail proper. Follow the paved path into the gulch. (You can start here if the campground gate is open and parking is available.)

1.7   The stream forms a small cataract.

2.2   Reach the end of the paved trail and the junctions of the Waterfall Trail, North Trail, and Falls Loop Trail. Follow the signs for the Waterfall Trail, a dirt track that climbs directly up the gulch.

2.4   Climb a set of stairs and cross a footbridge over a side stream.

2.6   Climb another set of steps to another footbridge.

2.8   Reach Russian Gulch Falls. Check out the sights from the bridge at the base or from viewpoints on the trails just above the falls. Retrace your steps.

5.6   Arrive back at the trailhead.

Options: You can stretch your hike and your exploration of Russian Gulch by continuing past the waterfall to pick up the Falls Loop Trail. Another option is to follow the hiker's-only North Trail, which departs from the campground and meets up with Fern Canyon Trail where the pavement ends.

59 Stornetta Falls

Walk along the edge of the continent to a seasonal fall that spills over a steep bluff into the Pacific.

Height: About 200 feet
Beauty rating: ★★★★
Distance: 1.8 miles out and back
Difficulty: Easy
Best season: Winter and early spring
County: Mendocino
Trailhead amenities: Portable toilets and information signboard

Land status: Bureau of Land Management
Maps: USGS Point Arena CA; map on the Stornetta Public Lands site online
Trail contact: Bureau of Land Management, Ukiah Field Office, 2550 N. State St., Ukiah, CA 95482; (707) 468-4000; www.blm.gov/ca/st/en/fo/ukiah/stornetta.html

Finding the trailhead: From Point Arena head north on CA 1 for about 2.5 miles to Lighthouse Road. Turn left (west) onto Lighthouse Road and go 1.3 miles to the roadside trailhead and parking pullout on the left. About ten cars can park in the pullout, with additional parking available alongside the road (be sure to pull clear of the traffic lane). GPS: N38 56.421' / W123 43.780'

The Hike

Stornetta Public Lands, which stretches along the coastline north of Point Arena, is a relatively new addition to California's parklands. It's part of the California Coastal National Monument, established in 2000 to protect islands and rocks along the state's coastline. Development of this pocket of the monument, administered by the Bureau of Land Management, is minimal, with a single track wandering along the edges of bluffs that drop several hundred feet into the Pacific Ocean. It's an edge-of-the-continent extravaganza, with views stretching north to the Point Arena Lighthouse, south into Point Arena, east into the coastal ranges, and west—oh, west—over Sea Lion Rocks to the endless horizon.

The Stornetta waterfall is fed by a slender, perennial stream that pours off the edge of the bluffs near trail's end. Rainfall charges the watershed, so time your visit for the winter or after a healthy springtime rainstorm. The stream pours through a cleft in the bluff top, and the fall, which spills into that cleft, is best viewed by circling around on the bluff arcing west (seaside) of the stream.

The waterfall is about a mile from the trailhead and reached via a rough, flat path beaten into the grass by hikers' boots and delineated with four-foot-high brown trail markers. Watch for sinkholes, which form when the tides erode the bluffs. Avoid the holes, and avoid getting too close to the edges of the bluffs themselves, which are also prone to erosion. Staying clear is not a hardship, however, because the views are endless no matter where you stand. Take in the falls, take in the vistas, take in the wind,

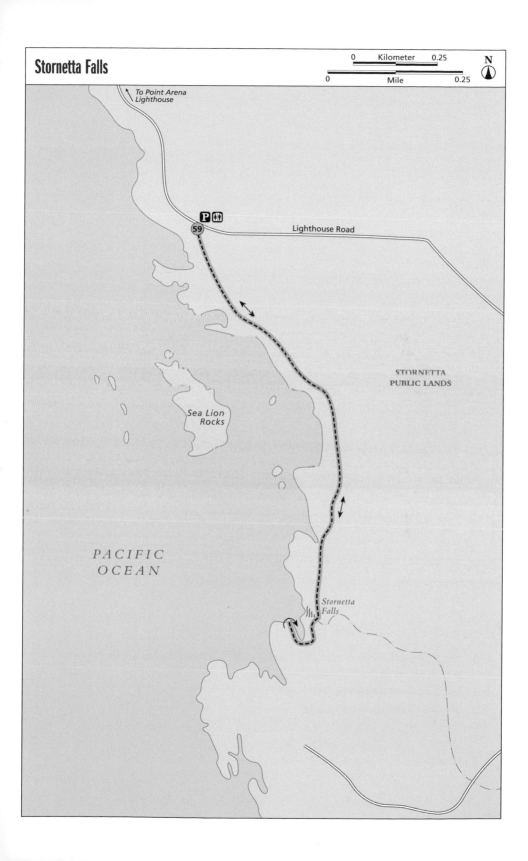

Stornetta Falls

0   Kilometer   0.25

0   Mile   0.25

N

To Point Arena
Lighthouse

59

Lighthouse Road

STORNETTA
PUBLIC LANDS

Sea Lion
Rocks

PACIFIC
OCEAN

Stornetta
Falls

Water flows gently over the edge of the bluffs at Stornetta Falls.

and then return as you came. ***Note:*** Erosion on the bluff had focused the stream/waterfall into a cleft as of mid–2015. Future geologic shifts may expose the fall in a different way.

Miles and Directions

0.0   Pass through the stile and head off across the bluffs, following the track beaten into the turf and the slender, widely spaced trail markers.

0.5   Pass a cluster of wind-whipped cypresses.

0.7   Cross the stream above the waterfall.

0.9   Curl around on the bluff west of the waterfall, looking back east to view the stream as it meets the cliff. Retrace your steps.

1.8   Arrive back at the trailhead.

San Francisco Bay Area

Most of the falls in the Bay Area are seasonal, best viewed in winter and late spring, when rains have saturated the hillsides and runoff flows into streams and creeks. The North Bay, and particularly Marin County, brings in the prize for the most waterfall hikes, while Uvas Canyon, in the South Bay, takes home a ribbon for the greatest concentration of falls on a single trail loop. San Francisco is the obvious hub of the region, with San Rafael the major city in the North Bay, Oakland in the East Bay, and San Jose in the South Bay. A web of major highways, including US 101, I-80, I-680, and I-280, link Bay Area cities, parks, and waterfalls.

Wild sweet pea blooms along the trail to Cataract Falls (hike 66).

60 Sugarloaf Fall

An easy loop in a Wine Country park leads through meadowland and woodland to a seasonal cascade near the headwaters of Sonoma Creek.

Height: 25 feet
Beauty rating: ★★★
Distance: 2.0-mile loop and spur
Difficulty: Easy
Best season: Winter and spring
County: Sonoma
Trailhead amenities: Restrooms and an information signboard at the trailhead. Water, information, picnic sites, a campground, and a visitor center are nearby. The park is also home to the Robert Ferguson Observatory, which houses several telescopes and is open on a limited basis. A fee is charged.

Land status: Sugarloaf Ridge State Park
Maps: USGS Kenwood CA; park map available at the entrance kiosk and online
Trail contact: Sugarloaf Ridge State Park, 2605 Adobe Canyon Rd., Kenwood, CA 95452; (707) 833-5712; www.sugarloafpark.org.

Finding the trailhead: From CA 12 in Kenwood, head east on Adobe Canyon Road. Travel 4.7 miles up the scenic roadway, passing the park boundary sign, to the entry kiosk. The parking area is 0.1 mile past the kiosk on the left. GPS: N38 26.279' / W122 30.862'

The Hike

Sugarloaf Fall, also called the Canyon Trail waterfall and the Sonoma Creek waterfall, is tucked in a verdant canyon on the lower slopes of Bald Mountain. It's a pretty little seasonal cascade, strengthened by winter rains and typically dry by late June, with a pool at its base and a thick green canopy overhead.

Hiking directly to the fall is a relatively straightforward affair, but it would be a shame to limit your visit to this unique regional park to that experience. One aspect of that uniqueness is the park's astronomical focus: Not only is it home to the Robert Ferguson Observatory and its telescopes, it also features a Planet Walk, a moderately difficult hike that scales the solar system to walking distance. Another unusual feature: Sugarloaf Ridge is operated by Team Sugarloaf, a partnership of nonprofits led by the Sonoma Ecology Center, which took over operation of the park when it was threatened with closure by a statewide funding scandal that erupted in 2012. Team Sugarloaf's operating agreement is in place through 2019.

The Canyon Trail leads directly down to the fall from near the entrance station, but a pleasant loop that incorporates a bit of meadow and some nice views down the valley toward the vineyards of Kenwood is described.

Begin by hiking up the broad Stern Trail, which cruises through grassland that is liberally peppered with wildflowers in the spring and burnished gold in late summer and fall. This graded, gravel, walk-and-talk stretch also features great views down Adobe Canyon toward Kenwood.

Sonoma Creek cascades from its headwaters in Sugarloaf Ridge State Park to the valley floor.

Leave the Stern Trail for the narrow Pony Gate Trail, dropping through more grassland to the junction with the Canyon Trail. You'll remain on the Canyon Trail for the remainder of the hike, dropping first through an open oak woodland and then down onto the park road. Cross the road to the sign on the creekside and continue the descent in a woodland of oak and bay laurel with a more riparian flair, its understory composed of ferns and poison oak, and the occasional maple entering the mix.

The trail parallels a seasonal stream as it drops into the canyon. The unsigned trail to the fall branches left (south) off the main Canyon Trail at 1.3 miles, but it's clear and well used. Scramble down a final stretch to poolside; the fall rumbles over large rocks at the head of the narrow, darkly green dell.

To return to the trailhead, retrace your steps to the junction of the Canyon Trail with the park road. Turn right onto the park road and follow it up, past the entrance kiosk, to the trailhead and parking area.

Miles and Directions

0.0 From the parking lot walk down the park road toward the entrance kiosk for less than 0.1 mile to a signed junction with the Stern Trail/Bay Area Ridge Trail. Turn right onto the dirt road and begin a moderate climb.

0.6 At the signed junction with the Pony Gate Trail, turn left and follow the singletrack down through the grasses.

0.75 At the signed junction go left onto the Canyon Trail. Cross a streamlet that flows only in the wet season.

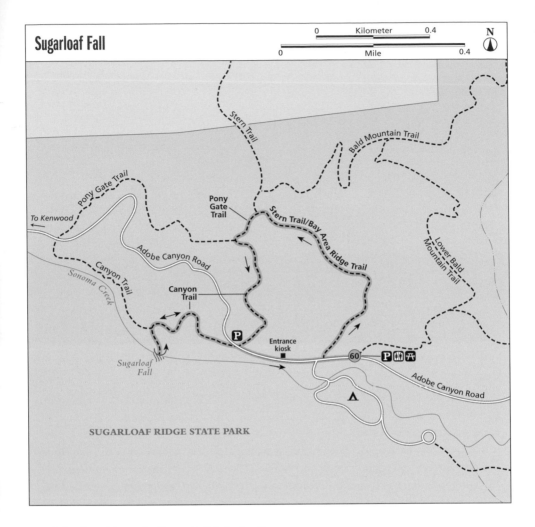

Sugarloaf Fall

0.9 Stay right on the Canyon Trail, following the arrow.

1.1 Drop into the parking area for the Canyon Trail. Cross the park road and pick up the trail, which drops into the ravine cradling the creek.

1.3 At the unsigned trail junction, turn sharply left on the well-used trail that descends toward Sonoma Creek.

1.4 Reach the waterfall. Take it all in; then retrace your steps to the park road.

1.7 Turn right and follow the park road toward the entrance station.

2.0 Arrive back at the trailhead.

Option: To make a slightly longer loop, you can stay right on the Pony Gate Trail at the first junction, and head downhill for 0.8 mile to the park road. Cross the road and head downhill about 25 yards to the Canyon Trail. Follow the Canyon Trail uphill to the falls in 0.2 mile, then continue up the Canyon Trail to the upper road junction and trailhead. Total distance is about 2.6 miles.

61 Bouverie Falls

Charged by rainfall in the Mayacamas Mountains, this waterfall is one of many headliners along the trails in this well-tended nature preserve.

Height: About 100 feet
Beauty rating: ★★★★
Distance: About 4.5 miles
Difficulty: Moderate
Best season: Late winter and spring
County: Sonoma
Trailhead amenities: Restrooms and information center
Land status: Nature preserve

Maps: USGS Glen Ellen CA; map available at the preserve
Trail contact: Audubon Canyon Ranch Bouverie Preserve, 13935 CA 12, Glen Ellen, CA 95442; (415) 868-9244; http://egret.org/visit_bouverie. Access is by appointment only. To secure a spot in a docent-led tour in spring or fall, send your name, address, phone number, and the number of people in your party to rsvp@egret.org. There is no fee, but donations are accepted.

Finding the trailhead: From downtown Sonoma follow CA 12/Sonoma Highway west toward Glen Ellen for about 6.5 miles. The signed preserve access road is on the right, about 0.3 mile east of the traffic signal at the junction of CA 12 and Arnold Drive (if you reach the signal, you've gone too far). Pass through the gate and follow the access road for about 0.5 mile to the parking area at the information center. GPS: N38 22.136' / W122 30.480'

The Hike

The lovely and secluded seasonal waterfall in the Bouverie Preserve, most vigorous toward the end of a winter with healthy rainfall, plummets down a brushy cliff in an alcove of the steep and heavily wooded Mayacamas Mountains. The hike to the fall is a stellar, docent-led immersion in the nature of the Sonoma Valley.

The 535-acre preserve is the legacy of architect David Bouverie, who welcomed a number of mid-twentieth-century writers and artists to his Valley of the Moon property, most famously food maven M.F.K. Fisher, who lived on the ranch for a time. Bouverie gifted the land to the nonprofit Audubon Canyon Ranch, setting it aside for both preservation and educational purposes. The preserve runs a sought-after nature program for schoolchildren; public access is restricted to guided weekend nature walks. The limited access ensures that the preserve is not overused, a hallmark of careful stewardship that allows the native ecosystems—riparian, chaparral, oak woodland—to retain natural values close to what was in the valley before development took place.

Trails within the preserve permit docents to lead visitors on a number of different routes, from easy to more strenuous. Reaching the waterfall is a common goal, and the docents headed out that way will make clear the destination. The route described

here is a long loop within the preserve, leading to other highlights as well as the waterfall.

From Gilman Hall (the information/visitor center), which is filled with educational displays, several trails lead back toward the Canyon Trail, a wide path that follows Stuart Creek deeper into the watershed. One of these routes, the Josephine Trail, is peppered with things that don't belong—plastic toys stashed in the crooks of trees and perched on rocks—that docents use to help sharpen students' observational skills.

Along the Canyon Trail check out the roadcut on the left. The homes of turret spiders, shaped like … turrets … jut from the earth. The first one is hard to find, but once spotted, suddenly they are everywhere along the cut. In winter and early spring, watch for the unofficial preserve mascot, the red-bellied newt, as it migrates down to Stuart Creek. On one hike in the preserve, the newts were so numerous we had to watch our step to avoid squishing them. Low, numbered posts along the creek denote paths leading to the streamside, where you can observe newts and other creatures in the waterway.

Beyond the junction with the trail that leads to the redwood grove, your docent will know the best way to proceed to the waterfall. The Canyon Trail was damaged by a landslide following the 2014 Napa earthquake; plans were in place to reroute the trail in 2015. Regardless of the route, it's a climb to the falls, either via the Connector Trail to the Rim Trail, which drops back into the canyon to the falls overlook, or via a more direct route. The route shown on the map links the Canyon Trail with the Rim Trail via switchbacks and staircases, and then follows the Rim Trail down to the waterfall overlook. Just follow the leader.

By any trail you'll reach the waterfall overlook at about the 2-mile mark. That same 2014 earthquake had an unexpected effect here: It punched the bedrock in such a way that streams in the North Bay region, including Stuart Creek, were recharged in the midst of the dry season and drought, and the waterfall was flowing even in October. After coursing down the cliff face for a long pitch, the final drop into the pool at the base is a free fall fronting a dark alcove. There's no access to the base of the falls, but the overlook is a great place to rest, snack, and recharge for the return leg of the loop.

Again, your return route to the trailhead may differ, but this loop follows the Rim Trail back up onto the mountainside, where views open down Stuart Canyon into the Sonoma Valley proper. The trail drops down to Cougar Pond, often dry in late season but a magnet for local wildlife, including mountain lions and bobcats, when water is available. Continue down to the Grandmother Oak, a massive specimen, and then up to a re-created Native camp, with bark hut, acorn granary, and sun shelter. A short side trip leads out to a viewpoint that, on a clear day, offers a stunning vista

◀ *Ordinarily dry by late season, the waterfall in the Bouverie Preserve was recharged after an earthquake in nearby Napa in 2014.*

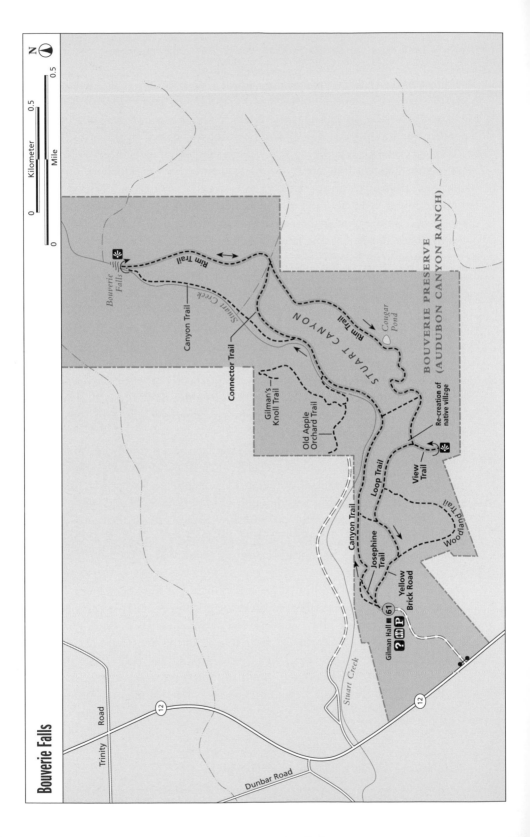

Bouverie Falls

south down the widening valley all the way to San Francisco Bay. A final downhill run leads into the meadowlands, where wildflowers bloom in profusion in season. The loop ends back at the information center and parking area.

Miles and Directions

0.0 Start at the information center, heading east on one of several trails that lead toward the Stuart Creek drainage.

0.3 Merge onto the Canyon Trail, paralleling Stuart Creek.

0.7 At the junction with the trail that leads to the right to the redwood grove, stay left on the Canyon Trail.

1.0 At the junction with the Connector Trail, head uphill via switchbacks and stairs. In 2014 plans were in place to reroute the Canyon Trail beyond this point. Your route from here to the waterfall may vary; your docent will know the way.

1.4 At the junction with the Rim Trail, head left and down toward the waterfall overlook.

2.0 Descend a wooden staircase to the waterfall overlook, which is to the right. Check out the waterfall, and then return to the staircase and retrace your steps along the Rim Trail.

2.6 Back at the junction with the Connector Trail, continue straight on the Rim Trail.

3.4 Pass Cougar Pond. Continue downhill on the Rim Trail.

3.5 Arrive at the junction with the Loop Trail. Go left to the Grandmother Oak; a right-hand turn leads to the redwood grove and the Canyon Trail. When you reach the Grandmother Oak, continue uphill to the left, circling around to the mock Native camp.

3.7 Follow the spur trail to the viewpoint at its end, and then return to the main route and go left. Stay on the main track up and over a last hill, staying right at junctions toward Gilman Hall.

4.5 Arrive back at the trailhead.

62 Indian Valley Falls

A pleasant trail winding through oak woodland leads to this seasonal waterfall.

Height: 25 feet
Beauty rating: ★★★
Distance: 2.9-mile lollipop
Difficulty: Easy
Best season: Winter and spring
County: Marin
Trailhead amenities: Restrooms behind the ball fields; information signboard

Land status: Indian Valley Open Space Preserve
Maps: USGS Petaluma CA; online at www.marincountyparks.org
Trail contact: Marin County Parks Administrative Office, Marin County Civic Center, 3501 Civic Center Dr., Ste. 260, San Rafael, CA 94903; (415) 473-6387; www.marincounty parks.org

Finding the trailhead: From US 101 in Novato, take the Ignacio Valley exit. Follow Ignacio Boulevard for about 2.5 miles to the Indian Valley campus of the College of Marin. Proceed through the campus to the road's end in the parking lots for the campus ball fields. An information signboard marks the informal trail, which passes behind the ball fields before reaching the trails of the preserve proper. GPS (parking at the ball fields): N38 04.602' / W122 34.925'

The Hike

One of several seasonal waterfalls in Novato-area open space parks, the no-name waterfall in the Indian Valley Open Space Preserve is reached via a pleasant loop hike with some of the friendliest switchbacks you'll ever encounter on a trail. It's a modest little fall, only about 25 feet high and entirely fed by rainwater (which means it's typically dry by summertime), but the loop trail that leads past the fall is a pleasant immersion in a pocket of oak woodland.

The route begins by climbing past the gardens of the Indian Valley campus of the College of Marin to Pacheco Pond. The pond is small and reed-lined, with mallards and other waterfowl enjoying the year-round water source. This makes a nice, short-hike destination in itself.

From the pond the route switchbacks gently uphill, winding through well-spaced oaks, red-barked manzanita, and wildflowers in season. The grade is gentle enough that walking and talking is easy, making this a premier Sunday afternoon walk with family and friends. The first set of switchbacks leads to a long curve through a gully, and then to a second set of switchbacks that ends at a four-way junction in a saddle.

The descent to the waterfall is as easy as the climb, following a no-name stream down a steep ravine. Oaks and bay laurels provide abundant shade, and moisture prompts blooms of ferns and mushrooms alongside the path. Negotiate a series of stream crossings as you descend, which may be slippery or tricky depending on water flow. The stream is a constant, whether flowing strongly, trickling, or merely a dry bed.

The namesake feature of the Waterfall Trail in Indian Valley.

The final stream crossing is just beyond the junction with the Susan Alexander Trail; this is also the top of the falls, which are just downstream and accessible via short, steep side trails that drop to the streamside. The falls drop about 25 feet over a slab into the shady streambed below.

To finish the loop, continue downstream, cross a bridge, and then meet the broad Indian Valley Fire Road. Turn right onto the road and loop back to the trailhead at the ball fields.

Miles and Directions

0.0 Start by walking west on the Indian Valley Fire Road, which skirts the north (right) side of the ball fields.

0.1 At the Y-intersection stay left.

0.2 Pass around the gate and go left, climbing the steep, unsigned Pacheco Pond Fire Road.

0.4 Stay straight on the broad track at the junction with the Jack Burgi Trail, which breaks to the right.

0.6 At the signed junction with the Waterfall Trail, go left and uphill.

0.7 Reach Pacheco Pond. Stay left, circling the pond's southeast shore.

0.8 At the signed junction at the far end of the pond, go left on the Waterfall Trail and begin climbing easy switchbacks.

1.4 The switchbacks end at a four-way junction in a saddle. Take a gentle left (not a hard left) onto the signed Waterfall Trail.

1.7 Make the first stream crossing.

1.8 A set of stone steps leads to the second stream crossing. Three more stream crossings pass in quick succession.

2.1 At the signed junction with the Susan Alexander Trail, stay right on the Waterfall Trail.

2.2 Cross the stream and drop down use trails on the left to view the waterfall. Return to the main track and go left to finish the loop.

2.4 Cross a bridge.

2.5 Pass the junction with the Clark-Melone Trail and then turn right onto the Indian Valley Fire Road.

2.9 Arrive back at the trailhead.

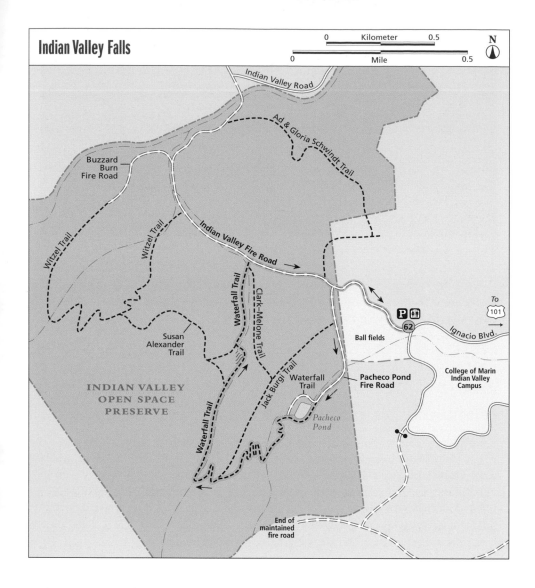

0   Kilometer   0.5

0   Mile   0.5

N

Indian Valley Road

Ad & Gloria Schwindt Trail

Buzzard Burn Fire Road

Witzel Trail

Witzel Trail

Indian Valley Fire Road

Waterfall Trail

Clark-Melone Trail

Susan Alexander Trail

Jack Burgi Trail

Waterfall Trail

Waterfall Trail

INDIAN VALLEY OPEN SPACE PRESERVE

Ball fields

Pacheco Pond Fire Road

Pacheco Pond

Waterfall Trail

College of Marin Indian Valley Campus

Ignacio Blvd.

To 101

P 62

End of maintained fire road

Options: Two other Marin County Open Space parks in Novato feature short hikes to seasonal waterfalls, both best just after heavy rains.

Pacheco Creek Falls, about 25 feet high, is in the Pacheco Valle Open Space Preserve; the trailhead is at the Marin County Open Space gate at the intersection of Alameda Del Prado and Clay Court, off US 101.

Fairway Falls (aka Arroyo de San Jose Falls) is in the Ignacio Valley Open Space Preserve, adjacent to the Indian Valley preserve but not linked by a trail. To reach the trailhead, follow Ignacio Boulevard west from US 101 to Fairway Drive. Turn left onto Fairway Drive; the trailhead is at the gate at the end of the road. The first fall, about 30 feet high, is an easy half-mile walk from the trailhead. Other cataracts are farther up the creek.

63 Cascade Falls

This slender waterfall tumbles down Cascade Creek in one of Marin County's tucked-away open space preserves.

Height: 50 feet
Beauty rating: ★★★
Distance: 1.8 miles out and back (or lollipop)
Difficulty: Easy
Best season: Spring and early summer
County: Marin
Trailhead amenities: None

Land status: Elliott Nature Preserve/Cascade Canyon Open Space Preserve
Maps: USGS San Rafael CA; Cascade Canyon Open Space map available online
Trail contact: Marin County Open Space; (415) 507-2816; www.marincountyparks.org

Finding the trailhead: From US 101 in Larkspur, take the Sir Francis Drake Boulevard exit. Head west on Sir Francis Drake for about 3.5 miles to Fairfax; a quick left at the Fairfax sign and then a quick right will land you on Broadway. From the junction of Broadway and Bolinas Road in downtown, head west on Bolinas Road for 0.5 mile to the stop sign at the junction with Cascade Drive and Frustuck Drive. Take the middle right, through the Cascade Gates, onto Cascade Drive. Follow the narrow, winding residential road for about 1.5 miles to its end at the gate for Elliott Nature Preserve. Park carefully along the narrow roadway. GPS: N37 58.691' / W122 36.843'

The Hike

Marin County has been dealt a generous hand when it comes to seasonal waterfalls, and many of these are neighborhood treasures. Such is the case with Cascade Falls in Fairfax: It happens to be the waterfall in my childhood neighborhood. A quick trip down to the end of the Cascades and into what was then called Elliott's property, then a splash through the sometimes vigorous fords of San Anselmo Creek to the base of Repack (a famous downhill mountain bike run), then what was essentially a bushwhack through fern and poison oak to the cascade itself ... a trail I've traveled many times, both on foot and on a fat-tire bike.

Today the journey to Cascade Falls is considerably more civilized. Now formally ensconced in Elliott Nature Preserve, part of the Cascade Canyon Open Space Preserve, the hike blends dirt singletracks and fire roads to access the falls. The creek crossings remain the most challenging obstacle: Check out access before you head into the canyon. If the water is flowing fast and high in the creek, the fords may be impassable; access is also restricted at times to allow for steelhead spawning.

The hike begins at the gate at the end of Cascade Drive. The Cascade Fire Road leads into the preserve. At the Y-junction not far from the gate, go right on the High Water Trail (for hikers only) and follow the narrow singletrack as it traces the creek,

Looking down from the top of Cascade Falls into Cascade Creek.

which flows on the left. Stay on the High Water Trail at all junctions, crossing a couple of footbridges before the trail merges with the Cascade Fire Road again.

Pass the Cut Trail and then follow the fire road down to a bridge spanning Cascade Creek, just above its confluence with San Anselmo Creek. On the other side of the bridge, a left-hand turn on the fire road heads up the Repack grade, stage of a famous series of downhill mountain bike races in the late 1970s and early 1980s. The grade got its name because cyclists would have to repack their drum brakes after making the descent, a phenomenon I have firsthand experience with.

Turn right on the unmarked singletrack to reach the falls, now paralleling Cascade Creek, which rumbles through a rocky bed on the right. Native bunchgrasses grow close to the waterway, while poison oak flourishes alongside the trail and oaks provide a shady emerald canopy overhead. Social trails break right to the streamside, but to reach the fall, stay on the main path. Over the years foot traffic has polished some of the soapstone in the treadway.

Near the fall both canyon and trail narrow. Climb a short flight of polished stone steps to reach the lower overview of the cascade, which spills through several pools before plunging over an outcropping, a drop of about 50 feet total, into the

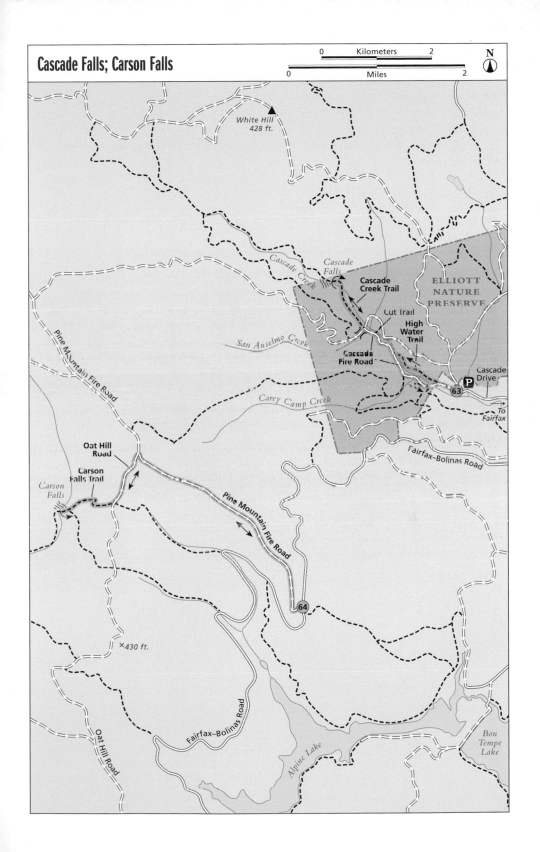

Cascade Falls; Carson Falls

Kilometers
0   2

Miles
0   2

N

White Hill
428 ft.

Cascade Creek

Cascade
Falls

Cascade
Creek Trail

Cut Trail

High
Water
Trail

ELLIOTT
NATURE
PRESERVE

San Anselmo Creek

Cascade
Fire Road

Cascade
Drive

63

To
Fairfax

Pine Mountain Fire Road

Carey Camp Creek

Fairfax–Bolinas Road

Oat Hill
Road

Carson
Falls Trail

Carson
Falls

Pine Mountain Fire Road

64

×430 ft.

Oat Hill Road

Fairfax–Bolinas Road

Alpine Lake

Bon
Tempe
Lake

creek below. A set of wooden stairs, a boardwalk, and a bit of a rock scramble lead to the top of the falls, where the creek mellows and the trail narrows even more. This is the turnaround.

You can return as you came or follow the Cascade Fire Road back to the trailhead, fording San Anselmo Creek several times as you head downstream. Skillful rock-hopping may keep your boots dry, but particularly when the water is high, prepare to get wet.

Miles and Directions

0.0 Start by heading down the Cascade Fire Road. At the Y less than 0.1 mile past the gate, go right on the High Water Trail (hikers only).

0.2 At the four-way junction at the ford, stay right on the signed High Water Trail.

0.3 Meet the Cascade Fire Road and continue to the right, hiking up the road.

0.4 Pass the Cut Trail, remaining on the Cascade Fire Road.

0.5 Cross the wooden footbridge that spans Cascade Creek and then turn right onto the unmarked trail leading up alongside the creek. A left-hand turn leads up the Repack grade.

0.9 Climb stone and wooden stairs up to and then alongside the Cascade Falls to the top of the rock outcropping. When ready, return as you came or follow the Cascade Fire Road back to the trailhead to complete a lollipop loop.

1.4 If you have chosen to make the loop instead of taking the High Water Trail to the left, stay right on the Cascade Fire Road. You may share this wide route with mountain bikers, but there is plenty of space for all users.

1.5 At the junction with the Canyon Trail, stay left and ford San Anselmo Creek. You'll ford the creek several more times as you continue downstream toward the junction with the High Water Trail and the trailhead.

1.8 Arrive back at the trailhead.

64 Carson Falls

A hike to this seasonal waterfall features superlative views. The waterfall also flows through the breeding ground of the rare foothill yellow-legged frog, which may be seen clinging to the rocks in the pool at the base.

See map on page 215.
Height: 150 feet
Beauty rating: ★★★★
Distance: 3.8 miles out and back
Difficulty: Moderate
Best season: Winter and spring
County: Marin
Trailhead amenities: None. Leashed dogs are permitted on the trail.
Land status: Marin Municipal Water District

Maps: USGS Bolinas CA; Marin Municipal Water District/Mount Tamalpais Watershed trail map available online at marinwater.org/DocumentCenter/View/160 (black and white) or www.marinwater.org/DocumentCenter/View/159 (color)
Trail contact: Marin Municipal Water District, 220 Nellen Ave., Corte Madera, CA 94925; (415) 945-1180 (ranger) or (415) 945-1400 (customer service); marinwater.org

Finding the trailhead: From US 101 in Larkspur, take the Sir Francis Drake Boulevard exit. Head west on Sir Francis Drake for about 5.5 miles to Fairfax; a quick left at the Fairfax sign and then a quick right will land you on Broadway. From the junction of Broadway and Bolinas Road in downtown, head west on Bolinas Road (which becomes the Fairfax-Bolinas Road) for about 3.8 miles to the parking area at the top of the hill above the Meadow Club golf course. If you reach the steep descent toward Alpine Lake, you've gone too far. Parking for about twenty cars is located across the road from the trailhead. GPS: N37 57.834' / W122 37.511'

The Hike

It's amazing how two waterfalls in the same watershed, located just a few miles from each other, can have such different settings. Carson Falls, facing west, is surrounded by grassland, semiarid as the season creeps into summer and drying to a trickle by August. Meanwhile, the canyon holding Cataract Falls, facing north, stays moist and green year-round, even as the cataracts dry out. Which is better? Depends on what you are looking for …

For a spring wildflower display, Carson Falls can't be beat, with the rolling coastal grasslands erupting in lupine and poppy as the days grow longer. The hike to Carson Falls also includes spectacular views south and west across the woodlands of the watershed to Mount Tamalpais in perfect profile, especially spectacular when the fog begins to spill over the ridges. On clear days views open north beyond Pine Mountain to Loma Alta and Mount St. Helena, and southeast across sprawling San Francisco Bay to Mount Diablo.

The fall itself spills down a narrow rocky canyon near the headwaters of Little Carson Creek, tumbling over several benches before a final 40-foot drop into a small

pool. The pool is where you might be able to spot the foothill yellow-legged frog. Though the falls may be dry by midsummer, which is just about when the hike up the exposed Pine Mountain Fire Road becomes a sunbaked slog, the pool may hold water for weeks longer, and the frogs may be spotted into August.

Begin by climbing on the broad Pine Mountain Fire Road. Popular with mountain bikers, the route is wide enough to accommodate all users. Stay right and aware; cyclists typically warn you of their approach, and the crunch of their tires on the rocky road may give them away as well, but they move swiftly on the downhill. I'd call this a walk-and-talk stretch, except that it's relatively steep, so heavy breathing may preclude conversation.

You'll know you're nearing the top of the climb when you reach a telephone line, which rebounds across the road several times before the ascent mellows and the descent begins. At the signed junction with Oat Hill Road, another fire road with a sign pointing to Carson Falls, go left. The descent continues to a saddle, where a serpentine outcropping rises greenish gray among the grasses. At the trail junction in the saddle, pick up the signed Carson Falls Trail. The trail winds briefly through grassland and then drops via four switchbacks through oak woodland in the Little Carson Creek canyon. Emerge from under the canopy at a trail Y. The right path leads past a sign describing the foothill yellow-legged frog to rock outcroppings looking down onto the fall and out across the forested ridges of Mount Tam's watershed. The left trail crosses a bridge over the stream and then descends to overlooks on the opposite side of the canyon.

Though the Little Carson Trail continues, linking to other routes within the watershed to create long loops, the waterfall overlooks are the turnaround. Explore, and then return as you came, enjoying the views on the walk down the Pine Mountain Fire Road.

Miles and Directions

0.0 Begin by walking across the Fairfax-Bolinas Road. Pass the gate and the information signboard and head up the Pine Mountain Fire Road.

0.7 Meet the telephone line, which crosses the road several times.

1.2 At the junction, turn left onto the signed Oat Hill Road and continue steeply downhill.

1.5 In the saddle, go right onto the signed Carson Falls Trail.

1.9 Reach the overlooks for Carson Falls. Explore; then return as you came.

3.8 Arrive back at the trailhead.

◀ *Waterfall to mossy streak: Carson Falls shows the effect of prolonged drought.*

65 Stairstep Falls

Swathed in dense riparian foliage, Stairstep Falls descends past a small viewing area to feed Devil's Gulch and Lagunitas Creek.

Height: 40 feet
Beauty rating: ★★★
Distance: 2.8 miles out and back
Difficulty: Easy
Best season: Late winter and spring
County: Marin
Trailhead amenities: None. The parking area along Sir Francis Drake Boulevard accommodates about twenty-five cars. All amenities, including restrooms, water, picnic sites, and a campground, are located 1 mile east of the trailhead on Sir Francis Drake Boulevard at Camp Taylor.

Land status: Samuel P. Taylor State Park
Maps: USGS San Geronimo CA; state park map available online and at the park's main entrance
Trail contact: Samuel P. Taylor State Park, 8889 Sir Francis Drake Blvd. (main entrance), Lagunitas, CA 94938; (415) 488-9897; www.parks.ca.gov

Finding the trailhead: From US 101 in Larkspur, take the Sir Francis Drake Boulevard exit. Follow Sir Francis Drake Boulevard through the east Marin towns of Kentfield, San Anselmo, and Fairfax; continue into West Marin, through the San Geronimo Valley and into Samuel P. Taylor State Park. The main park entrance is about 10 miles west of Fairfax. The Devil's Gulch trailhead is 3 miles beyond the east boundary of the park and 1 mile east of Camp Taylor. Parking for about twenty-five cars is on the west side of the road; the trailhead is across Sir Francis Drake on the east. GPS: N38 01.790' / W122 44.221'

The Hike

Stairstep Falls is tucked away in an overgrown crevice in a fabulous state park. Reaching the hidden falls involves a steady, easy climb broken by long, gentle traverses. The falls are on a side stream feeding Devil's Gulch, which flows peacefully to its confluence with Lagunitas Creek, an environmental success story in that, after many years, it finally welcomes coho salmon back to spawn in winter.

The Stairstep Falls Trail is one of the easiest and most pleasant in Samuel P. Taylor State Park, which also hosts stands of redwoods, a scenic and popular campground, and a trail system that includes the paved Cross Marin Trail and a stiff climb to the top of Barnabe Peak, at more than 1,400 feet. Lagunitas Creek, aka Papermill Creek, was the site of one-time argonaut Samuel P. Taylor's paper mill, touted in park literature as the first paper mill on the West Coast. The creek is the soul of the park, with glassy water pooling in swimming holes that delight on hot summer days.

The falls themselves are slender, toppling from step to green step, hemmed in by steep walls overgrown with sword fern, poison oak, and moss, with a thick canopy of oak, madrone, bay laurel, and Douglas fir interwoven overhead. Stairstep is seasonal,

Artful signs alongside the trail to Stairstep Falls remind hikers that Devil's Gulch and Lagunitas Creek are spawning grounds for steelhead.

by midsummer thinning to a trickle that is seen more than heard, so it's best enjoyed in winter after a series of soaking rains.

Begin by walking up the paved Devil's Gulch Road toward the tiny camping area. You can hitch down onto a creekside path not far up the road or drop down to the creek at the sign in the campground (if you reach the end of the pavement at a gate, you've gone too far). Both routes lead to a bridge crossing Devils Gulch Creek, where interpretative signs describe the steelhead and coho that return to the stream each year to spawn. Cross the bridge and head left on Bill's Trail, a gentle climb alongside the creek with a pair of smaller bridges spanning side streams that drop into the main waterway. The shade is thick and lush on these north- and west-facing slopes, making the walking pleasant even on hot summer days. The gulch drops away and out of sight to the left as you approach the spur to Stairstep Falls.

The Stairstep Falls Trail splits left from Bill's Trail after a little more than a mile's climb, curling around a fold in the mountainside and narrowing to singletrack. A

Stairstep Falls

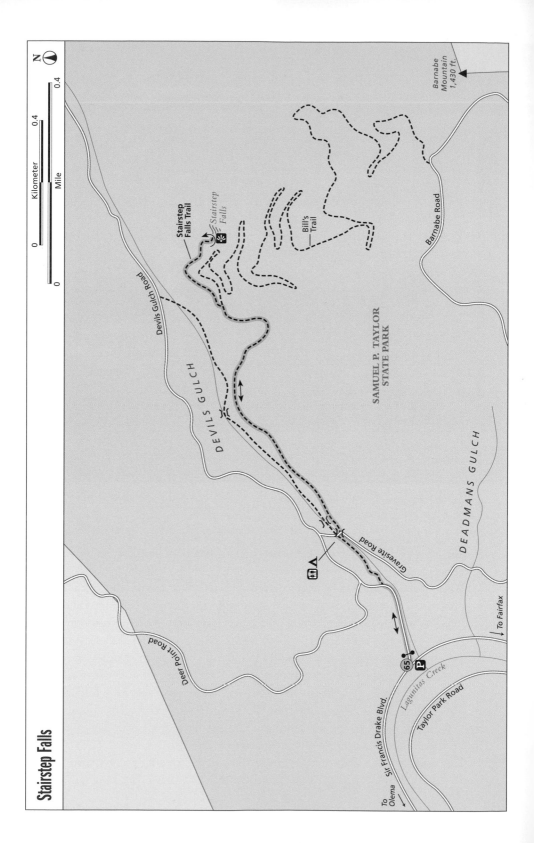

N

Kilometer

Mile

0   0.4   0.4

Barnabe Mountain
1,430 ft.

Barnabe Road

Stairstep Falls Trail

Stairstep Falls

Bill's Trail

Devils Gulch Road

DEVILS GULCH

SAMUEL P. TAYLOR
STATE PARK

DEADMANS GULCH

Gravesite Road

Deer Front Road

65

Lagunitas Creek

Sir Francis Drake Blvd.

Taylor Park Road

To Olema

To Fairfax

short descent leads to the fenced falls overlook, with a bench. Take a break in the fairy forest setting then return as you came.

(***Note:*** Bill's Trail, which provides access to the Stairstep Falls Trail, was closed for construction beginning in August 2014. Construction, which will benefit all trail users, is expected to be completed sometime in 2017. Contact the park to ensure access.)

Miles and Directions

0.0 Begin by carefully crossing Sir Francis Drake Boulevard to the signed Devil's Gulch Road and walking up the shady paved street toward the campground.

0.1 Reach the singletrack trail that parallels both Devil's Gulch and the campground road. Either route leads to the bridge crossing Devil's Gulch.

0.25 If you are following the pavement, pass the group horse camp and corral (with restroom).

0.4 Just beyond the first campsite, a trail sign marks an access path down to the creek. Meet the streamside trail and then cross the bridge over the gulch. On the far side of the bridge, go left onto Bill's Trail. A right turn leads to Barnabe Trail and the Gravesite Road back to the main campground in the park.

0.5 Cross a second bridge.

1.0 Cross a third bridge.

1.1 At the unsigned trail junction, go left onto the Stairstep Falls Trail. A right turn heads up onto the exposed summit of Barnabe Peak via Bill's Trail.

1.4 Reach Stairstep Falls. Enjoy the sights from the overlook, and then return as you came.

2.4 On the far side of the bridge over Devil's Gulch, stay left on the singletrack trail that parallels the creek, following it downstream toward Lagunitas Creek and Sir Francis Drake Boulevard.

2.8 Arrive back at the trailhead.

66 Cataract Falls

A challenging but spectacular trail leads up along Cataract Creek, passing a series of waterfalls as it climbs from Alpine Lake to Laurel Dell.

Height: A series of small waterfalls, some 20 to 25 feet tall

Beauty rating: ★★★★

Distance: 4.6 miles out and back

Difficulty: Strenuous

Best season: Winter and spring

County: Marin

Trailhead amenities: None. Park carefully on the shoulders of winding Fairfax-Bolinas Road near the trailhead. Leashed dogs are permitted.

Land status: Marin Municipal Water District

Maps: USGS Bolinas CA; Marin Municipal Water District/Mount Tamalpais Watershed trail map available online at marinwater.org/DocumentCenter/View/160 (black and white) or www.marinwater.org/DocumentCenter/View/159 (color)

Trail contact: Marin Municipal Water District, 220 Nellen Ave., Corte Madera, CA 94925; (415) 945-1180 (ranger) or (415) 945-1400 (customer service); marinwater.org

Finding the trailhead: From US 101 in Larkspur, take the Sir Francis Drake Boulevard exit. Head west on Sir Francis Drake for about 5.5 miles to Fairfax; a quick left at the Fairfax sign and then a quick right will land you on Broadway. From the junction of Broadway and Bolinas Road in downtown, head west on Bolinas Road (which becomes the Fairfax-Bolinas Road) for about 8 miles to a hairpin turn just beyond the Alpine Lake Dam. Park carefully alongside the roadway. GPS: N37 56.193' / W122 38.280'

The Hike

Given sufficient rainfall, any number of ephemeral cascades can be found in the steep gullies of the Mount Tamalpais Watershed. But few carry the notoriety of the falls found along the Cataract Trail, which climbs beside Cataract Creek above Alpine Lake, one of five reservoirs on the mountain's flanks.

A relatively challenging trail traces Cataract Creek as it plunges about 1,000 feet from Laurel Dell to Alpine Lake. Artfully combining switchbacks with stone and wooden staircases, the trail traverses steep slopes shaded by redwoods, laurels, and oaks through an understory lush with sword fern and bracken fern, and glowing with moss.

The upside-down route begins innocuously, traversing easily above the shoreline of Alpine Lake, the biggest reservoir in the Tamalpais watershed. You'll encounter the first staircase less than a half mile into the hike, and it's all uphill from here.

Cataract Falls spills down a long ravine on the slopes of Mount Tamalpais. ▶

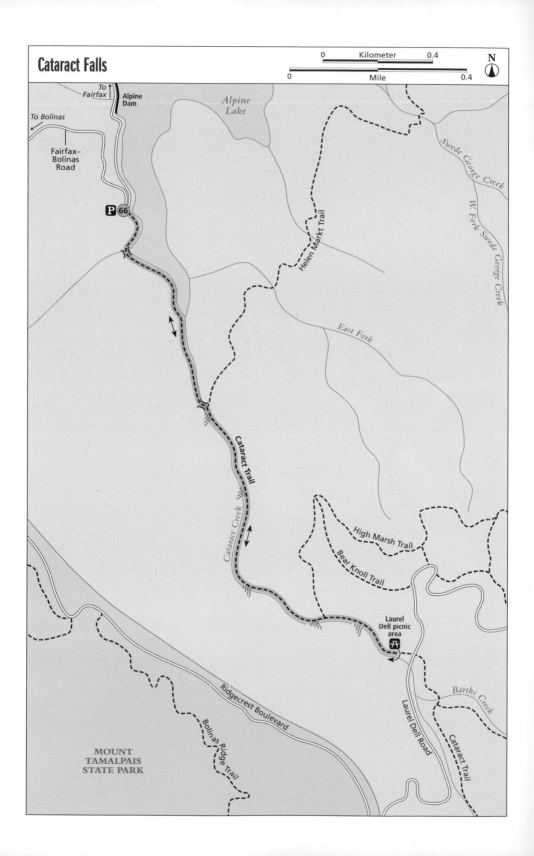

Cataract Falls

To Fairfax

To Fairfax

Alpine Dam

Alpine Lake

To Bolinas

Fairfax–
Bolinas
Road

P 66

Swede George Creek

W. Fork Swede George Creek

Helen Markt Trail

East Fork

Cataract Trail

Cataract Creek

High Marsh Trail

Bear Knoll Trail

Laurel Dell picnic area

Ridgecrest Boulevard

Barths Creek

Laurel Dell Road

Bolinas Ridge Trail

Cataract Trail

MOUNT
TAMALPAIS
STATE PARK

Some of the steps have significant rises, but in general they mitigate the climb, as does the sound of the creek flowing alongside, whether a tinkle, a rumble, or a roar. Overlooks at switchbacks along the lower part of the climb allow climbers to take breaks with views.

At about 1 mile the route crosses the creek via a split-log bridge. Round a switchback, pass a Cataract Trail marker, and take a break by stepping off the trail to enjoy a 10-foot plunge into a clear pool; in warm weather, water flows permitting, this is a nice place to dip your feet. Above the pool the trail becomes a moderate streamside ramble, the creek dancing from pool to pool on the right and the trail bordered by primordial sword fern.

Another set of staircases, the first arcing around a rock outcropping and the second featuring a metal rail, lead up to a second pool plunge, this one about 25 feet high. Take another break; then climb another staircase and round more switchbacks to yet another short fall and pool, this one reached via a staircase that breaks right from the main trail.

Beyond the junction with the High Marsh Trail, the Cataract Trail mellows. It's a short jaunt to the turnaround at Laurel Dell, with picnic sites, restrooms, and other amenities. Take a break in the dell, and then retrace your steps to the trailhead. It's all downhill, but take care on the descent, especially in wet weather, as the steps and trail surface may be slick.

More than 130 miles of trails and fire roads lace through the Mount Tamalpais watershed, allowing hikers to piece together a number of longer hikes and loops that include the Cataract Trail. Download the trail map and customize a longer route as time and fitness permit.

Miles and Directions

0.0 Start at the gated trailhead, passing information signs and heading gently uphill along an arm of Alpine Lake.

0.1 Cross the bridge over a side stream.

0.3 Arrive at the first set of stairs and begin the relentless but lovely climb.

0.6 Cross a bridge over a second feeder stream.

0.75 Pass a couple of switchbacks offering overlooks of small cascades.

1.0 Cross Cataract Creek on a split-log footbridge. Round a switchback, pass a Cataract Trail signpost, and reach an overlook of a plunge that drops about 10 feet into a pool.

1.7 Climb a staircase around a rock outcropping, a second staircase with a metal rail, and reach a 25-foot plunge into a pool.

2.0 A staircase breaks off the main trail to the right, down to another short fall and pool.

2.1 At the junction with the High Marsh Trail, stay right on the Cataract Trail.

2.3 Reach Laurel Dell. This is the turnaround; retrace your steps.

4.6 Arrive back at the trailhead.

67 Alamere Falls

A long, lovely coastal ramble leads to Alamere Falls, which drops directly onto Wildcat Beach in the Point Reyes National Seashore.

Height: 50 feet, with shorter cascades above
Beauty rating: ★★★★★
Distance: 8.5 miles out and back
Difficulty: Moderate, strenuous at the end
Best season: Spring and early summer
County: Marin
Trailhead amenities: Restrooms, trash cans, and information signboards. The parking area fills early on sunny weekends; additional parking along gravel access road
Land status: Point Reyes National Seashore
Maps: USGS Double Point CA; Point Reyes National Seashore map available at the Bear Valley Visitor Center and online

Trail contact: Point Reyes National Seashore, Bear Valley Visitor Center; (415) 464-5100; www.nps.gov/pore
Special considerations: Many cliffs and bluffs in Point Reyes National Seashore are composed of friable rocks and are quite unstable. Rockfalls and slumps occur regularly, so visitors should stay several meters away from the edges and bases of cliffs. Due to the crumbly nature of the rocks, climbing within the seashore is discouraged.

Finding the trailhead: From US 101 in Larkspur, take the Sir Francis Drake Boulevard exit. Follow Sir Francis Drake Boulevard through the east Marin towns of Kentfield, San Anselmo, and Fairfax; continue into West Marin, through the San Geronimo Valley and Samuel P. Taylor State Park to the junction with CA 1 in Olema. Turn left onto CA 1 and drive 9 miles south, toward Bolinas and Stinson Beach. Where the road forks at the Bolinas Lagoon, stay right on the unsigned Olema-Bolinas Road into Bolinas. Travel 1.3 miles to the stop sign at Horseshoe Hill Road; stay left (southbound) on the Olema-Bolinas Road. At the junction with Mesa Road, turn right and follow Mesa Road for 4.5 miles to its end at the Palomarin Trailhead, passing the Point Reyes Bird Observatory at 3.9 miles. GPS: N37 56.038' / W122 44.822'

The Hike

Alamere Falls, like a wild rose, displays its beauty without reservation but is prickly and difficult to reach. When engorged with winter rains the waters run muddy and swift, tumbling over a series of terraces before taking the final plunge onto Wildcat Beach, and filling the air with a turbulent roar that harmonizes with the surf pounding the strand.

The route begins by climbing a short staircase adjacent to the restrooms. The broad Coast Trail immediately turns north and enters a glade of eucalyptus, passing several information signs and the trail that leads left (west) to Palomarin Beach.

Beyond the eucalyptus the Coast Trail follows the contours of the coastline, weaving inland through gullies and out onto the bluffs overlooking the ocean for more

A series of cataracts builds toward a final plunge over Alamere Falls.

than a mile before climbing steeply up and inland. Round a couple of sweeping curves and ascend past a steep, rocky ravine on the right, and then pass through a cleft between the two hillsides to a saddle. The climb is done.

From the saddle, drop to the Lake Ranch Trail junction, which breaks off to the right (northeast). Stay left on the Coast Trail, passing a series of ponds and vernal pools as the trail drops to Bass Lake. A footpath to the lakeshore breaks off to the left before the Coast Trail begins to climb away from the water through a thick mixed evergreen forest.

The Coast Trail flattens above the Bass Lake basin and arcs westward. Pass the closed trail to Crystal Lake; then pass out of the dense woodlands back into coastal scrub. Pelican Lake lies cupped in a bowl below and to the left (west), and a snapshot of the ocean can be seen through a V-shaped break in the bluffs.

The easy descent continues, shaded in spots by thickets of broom and scrub, and the sounds of the nearby surf are carried up to the trail by the wind. Pass an unmarked social trail that breaks off to the left toward the Double Point Overlook. The trail to Alamere Falls branches off to the left (west) about 100 feet beyond, at about 3.75

Alamere Falls

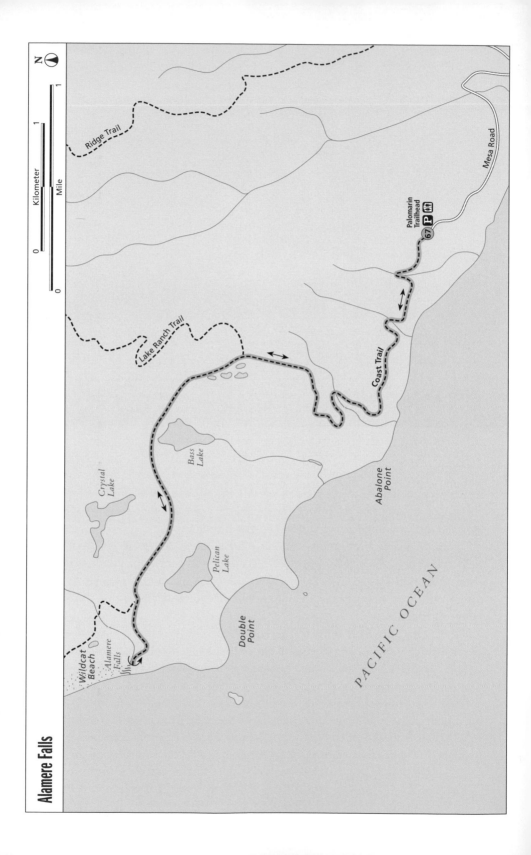

miles. Watch carefully for the trail and trail sign, as both blend into the landscape and could be missed.

Thick brambles of coyote brush encroach on the eroded singletrack trail, but it's clear and easy to follow. Alamere Creek runs through the willow-choked basin to the right (north). The track heads downhill and, given both the ruts and pitch, is deceptively difficult. Pass through head-high bowers of thick brush to the brink of the falls, where the path is no longer deceptively difficult—it's plainly so, skittering down an eroded cliff adjacent to the upper reaches of the falls. It's a hands-on affair that's not for the hiking neophyte.

Pick your way down onto terraces misted by the adjacent falls; these rocky platforms overlook both the ocean and the cascades. The most spectacular plunge of the fall flows over the terrace and then drops the final 50 feet or so to Wildcat Beach. You may see hikers descending to the beach below: *Do not attempt this from the upper terrace.* The bluffs are subject to erosion, and in the wake of a 2014 tragedy at nearby Arch Rock, park officials warn hikers away from the edges of the cliffs. To approach the base of the falls, hike down the beach from Wildcat Camp (about 3 miles round-trip, accessible at low tide).

From the terrace, views open westward across the Pacific and back eastward onto the tumbling cascades. Whether you settle on the rocks along the upper cascades or rest on the beach at the base, Alamere Falls is an invigorating destination. Water is everywhere—washing the sand, tumbling from the cliffs, cascading through channels. When you can tear yourself away, retrace your steps.

Miles and Directions

0.0 Start at the Palomarin Trailhead, climbing the stairs next to the restrooms and turning left onto the Coast Trail.

0.1 At the junction with the Palomarin Beach Trail, stay right (straight) on the Coast Trail.

0.6 Cross the first footbridge.

1.4 Cross the second footbridge.

1.6 Round a switchback and head uphill and inland.

2.25 At the junction with the Lake Ranch Trail, stay left (straight) on the Coast Trail.

2.75 Pass scenic Bass Lake.

3.2 Pass a closed trail, remaining on the Coast Trail.

3.75 At the signed junction turn left onto the narrow trail to Alamere Falls.

4.25 Scramble down the steep trail to the bluff top between the Alamere Creek cascades and the top of Alamere Falls. This is the turnaround, though another steep scramble down the 50-foot cliff will drop you onto Wildcat Beach. Enjoy the amazing views; then return as you came.

8.5 Arrive back at the trailhead.

68 Dawn Falls

This seasonal waterfall lies in a secluded canyon shaded by stands of redwoods.

Height: 30 feet
Beauty rating: ★★★★
Distance: 1.2 miles out and back to the falls; 3.8 miles out and back to the dam and bridge turnaround
Difficulty: Easy
Best season: Winter and spring
County: Marin

Trailhead amenities: Information signboard with preserve map. Park carefully alongside the roadway at the trailhead.
Land status: Baltimore Canyon Open Space Preserve
Maps: USGS San Rafael CA; Baltimore Canyon Open Space Preserve map available online
Trail contact: Marin County Open Space; (415) 507-2816; www.marincountyparks.org

Finding the trailhead: From US 101 in Larkspur, take the Sir Francis Drake Boulevard exit. Head west on Sir Francis Drake Boulevard for about 2 miles to College Avenue in Kentfield. Turn left onto College Avenue and go 0.4 mile to Woodland Avenue. Turn right onto Woodland Avenue and go 0.2 mile to Evergreen Drive. Turn left onto Evergreen Drive and climb for 0.9 mile to Crown Road. Turn left onto Crown Road and go 0.1 mile to the gate and trailhead at the end of the road. GPS: N37 56.448' / W122 33.636'

The Hike

Dawn Falls may be the goal, but Mount Tamalpais, Marin County's Sleeping Lady, is the dominant feature on this hike. Views of the summit dominate at the outset, and even as the nose of the Lady slips from view, the dense oak and laurel forest that makes up her gown is all-encompassing. The falls are tucked along Larkspur Creek in one of the mountain's deep green folds, fed by seasonal rainfall and dry by midsummer.

Begin by walking along the wide Southern Marin Line Fire Road, which curls south into the 196-acre Baltimore Canyon Open Space Preserve. The woods that cling to the steep hills are second growth; the old growth was harvested near the turn of the twentieth century to provide lumber for a burgeoning San Francisco. The redwoods that thrive in remote dells on the mountain slopes were a hot commodity, as the lumber was rot-resistant and unappealing to pests, including termites.

Pass a junction with the Hoo-Koo-E-Koo Trail, staying left on the Southern Marin Line Fire Road to its junction with the Dawn Falls Trail at 0.3 mile. An obvious trail sign designates the right-hand leg of the Dawn Falls route, which climbs higher onto the mountain and connects to the Hoo-Koo-E-Koo. Look left for the leg of trail that heads down to Dawn Falls, descending flights of wooden steps and switchbacks into the shady canyon that cradles Larkspur Creek.

A grand stand of redwoods flourishes at the base of Dawn Falls. ▶

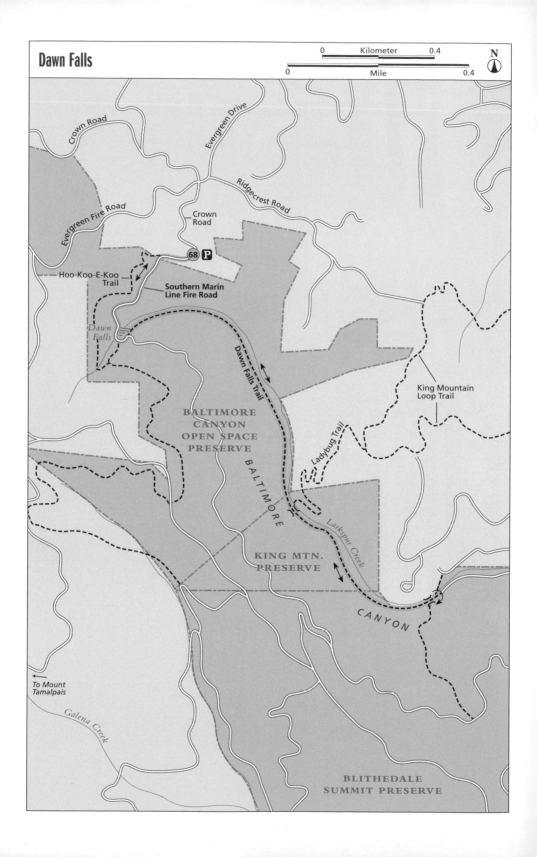

Dawn Falls

0   Kilometer   0.4
0   Mile   0.4

N

Crown Road

Evergreen Drive

Ridgecrest Road

Evergreen Fire Road

Crown Road

68 P

Hoo-Koo-E-Koo Trail

Southern Marin Line Fire Road

Dawn Falls

Dawn Falls Trail

King Mountain Loop Trail

BALTIMORE CANYON OPEN SPACE PRESERVE

BALTIMORE

Ladybug Trail

Larkspur Creek

KING MTN. PRESERVE

CANYON

To Mount Tamalpais

Galena Creek

BLITHEDALE SUMMIT PRESERVE

The falls lie just downstream of the last switchback, tumbling about 30 feet over an inverted cliff into the creek bed below. If you are simply bagging waterfalls, you can turn around here, but the trail downstream from the falls is lovely, worthwhile, and qualifies as a premier day hike.

To continue, drop around another switchback into a magical streamside clearing surrounded by towering redwoods. Less than 0.1 mile farther, the redwoods give way to leafy oak woodland, with a thick understory of fern and wildflowers in season. This, in turn, gives way to a forest of fragrant bay laurel, and then back again, seamless transitions between the dominant tree and understory. Even when the falls disappoint, sucked dry by sunshine and summer, the descent through the forest is enchanting.

Pass the bridge at the junction with the Ladybug Trail. The remnants of an old dam lie beyond the bridge; according to preserve literature, the structure was blown up following a drowning in the reservoir it contained. As you near the turnaround point for this route, neighborhood homes can be seen, perched on the widening canyon slopes above the creek.

A bridge that leads up into the neighborhood marks the turnaround. Return as you came or make a loop by connecting back to the Southern Marin Line Fire Road via the Barbara Springs Trail.

The Dawn Falls Trail links to a number of other trails on both Marin County Open Space land (the neighboring Blithedale Summit and Camino Alto Open Space Preserves) and within the Mount Tamalpais Watershed. A left turn on the Dawn Falls Trail from the Southern Marin Line Fire Road deposits you on the Hoo-Koo-E-Koo Trail, a favorite of pioneering mountain bikers before singletrack routes on the mountain were closed to fat-tire bikes. The Hoo-Koo-E-Koo Trail, then Fire Road, leads up onto the Old Railroad Grade, which climbs to the east peak of the mountain and presents fabulous views of San Pablo Bay, Ring Mountain, and the Richmond San Rafael Bridge.

Miles and Directions

0.0 Start by passing the gate and following the flat, easy Southern Marin Line Fire Road.

0.1 Pass a junction with the Hoo-Koo-E-Koo Trail, staying left on the Southern Marin Line Fire Road.

0.3 At the junction with the Dawn Falls Trail, go left and down two flights of wooden steps.

0.6 Reach Dawn Falls. This can be the turnaround, but the route continues downstream.

0.8 Switchback down into a redwood grove below the falls.

0.9 The redwoods give way to oak woodland as the trail flattens.

1.4 Reach the bridge at the junction with the Ladybug Trail.

1.7 Pass the remnants of a dam and an old fence line.

1.9 Reach a bridge that spans Larkspur Creek and offers access to a path leading up into the surrounding neighborhood. This is the turnaround point; retrace your steps.

3.8 Arrive back at the trailhead.

69 Huntington Falls

Stuck in the city and in need of falling water? Huntington Falls may be man-made, but the waterfall will serve in a pinch, as will the short hike around Strawberry Hill and Stow Lake in Golden Gate Park.

Height: About 420 feet
Beauty rating: ★★★
Distance: 1.4-mile double loop
Difficulty: Easy
Best season: Year-round
County: San Francisco
Trailhead amenities: Snack bar, restrooms, information, and boat rentals at the Boathouse on Stow Lake
Land status: Golden Gate Park
Maps: USGS San Francisco North CA; down-loadable and interactive maps of Golden Gate Park, including Stow Lake, are available at www.golden-gate-park.com/map.html
Trail contact: San Francisco Recreation and Parks Department, McLaren Lodge in Golden Gate Park, 501 Stanyan St., San Francisco, CA 94117; (415) 831-2700; sfrecpark.org. Get lots of park-specific information at Golden Gate Park, www.golden-gate-park.com, or at sfrecpark.org/parks-open-spaces/golden-gate-park-guide/. San Francisco Convention and Visitors Bureau, 900 Market St., Hallidie Plaza, San Francisco, CA 94102-2804; (415) 391-2000; www.sanfrancisco.travel

Finding the trailhead: From I-80 westbound and/or US 101 northbound in downtown San Francisco, follow US 101 north to the Fell/Laguna exit. Drive about 1.5 miles west on Fell Street. Fell turns into John F. Kennedy Drive at the intersection with Stanyan Street. Continue on John F. Kennedy Drive, one of Golden Gate Park's main roadways, to Stow Lake Drive, the short access road to Stow Lake.

From the San Francisco Peninsula, take I-280 northbound to the Golden Gate Bridge/19th Avenue exit (stay in the left-hand lanes of the freeway). Continue on CA 1 northbound for almost 5 miles, following Junipero Serra Boulevard, 19th Avenue, and Park Presidio through Golden Gate Park. On the northern boundary of the park, turn right onto Fulton Street, go 3.5 blocks, and turn right onto 10th Avenue. At the next stop sign, turn left onto John F. Kennedy Drive and follow it west to the Stow Lake access drive.

From the Golden Gate Bridge, stay right on the Park Presidio/19th Avenue off-ramp and drive about 2 miles south on Park Presidio Boulevard. One block before Golden Gate Park's northern boundary, turn right onto Cabrillo Street and then make an immediate left turn onto 14th Avenue. Drive 1 block and turn left onto Fulton Street. Cross Park Presidio and continue on Fulton for 3.5 blocks. Turn right onto 10th Avenue. At the next stop sign, turn left onto John F. Kennedy Drive and go west to Stow Lake.

Parking is available along John F. Kennedy Drive and around Stow Lake, but may be difficult to find on weekends. John F. Kennedy Drive is closed to auto traffic for half days on Sat and all day Sun (no parking permitted alongside the road either) from Stanyan Street to Park Presidio. You may have to park farther afield, but there is plenty to see in other parts of Golden Gate Park as you walk to Stow Lake and the falls. GPS (boathouse): N37 46.236' / W122 28.640'

Man-made Huntington Falls flows into Stow Lake at the Golden Gate Pavilion.

The Hike

Exploring Golden Gate Park—3 miles long and a handful of blocks wide, a linear swipe of green space linking San Francisco's city streets to Ocean Beach and the Pacific—is a pleasure whether you live in the City by the Bay or are just visiting. Park visitors enjoy a variety of activities: strolling through the Japanese Tea Garden and the Conservatory of Flowers; taking in the exhibits at the deYoung Museum and the California Academy of Sciences; wandering through redwood groves, rhododendron dells, botanical gardens, or grassy meadows. Huntington Falls is one highlight among many, and is an easy waterfall escape from big-city busy-ness.

To view the falls, simply follow the easy dirt path that encircles Strawberry Hill, an "island" in the middle of Stow Lake. Navigation is not a challenge: From the paved path that encircles the lake, cross the concrete Roman Bridge and follow the path around, staying right as you circumnavigate the island. Paths and staircases also lead to the summit of Strawberry Hill, where you can enjoy views of the city and surroundings, as well as the "headwaters" of Huntington Falls. At the base of the falls, near the Golden Gate Pavilion—a gift to San Francisco from its sister city, Taipei, Taiwan—the path crosses the pool at the base of the falls via artfully placed stepping stones, which also allow more intimate access to the artificial cascade.

After you've seen the falls up close, take the longer, paved loop around Stow Lake. The people-watching is great, as are views across the lake and above the canopy of the park's trees into the hillside neighborhoods of the city. Look for turtles sunning themselves in the shallows along the lakeshore and ducks, geese, and swans clustering around folks tossing crusts of bread.

Miles and Directions

0.0 Start at the boathouse, heading left on the paved lakeside path.

0.2 Reach the paved path/road that veers right at the concrete Roman Bridge. Cross the bridge and turn right onto the broad dirt trail that circles the base of Strawberry Hill. Stay to the right as you circumnavigate the island, unless you want to take one of the paths or stairways that lead left and steeply up to the top of the hill.

0.4 Pass the stone Rustic Bridge, the ornate Golden Gate Pavilion, and the tumble of Huntington Falls.

0.5 Complete the loop around Strawberry Hill. Cross the Roman Bridge to the main lake path. You can go either way; the path is described in a clockwise direction, heading right from the bridge.

0.8 Reach the far end of the lake and enjoy the views back to Strawberry Hill.

0.9 An unpaved side trail leads left (south) and down to Martin Luther King Jr. Boulevard. Continue straight on the lakeside path.

1.1 Pass the Rustic Bridge to Strawberry Hill.

1.4 Arrive back at the trailhead.

THE EVOLUTION OF A CITY PARK

Both Golden Gate Park and Huntington Falls were imposed on a landscape that once was little more than sand dunes whipped by winds blowing off the nearby Pacific. The acreage was chosen as the park site in the 1860s; shortly thereafter civil engineer William Hammond Hall, the park's designer and first superintendent, began the long transformation process by planting beach grasses, lupine, and barley to stabilize the sand. More than 200,000 trees have been planted since, creating an unnatural but lovely oasis.

The park's second superintendent, Scottish garden designer John McLaren, carried on in Hall's tradition: He oversaw the creation of many of the park's features, including Huntington Falls. The idea for the falls, according to park literature, was inspired by a trip McLaren took to the Sierra with legendary naturalist John Muir. The waterfall is named for Collis Huntington, a railroad baron who ponied up a generous sum in support of the project.

70 Martin Luther King Jr. Memorial Waterfall

Downtown San Francisco encompasses more than a bustling financial and shopping district; it's also home to Yerba Buena Gardens and its man-made memorial waterfall, an inspirational diversion in the heart of the city.

Height: 20 feet
Beauty rating: ★★★
Distance: About 0.2 mile to tour
Difficulty: Easy
Best season: Year-round
County: San Francisco
Trailhead amenities: Restrooms, trash cans, gardens, museums, cafes . . . you name it, you can find it at the gardens or on adjacent city streets.

Land status: Yerba Buena Gardens
Maps: USGS San Francisco North CA; yerbabuenagardens.com/map/
Trail contact: Yerba Buena Gardens, 750 Howard St., San Francisco, CA 94103; (415) 820-3550; yerbabuenagardens.com. San Francisco Convention and Visitors Bureau, 900 Market St., Hallidie Plaza, San Francisco, CA 94102-2804; (415) 391-2000; www.sanfrancisco.travel.

Finding the trailhead: From I-80 westbound in downtown San Francisco, take the Fremont Street exit. Take an immediate left from Fremont onto Howard Street. Get into the right lane; drive 2 blocks and turn right onto Third Street. The gardens are on the left.

From the Golden Gate Bridge, continue south on US 101/Presidio Parkway, staying right onto Lombard Street. Drive about 1 mile on Lombard Street and then turn right on Van Ness Avenue. Follow Van Ness to Golden Gate Avenue and turn left. Follow Golden Gate, which crosses Market Street onto Sixth Street. Follow Sixth Street for 3 blocks to Folsom Street and turn left. Follow Folsom up to Third Street; turn left onto Third Street to reach the garden.

You can find parking at the Fifth & Mission/Yerba Buena Gardens Garage at Fifth and Mission Streets, 1 block south of Market Street; there are other parking garages nearby as well. Public transportation, both by bus and municipal railway, is also available. GPS: N37 47.085' / W122 24.162'

Viewing the Falls

The 20-foot-high, 50-foot-wide sheet of water that washes over the stone and glass memorial to Martin Luther King Jr. in Yerba Buena Gardens radiates power, peace, and hope. The lack of a monumental natural setting doesn't hinder this waterfall's ability to inspire: It invokes turbulence and cleansing, both central to the legacy of the great man it honors, and it brings people together, no matter their own legacies, which was what the great man wanted.

Framed in granite from the Sierra, the glass panels in the shade of the grotto behind the falling water are etched with quotes from the civil rights era and its iconic leader, translated into the many languages of San Francisco's residents and visitors. Called Revelations, the memorial is intended by its creators to educate, empower, and renew those walking on the bridge beneath the cascade and reading King's words.

Walk behind the waterfall in Yerba Buena Gardens to witness the legacy of America's great civil rights leader.

After touring the grotto, take either of the ramps flanking the waterfall to the upper level, which overlooks the garden and surrounding cityscape, including the distinctive striped tower of the San Francisco Museum of Modern Art and St. Patrick Church, in the shadow of the towering San Francisco Marriot Marquis.

Yerba Buena Gardens, a dollop of open space in the midst of an urban wonderland, is worthy of further exploration. Set atop a part of the giant Moscone Convention Center and across the street from the San Francisco Museum of Modern Art, the gardens encompass the Yerba Buena Center for the Arts, including art galleries and forums for the performing arts and theater, an outdoor stage, a collection of public sculptures (including a large glass sculpture of a boat hull, called Seasons of the Sea Adrift, which erupts from the east plaza), and an inviting lawn encircled by the paved esplanade. The site also encompasses Reiko Goto's butterfly garden, designed to attract several species of butterflies native to the Bay Area; a garden featuring flowers from each of San Francisco's thirteen sister cities; a children's play area; and a labyrinth.

71 Brooks Creek Falls

A loop through history also offers views of seasonal Brooks Creek Falls.

Height: 175 feet
Beauty rating: ★★★
Distance: 2.5-mile loop
Difficulty: Moderate due to some steep climbs
Best season: Winter and early spring
County: San Mateo
Trailhead amenities: Restrooms, picnic sites, water, trash cans, and visitor center. A fee is charged.
Land status: San Pedro Valley Park

Maps: USGS Montara Mountain CA; San Pedro Valley County Park brochure and map available online at parks.smcgov.org and at the trailhead
Trail contact: San Pedro Valley County Park, 600 Oddstad Blvd., Pacifica, CA 94044; (650) 355-8289. San Mateo County Department of Parks, 455 County Center, 4th Fl., Redwood City, CA 94063; (650) 363-4020; parks. smcgov.org.

Finding the trailhead: To reach the park from CA 1 in Pacifica, go east on Linda Mar for 1.9 miles to its end at Oddstad Road. Turn right (south) on Oddstad and go 1 block to the park entrance on the left (east). Park in the lot near the visitor center. The trailhead is located behind the Old Trout Farm restrooms. GPS: N37 34.688' / W122 28.558'

The Hike

The seasonal falls on Brooks Creek can't be reached directly, but a nice loop hike through coastal San Pedro Valley County Park offers unimpeded views of the narrow 175-foot ribbon, a striking splash of white amid green scrub when swollen with rainfall. When the falls dry up in summer, the stained cliff still draws the eye, a streak of dark amid scrub dried by the season.

But even when the rains don't fall, fog and moist ocean breezes, a weather mainstay in Pacifica, regularly blow into the hollows of coastal hills. That incessant moisture supports the lush coastal scrub that pillows the lower slopes of Montara Mountain and helps to sustain flows in San Pedro Creek and Brooks Creek, which wind through alder and willow to the San Pedro Valley floor.

In addition to the falls, the county park preserves a significant historical site. In 1769, Don Gaspar de Portola's colonial expedition overshot its destination, Monterey Bay, forging northward through alien country to "discover" the enormous body of water that is San Francisco Bay. Portola's exploration of the area included a visit to the fruitful San Pedro Valley; after Mission Dolores and Yerba Buena were established farther inland on the peninsula, the oceanside valley became an important supply outpost, providing food and cattle for the settlement.

The fragrant eucalyptus forest on the foot of the ridge also links back in time. The quick-growing Australian natives were brought to California in the mid-1800s as a lumber source; when the trees proved too brittle, they were planted as windbreaks on coastal farms and ranches. These days the aging trees are being cut down in many Bay Area locales, as they have a tendency to drop limbs on roadways. And the Old Trout Farm Trail is named for—you guessed it—a trout farm that operated on the valley floor into the early 1960s.

This loop, which includes a portion of the Montara Mountain Trail, begins by climbing steadily through mixed forest and coastal scrub, sharing the route of the Old Trout Farm Trail for a stretch before leaving that behind near the bottom of a eucalyptus-shaded hollow.

Tracing the Brooks Creek drainage, the creek can be heard, if not seen, as it cascades down a tree-clogged bed. Views of Brooks Creek Falls appear near the mid-point of the ascent, full and white in the rainy months and typically dry by early summer. A bench offers a comfortable viewing perch. You can turn around here, but the loop is well worth finishing. Just continue uphill and try not to envy the broad-winged birds—crows, hawks, turkey vultures—that ride the thermals generated in the sheltered valley. They climb the easy way …

The trail arcs south and west via switchbacks to the Montara Mountain Trail at the apex of the loop. It's all downhill from here, as the path drops northward along a ridge. Views open periodically of Pacifica and the Pacific. The cotton-ball clusters of lace lichen that hang from the limbs of manzanita and oak are indicators of the cleanliness of the air on the mountain.

On the lower reaches of the ridge, a eucalyptus forest shades the trail. Switchbacks flip from ocean views amid scrub to no views in the woods. More than a half-dozen switchbacks later, you'll reach the park's paved service road, which is just above the trail-head. A short hop through a last stand of eucalyptus and you are back in the parking lot.

Miles and Directions

0.0 Start behind the restrooms and the picnic area. At the trail junction go left (south) on the Old Trout Farm Trail (also the Brooks Creek Falls Trail).

0.1 Pass a trail marker amid ferns, poison oak, firs, oaks, and eucalyptus.

0.3 Reach a closed trail that departs to the left; stay right (south) on the Old Trout Farm Trail. About 50 feet beyond stay right (south) again on the Brooks Creek Falls Trail. The Trout Farm Trail drops down to the left.

0.5 Cross the moist head of a ravine at a couple of posts; this may involve negotiating water in the winter months.

0.7 Leave the forest for scrubland.

0.8 Cross a bridge over a gully.

0.9 View the waterfall from the bench. Round a few switchbacks as the trail swings first south and then west and then flattens atop the ridge.

1.2 Arrive at the Montara Mountain Trail junction, with a bench and panoramic views of Pacifica and the ocean beyond. Go right (north) on the Montara Mountain Trail, starting the descent.

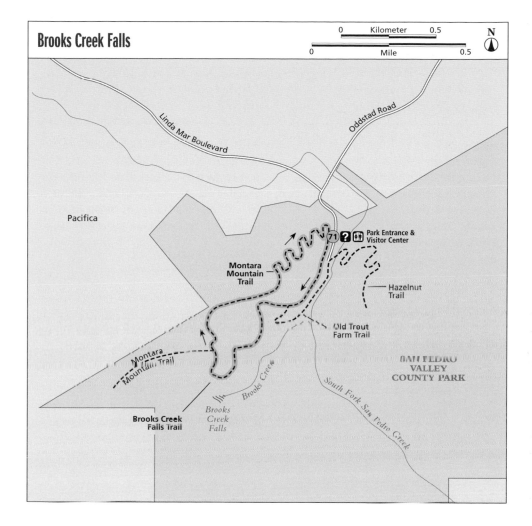

Brooks Creek Falls

0 — Kilometer — 0.5

0 — Mile — 0.5

N

Linda Mar Boulevard

Oddstad Road

Pacifica

71 ? Park Entrance & Visitor Center

Montara Mountain Trail

Hazelnut Trail

Old Trout Farm Trail

Montara Mountain Trail

SAN PEDRO VALLEY COUNTY PARK

Brooks Creek

South Fork San Pedro Creek

Brooks Creek Falls Trail

Brooks Creek Falls

1.3 Pass a "pullout" with a bench just before the first of many switchbacks.

1.5 Reach the first eucalyptus.

1.7 In the eucalyptus forest proper, the trail splits, with the upper route leading to a viewing bench. Stay left on the lower track. Seven switchbacks moderate the descent.

2.4 Reach the paved park service road and a trail sign. Cross the road and follow the path down to the first trail junction behind the Old Trout Farm restrooms. Go left and down to the trailhead and parking area.

2.5 Arrive back at the trailhead.

72 Castle Rock Falls

Follow forested trails past weirdly sculpted rock outcroppings to a waterfall that plunges 80 feet down a sheer face near the headwaters of Kings Creek.

Height: 80 feet
Beauty rating: ★★★★
Distance: 2.6-mile lollipop
Difficulty: Moderate
Best season: Winter and spring
County: Santa Cruz
Trailhead amenities: Pit toilets, trash cans, and information boards. Bring your own water.
Land status: Castle Rock State Park

Maps: USGS Santa Cruz CA; park map available online at www.parks.ca.gov
Trail contact: Castle Rock State Park, 15000 Skyline Blvd., Los Gatos, CA 95033; (408) 867-2952; www.parks.ca.gov. Portola and Castle Rock Foundation, 59 Washington St. #107, Santa Clara, CA 95050; www.portola andcastlerockfound.org.

Finding the trailhead: From I-280 in Cupertino take the CA 85 exit and head south on CA 85 to the Saratoga Avenue exit. Go right (south) onto Saratoga-Sunnyvale Road and continue for 2.4 miles to CA 9/Big Basin Way. Go right (west) on CA 9 for 7.3 miles to Skyline Boulevard/CA 35. Turn left (south) on Skyline Boulevard and travel 2.6 miles to the park entrance on the right (west).

Alternatively, from CA 17 in Los Gatos, take the Bear Creek/Black Road exit. Follow Montevina Road east for 0.3 mile to Black Road. Turn left onto Black Road and travel for 4.4 scenic, winding miles to Skyline Boulevard. Turn right (north) on Skyline Boulevard and go 3.7 miles to the park entrance, which is on the left (west). The trailhead is at the west boundary of the parking lot. GPS: N37 13.825' / W122 05.762'

The Hike

From the overhanging tafoni faces of Castle Rock to the observation deck jutting out over Castle Rock Falls, at the head of Kings Creek, the scenic destinations on this tour are enchanting.

Castle Rock, the park's high point, is more a palace for forest gnomes than for fairytale princesses. Perched on the crest of the Santa Cruz Mountains, its sandstone faces host a honeycomb of holds, shallow caves, and, on dry sunny days, crowds of climbers. Views are obscured by the dense forest that surrounds the rock and nearby sandstone outcroppings, but you can pull up a piece of the stone apron that surrounds the base and enjoy the athletic showmanship.

If you want views, head downhill and downstream, following the historic Saratoga Gap Trail to Castle Rock Falls. From the observation deck at the falls, views open across the ridgelines and forested hollows of the Santa Cruz range, with exposed rock outcroppings jutting from the canopy on the nearest slope to the north. Climbing

Castle Rock Falls, sapped by drought, as seen from the overlook platform.

routes lie on either side of the cascade, which stains a long slab diving into the Kings Creek watershed.

The trails linking the rock and the falls cruise through a dense woodland of pines and oaks, with very little sunlight filtering through. Mosses cling to the boulders lining the trails—at least to those faces that aren't used by climbers—and deadfall jams the creek above the falls. On a foggy day the atmosphere is primordial, with the slightest wind shifting the boughs overhead and rocks looming out of the woods suddenly, like giant trolls.

The elevation change from the trek's high point at Castle Rock to its low point at Castle Rock Falls feels significant but is not particularly strenuous. Slopes are moderate and easily tackled by hikers who watch their pace. And the observation deck is a perfect place to take a break and have a snack before tackling the ascent to the trailhead.

Miles and Directions

0.0 Start by heading left (south) and uphill on the trail to Castle Rock. A trail sign about 50 yards farther directs you right and up on the forested singletrack.

0.2 At the trail junction above the Isabella Soria and Nina Bingham Memorial Grove, go right (north) on the Castle Rock Trail, now a dirt road. Rock formations dot the forest to the left (southwest).

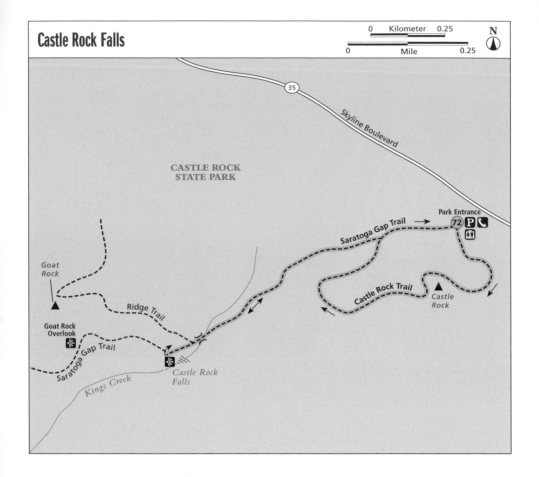

Castle Rock Falls

CASTLE ROCK
STATE PARK

Skyline Boulevard

Park Entrance

Saratoga Gap Trail →

Goat
Rock

Ridge Trail

Castle Rock Trail

Castle
Rock

Goat Rock
Overlook

Saratoga Gap Trail

Castle Rock
Falls

Kings Creek

0.3 Arrive at Castle Rock, which rises to the north of a large clearing. An outhouse is to the right (east). A trail marker points the way north to Saratoga Gap Trail. The singletrack curls around the base of the rock, passing caves where climbers can hang like bats while they contemplate their next moves.

0.5 At the trail sign, switchback to the right and downhill toward the Saratoga Gap Trail. Trail signs keep you on track for the next half mile, as climbers' trails branch off the main route.

1.0 Cross a series of little wooden bridges to the intersection with the Saratoga Gap Trail. Go left (west) on the Saratoga Gap Trail toward Castle Rock Falls.

1.5 Cross a bridge to the junction of the Saratoga Gap and Ridge Trails. Go left (west) on the Saratoga Gap Trail to Castle Rock Falls.

1.7 Arrive at the falls overlook. After checking out the cascade and the views, retrace your steps.

2.4 At the junction of the Saratoga Gap and Castle Rock Trails, stay left (east) on the Saratoga Gap Trail, which ascends past a cavernous rock. Ignore the climbers' trail that leads to the rock.

2.6 Arrive back at the trailhead.

73 Berry Creek Falls

A long ramble down through redwood groves and along fern-filled creek beds leads to the platform overlooking sheltered Berry Creek Falls.

Height: 60 feet
Beauty rating: ★★★★
Distance: 9.6 miles out and back
Difficulty: Strenuous due to distance and elevation change
Best season: Winter and early spring
County: Santa Cruz
Trailhead amenities: Restrooms, water, trash cans, visitor center and store, amphitheater, and information signboards

Land status: Big Basin Redwoods State Park
Maps: USGS Santa Cruz CA; park map available online and at the park visitor center
Trail contact: Big Basin Redwoods State Park, 21600 Big Basin Way, Boulder Creek, CA 95006-9064; (831) 338-8860; www.parks.ca.gov

Finding the trailhead: From CA 85 in Saratoga, take the Saratoga Avenue exit. Go right (southwest) on Saratoga Avenue through town; Saratoga Avenue becomes CA 9. Continue on CA 9/Big Basin Way for about 7 miles to the junction with Skyline Boulevard/CA 35; cross Skyline to continue on CA 9 toward the state park. Travel another 14 miles to the junction of CA 9 and CA 236. Stay right on CA 236 into the park. Continue on CA 236 for about 9 miles to the park headquarters and trailhead. GPS: N37 10.311' / W122 13.329'

The Hike

A long meander down the Skyline to the Sea Trail, through glade after glade of majestic coast redwoods, leads to one of Big Basin Redwoods State Park's premier attractions, Berry Creek Falls. The platform overlooking the 60-foot fall, which fans out across the dark-rock face behind, is often crowded with appreciative visitors taking snapshots and enjoying lunch before beginning the long climb back to the trailhead.

The falls are a worthy destination, tucked in a narrow box canyon shaded by redwoods and flanked by slopes thick with fern and pocked with moss-covered rocks. And the trail is a worthy journey, the kind of walk in the woods that inspires deep thinking. No doubt many a hiker has solved the problems of the planet while winding down along Kelly Creek through the towering forest … and then contemplated the limitations of lung and leg as they've slogged back up and over the mountain crest.

The only confusing part of the route is at the outset, where a web of trails connects the various amenities around the park's hub. Head down behind the amphitheater, cross the creek via one of a pair of footbridges, and head to the left—downstream along Opal Creek on the Skyline to the Sea Trail. At a large trail sign, the Skyline to the Sea Trail breaks sharply right, crosses a drainage via a footbridge, and begins a relatively short, switchbacking climb over the ridge. Another trail sign points the way

Despite the relatively long hike in, Berry Creek Falls is a main draw in Big Basin Redwoods State Park.

at the trail junction on the ridge crest, with the Skyline to the Sea Trail beginning a long, snaking drop into and then along the Kelly Creek drainage toward the falls.

Signboards with maps have been installed at the various trail junctions, making it nearly impossible to lose the route. But there's really no reason to worry about that anyway, as the descent to the falls is intersected only twice, up high by the Sunset Connector Trail and at the midpoint by the Timms Creek Trail. Ferns, redwood sorrel, and moss bloom on the forest floor in late fall, winter, and spring, along with trillium and other seasonal blooms, and the trail weaves artfully through cuts in fallen trees, under fallen trees, and over fallen trees. Footbridges span seasonal streams that run down ravines in winter, and stone staircases mitigate steep pitches. It's a very pleasant ride, both uphill and down.

By the 2-mile mark, the trail parallels Kelly Creek, an engaging companion. The shade of the redwood canopy precludes thick riparian underbrush, so the sides of the stream—and some of the boulders midstream—are cloaked in mosses and ferns. An

Berry Creek Falls; Big Basin Redwoods Waterfalls

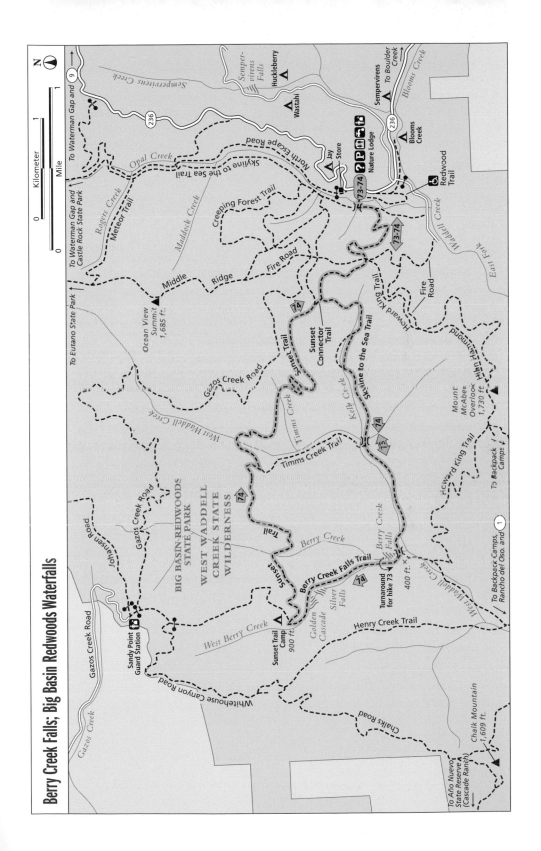

overlook on a large rock outcropping allows you to look down along the hollow, a green fold ringing with birdsong.

The long downhill ends at a crossing of Kelly Creek. Depending on when you visit, a seasonal bridge may be in place; otherwise make the crossing via boards and rock-hopping. A brief uphill follows, and then the trail drops into the Berry Creek drainage. A bench at a switchback offers a more distant view of the falls; then the trail drops across the creek and climbs briefly again to the overlook platform. The switch-backing path continues beyond the platform to the top of the falls and beyond, but this is the turnaround point. Take in the sights, and then return as you came.

Miles and Directions

0.0 Start by walking behind the amphitheater to the footbridge spanning Opal Creek (look left, though a second bridge to the right will do). Cross the bridge and go left on the Skyline to the Sea Trail.

0.3 At the trail junction at the footbridge, go right on the signed Skyline to the Sea Trail and begin to climb.

0.6 Cross another footbridge over a side stream.

1.0 Reach the crest of the ridge and a trail junction with a map signboard. Go right and down on the signed Skyline to the Sea Trail.

1.5 At the junction with the Sunset Connector Trail, stay left on the Skyline to the Sea Trail.

1.8 Cross a pair of footbridges as the trail curls through steep ravines.

2.5 Pass a closed trail and a map signboard. You'll pass the other end less than a half mile farther down the path.

3.4 At the bridge spanning Kelly Creek at the Timms Creek Trail junction, stay left on the Sky-line to the Sea Trail.

3.7 Pass through the John Sheridan Hartwell Jr. Memorial Grove, with a nice bench and a carpet of redwood sorrel in season.

4.2 A rock outcropping offers a great viewpoint overlooking the steep, shaded canyon. Drop down a stone staircase.

4.3 Cross Kelly Creek via a seasonal bridge or a more ramshackle arrangement of boards and rocks; then climb to the junction with the Berry Creek Trail. Go right on the Berry Creek Trail.

4.5 Pass a waterfall overlook with a bench at a switchback. Drop down to cross Berry Creek via a footbridge.

4.8 Reach the Berry Creek Falls overlook platform. Return as you came.

9.6 Arrive back at the trailhead.

Option: Big Basin Redwoods State Park is also home to Sempervirens Falls, a 20-foot spill on Sempervirens Creek and an easier destination for those seeking a fall but unable or unwilling to take on the challenges of getting to Berry Creek Falls or doing the waterfall loop. To reach these falls from park headquarters, pick up the Sequoia Trail, which parallels the park road south and then east, passing the Jay campground, before curling north to follow Sky Meadows Road and Sempervirens Creek north to the falls. The round-trip distance is about 3 miles.

74 Big Basin Redwoods Waterfalls

A varied trail loop links Big Basin Redwoods' main attraction, Berry Creek Falls, with the two equally stunning but less-visited falls that lie upstream. Silver Falls flies over a relatively sheer cliff into a small pool, while Golden Cascades tumbles over tiers near the apex of the loop.

See map on page 249.
Height: 60 feet (Berry Creek Falls); 50 feet (Silver Falls); 50 feet (Golden Falls)
Beauty rating: ★★★★★
Distance: 12.3-mile lollipop
Difficulty: Strenuous due to distance and elevation change
Best season: Winter and early spring
County: Santa Cruz

Trailhead amenities: Restrooms, water, trash cans, visitor center and store, amphitheater, and information signboards
Land status: Big Basin Redwoods State Park
Maps: USGS Santa Cruz CA; park map available online and at the park visitor center
Trail contact: Big Basin Redwoods State Park, 21600 Big Basin Way, Boulder Creek, CA 95006-9064; (831) 338-8860; www.parks.ca.gov

Finding the trailhead: From CA 85 in Saratoga, take the Saratoga Avenue exit. Go right (southwest) on Saratoga Avenue through town; Saratoga Avenue becomes CA 9. Continue on CA 9/Big Basin Way for about 7 miles to the junction with Skyline Boulevard/CA 35; cross Skyline to continue on CA 9 toward the state park. Travel another 14 miles to the junction of CA 9 and CA 236. Stay right on CA 236 into the park. Continue on CA 236 for about 9 miles to the park headquarters and trailhead. GPS: N37 10.311' / W122 13.329'

The Hike

This long loop, which takes in Berry Creek's three waterfalls before curling back toward home, is arguably outside the realm of a day hike. Indeed, it can be part of an overnight trip, because Sunset Camp lies along the route. But for hardy hikers who want to see what lies above lovely Berry Creek Falls, it's worth the effort. Just be sure you allot enough time to complete the whole loop in the span of a short winter's day.

The reward, beyond the whitewater fan of 60-foot Berry Creek Falls, with its sometimes crowded overlook platform, is a pair of equally stunning falls on a path less traveled. Silver Falls flies off a 50-foot cliff and lands in a dark pool; the trail leading up along the cliff face follows a narrow, spray-washed staircase etched into the dark stone. The Golden Cascades are a short distance above and beyond, slipping down two tiers of lower-angle slabs with a hint of gold color in the rock.

The loop starts with a long meander down the Skyline to the Sea Trail, through glade after glade of majestic coast redwoods, to one of Big Basin Redwoods State Park's premier attractions, Berry Creek Falls. The 60-foot cascade spills into a box canyon shaded by redwoods and crowded with ferns and moss; this is the turnaround

Golden Cascades is the last in line along the Big Basin Waterfalls Loop.

point for many hikers. But the other two falls are an easy climb above, and then the Sunset Trail rolls along the upper reaches of the forested ridges back to the crest.

Begin behind the park's amphitheater, crossing Opal Creek via one of a pair of footbridges and then heading left (downstream) along the creek on the Skyline to the Sea Trail. The Skyline to the Sea Trail breaks sharply right at a large trail sign, crosses a drainage via a footbridge, and begins the relatively short climb over the ridge. Another trail sign points the way at the junction on the ridge crest; take the Skyline to the Sea Trail down the Kelly Creek drainage.

Signboards with maps have been installed at the various trail junctions, making it nearly impossible to lose the route. Pass the junctions with the Sunset Connector Trail and the Timms Creek Trail as you descend. In the rainy season, moisture puffs up the mosses that have shriveled in the summer, and ferns, redwood sorrel, and trillium, along with other woodland flora, unfurl in season. The trail winding down the canyon is thoughtfully constructed, curling around, over, and through deadfall, incorporating stone steps to mitigate occasional steep sections, and negotiating ravines that run with seasonal stream via footbridges.

The long downhill ends with a crossing of Kelly Creek, either via a seasonal bridge or boards and rocks. Hike up and over into the Berry Creek drainage. The

The trail gets up close to Silver Falls, with a wire-rope railing providing sketchy security on the mist-slick steps.

Berry Creek Falls overlook is on the west side of the creek, a fine place for a break before beginning the long trek back to the trailhead.

From the overlook a brief climb along the stream leads to Silver Falls and the thrilling staircase with the wire-rope railing that climbs alongside. Another short meander leads from Silver Falls to the Golden Cascades, a more sprawling set of falls that fans out over warm-hued slabs. Another staircase, along with switchbacks, leads out of the Berry Creek drainage above the falls and to the junction with the Sunset Trail, the return route.

After nearly 6 miles of walking in the woods, the brief stretches of open space along the Sunset Trail offer welcome long-distance views. But this trail, too, passes predominantly through the forest, rolling in and out of folds in the ridgeline above the Kelly Creek drainage. Pass the top of the Timms Creek Trail and continue to the Sunset Connector Trail, which drops back to the Skyline to the Sea Trail, closing the loop. Retrace your steps from here.

Miles and Directions

0.0 Start by walking behind the amphitheater to the footbridge spanning Opal Creek (look left, though a second bridge to the right will do). Cross the bridge and go left on the Skyline to the Sea Trail.

0.3 At the trail junction at the footbridge, go right on the signed Skyline to the Sea Trail and begin to climb.

0.6 Cross another footbridge over a side stream.

1.0 Reach the crest of the ridge and a trail junction with a map signboard. Go right and down on the signed Skyline to the Sea Trail.

1.5 At the junction with the Sunset Connector Trail, stay left on the Skyline to the Sea Trail.

1.8 Cross a pair of footbridges as the trail curls through steep ravines.

2.5 Pass a closed trail and a map signboard. You'll pass the other end less than a half mile farther down the path.

3.4 Reach the bridge spanning Kelly Creek at the Timms Creek Trail junction; stay left on the Skyline to the Sea Trail.

3.7 Pass through the John Sheridan Hartwell Jr. Memorial Grove, with a nice bench and a carpet of redwood sorrel in season.

4.2 A rock outcropping offers a great viewpoint of the canyon. Drop down a stone staircase.

4.3 Cross Kelly Creek via a seasonal bridge or an arrangement of boards and rocks; then climb to the junction with the Berry Creek Trail. Go right on the Berry Creek Trail.

4.5 Pass a waterfall overlook with a bench at a switchback. Drop down to cross Berry Creek via a footbridge below the falls.

4.8 Reach the Berry Creek Falls overlook platform. Take in the falls; then continue up the switchbacking singletrack.

5.2 Cross a bridge over Berry Creek above Berry Creek Falls.

5.8 Arrive at Silver Falls. Climb the exposed section of trail up the cliff, skimming close to the funnel at the top of the falls.

6.2 Reach the two-tiered Golden Cascades. Switchbacks and steps lead away from the falls, gaining elevation quickly.

6.4 Arrive at the junction with the Sunset Trail. Turn right, heading east on the footpath. Pass the left-hand turn into Sunset Camp.

8.4 At the junction with the Timms Creek Trail, stay left on the Sunset Trail.

8.7 Cross a pair of footbridges as the Sunset Trail roller-coasters along the mountainside.

9.8 In the open saddle stay right on the Sunset Trail, dropping toward the Sunset Connector Trail.

10.8 At the signed junction go right on the Sunset Connector Trail. The connector ends on the Skyline to the Sea Trail; from here retrace your steps to the trailhead.

11.3 Reach the crest and begin the final descent toward the trailhead.

12.3 Arrive back to the trailhead.

75 Uvas Canyon Falls

Saturate the Bay Area with a couple of good rains, and Uvas Canyon practically blossoms with falls, cataracts, and cascades.

Height: Six named falls, the shortest being Little Falls at about 5 feet and the tallest being Lower Falls at about 40 feet
Beauty rating: ★★★★★
Distance: 2.7-mile lollipop
Difficulty: Easy
Best season: Winter and spring
County: Santa Clara

Trailhead amenities: Restrooms, picnic sites, information signboard, campground, and fee station
Land status: Uvas Canyon County Park
Maps: USGS Loma Prieta CA; maps available at the park and online
Trail contact: Santa Clara County Parks, Uvas Canyon, 8515 Croy Rd., Morgan Hill, CA 95037; (408) 779-9232; www.sccgov.org/sites/parks/parkfinder/Pages/UvasCanyon.aspx

Finding the trailhead: From San Jose head south on US 101 into Morgan Hill. Take the Bailey Avenue exit and head right (west) on Bailey Avenue for 3.2 miles to McKean Road. Turn left (south) on McKean Road (which becomes Uvas Road) for 6 miles to Croy Road. Turn right (west) on Croy Road for 4.4 miles, passing through the private Sveadal community, to the park's day-use parking lot. A fee is charged. GPS: N37 05.069' / W121 47.573'

The Hike

The surprise of Uvas Canyon is that a local park can boast a cluster of destination-worthy waterfalls. Making a comparison to Yosemite is a big stretch, but it's the only other place in NorCal where such a concentration of falls can be found in a compact setting. The scale is vastly smaller, and this canyon is smothered in oaks, bay laurels, ferns, and moss—no soaring granite domes. But douse the Santa Cruz Mountains in a good rain and head up the Waterfall Loop, and you'll pass cataract after cascade after waterfall after waterfall. It's really fun.

The Uvas Canyon falls surround year-round Swanson Creek. The park's Waterfall Loop Trail takes in five of the named falls in this park; this description includes a short out-and-back trek to Lower Falls. A seventh waterfall, Triple Falls, is located in a neighboring canyon.

Begin at the trail sign in the Black Oak picnic area. Arrows indicate the Waterfall Loop begins to the left and right as you face the sign, which is slightly confusing. To take the loop in a counterclockwise direction, matching the interpretive guide (downloadable from the park website), go right, walking down the paved road. Pass the junction with the trail to the Lower Falls (described later), climb a flight of stone steps, cross the bridge, and pass diminutive Granuja Falls. This is just the beginning …

Little Granuja Falls is one of six named cascades along the Waterfall Loop in Uvas Canyon.

Follow the broad signed trail uphill, staying right at the two junctions that follow (both lefts lead back to the parking area). The broad walk-and-talk track heads up alongside spring-fed (and ideally, rain-swollen) Swanson Creek, which rumbles in its bed to the left. The side trail to Black Rock Falls breaks right at 0.7 mile; climb a rustic set of stone steps into the side canyon to check out the sheet, which indeed pours about 30 feet down a black rock face. Round a switchback near the falls' base and follow the path back to meet the main loop trail. Continue uphill to a flat area in the forest. The trail to Knobcone Point breaks to the right, and a few feet beyond is the side trail to Basin Falls, also to the right. A short out-and-back walk leads to the base of this 25-foot spill, in a side canyon like Black Rock Falls before. Upper Falls is to the left, on Swanson Creek, a tiered spill tumbling about 20 feet.

The path back to the start of the loop follows the opposite side of Swanson Creek, reached via a bridge opposite the turn to Black Rock Falls. Cross the bridge and head downstream, now up-close to the watercourse, which tumbles over a series of short drops. Pass Little Falls and continue down to the remnants of a concrete dam just

Uvas Canyon Falls

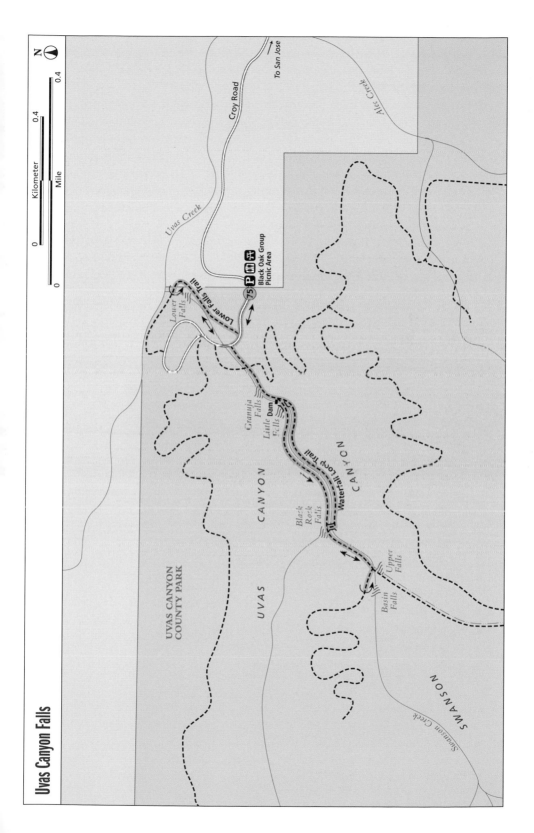

above the first bridge. Water levels permitting, rock-hop across the stream to gain the bridge and close the loop; the alternative is a scramble over the steep face above the dam and down to the bridge.

Back at the junction with the Lower Falls Trail, head down the wooden stairs and follow the narrow track that skims the hillside above the creek, again heading downstream. The trail descends to a flat area, climbs around a mossy rock outcropping, and drops down a steep staircase to the base of Lower Falls, which plunges about 30 feet over a low point in an eroded cliff. This locale is the most open along the route, with the denuded earth of the cliff face forming a small open bowl in the oak forest. Should the sun be shining and the day be warm, this makes an inviting place to picnic and, water levels permitting, hang out in the water.

Retrace your steps to the trailhead.

Miles and Directions

0.0   Begin by walking up past the restrooms to the sign in the Black Oak picnic area. Go right on the paved park road.

0.1   Pass the junction with signed trail to Lower Falls. Stay straight, climbing the stone steps and crossing the bridge on the signed Waterfall Loop.

0.2   Pass Granuja Falls. Stay right at the trail junctions that follow.

0.3   Cross the bridge below the dam, staying on the broad, obvious Waterfall Loop trail.

0.6   At the junction with the Black Rock Falls side trail, turn right and head up to the falls. To continue, climb the switchback and follow the path that parallels the main route.

0.7   Back on the main route, head right and uphill.

0.8   Pass the Maple Flat picnic area.

0.9   Reach a flat area. The Knobcone Point Trail breaks sharply right. Basin Falls is also to the right, up a short side trail. Upper Falls is to the left, in the main canyon. Explore; then retrace your steps to the junction with the Black Rock Falls side trail.

1.2   At the junction turn right, head around a switchback, and cross the bridge to reach the return route on the other side of Swanson Creek.

1.4   Pass Little Falls and cross a bridge.

1.6   At the dam rock-hop across the creek and regain the main trail, closing the loop. Cross the bridge and descend the stone steps.

1.8   Turn left onto the Lower Falls Trail.

1.9   At the unsigned junction stay straight on the trail to Lower Falls.

2.2   Cross a flat area, climb around a mossy rock outcropping, and descend a steep staircase.

2.3   Reach the base of Lower Falls. Retrace your steps.

2.7   Arrive back at the trailhead.

76 Abrigo Falls

This seasonal waterfall is reached via an easy walk through rolling coastal hills.

Height: About 25 feet
Beauty rating: ★★★
Distance: 3.2 miles
Difficulty: Easy
Best season: Late winter and early spring
County: Contra Costa
Trailhead amenities: Restrooms and picnic area

Land status: East Bay Regional Park
Maps: USGS Briones Valley CA; East Bay Regional Park District brochure and map available at the trailhead and at www.ebparks.org
Trail contact: East Bay Regional Park District, 2950 Peralta Oaks Ct., PO Box 5381, Oakland, CA 94605-0381; (888) EBPARKS; www.ebparks.org

Finding the trailhead: From CA 24 in Orinda, take the Orinda/Camino Pablo exit and head west, following Camino Pablo for 2.1 miles to its junction with Bear Creek Road. Make a right (east) turn on Bear Creek Road and go 5 miles to the signed access road for the Briones Regional Park Bear Creek Staging Area on the right (east). Follow the road for 0.4 mile to the park entry kiosk (a fee is charged). Park in the first lot, directly to the left of (behind) the entry kiosk. GPS: N37 55.640' / W122 09.504'

The Hike

This waterfall is no stunner. But these hills are parched much of the year, which makes water, and waterfalls, a sought-after break from the ordinary. The fall is only viable in a wet winter and is especially vigorous after a good rainstorm. And, as with many hikes to less-than-stellar seasonal waterfalls, it's not so much about the destination as getting there. Getting to Abrigo Falls is a pleasant walk in classic Bay Area park, with rolling, grass-covered hills opening on a fog-polished sky.

The route follows the Abrigo Valley Trail, a fire road, for its duration, with modest inclines and generous pockets of shade, especially at the outset. Abrigo Creek flows down and away to the left, behind a fence and blocked from view by a thick curtain of tangled oak and bay.

At about the half-mile mark, the road emerges from the woodland into open grassland, which comes alive in spring with poppies, lupine, vetch, and other native wildflowers. The grasses, however, are not native; they were transported to California on the hooves of Spanish horses and cattle centuries ago. Their bloom-and-rust cycle, vibrant green in winter and spring and drying to a crackly golden crunch in summer and fall, is as familiar to Bay Area residents as the June gloom (fog in summer), which predates the Spaniards by far.

The junction with the Mott Peak Trail is just before the 1-mile mark; stay on the Abrigo Valley Trail and pass the Maud Whalen camp, fenced off on the right. The

An easy walk through the East Bay hills leads to seasonal Abrigo Falls.

camp features a covered shelter, picnic tables, restrooms, and trash cans. The route continues through meadowland, with the open hills rolling away to the right and wooded hills (with a different, more northerly aspect) to the left.

Cross a creek, pass the junction with the Santos Trail, and continue through a second camp, Wee-Ta-Chi, also with restrooms, picnic facilities, and a covered shelter. The trail will gain altitude abruptly just beyond the camp, with the creek ravine steepening and growing darker on the right. Climb a short, steep pitch and watch on the right for the waterfall, which tumbles over a 25-foot cliff in the ravine. Thick foliage shields the view, but you can see and hear the fall from the trail. Dropping through the tangled woodland (complete with poison oak) to the streamside at the fall's base is not recommended. Also, be aware that in the rainy season, mud on the road, and the hillside, may be boot-sucking thick. When you've taken it all in, return as you came.

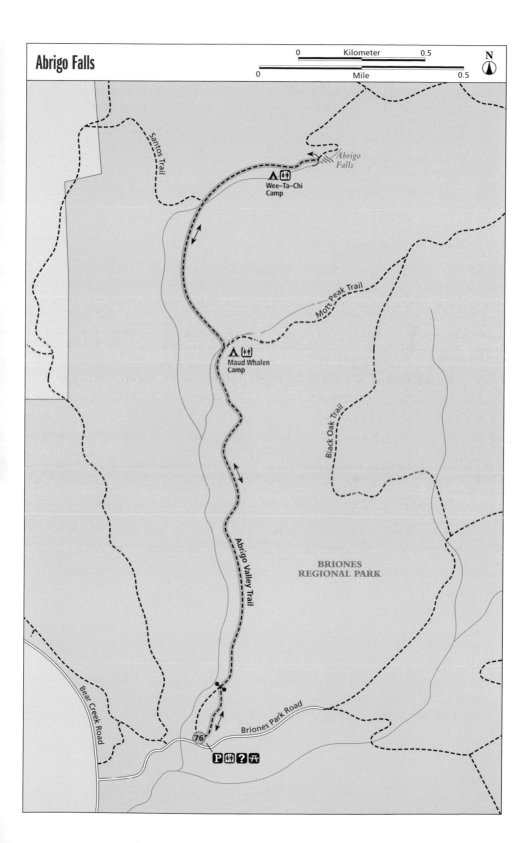

Abrigo Falls

0   Kilometer   0.5

0   Mile   0.5

N

Santos Trail

Abrigo Falls

Wee–Ta–Chi Camp

Mott Peak Trail

Maud Whalen Camp

Black Oak Trail

Abrigo Valley Trail

BRIONES REGIONAL PARK

Bear Creek Road

Briones Park Road

76

P

Miles and Directions

0.0 Start by following either of the trails that circle the meadow, walking up to the green gate that blocks vehicle traffic on the Abrigo Valley Trail (fire road). Pass the gate and head up the road.

0.5 Pass a bench and cross a seasonal stream; then climb a hill into open grassland.

0.9 At the junction with the Mott Peak Trail, go left on the Abrigo Valley Trail, passing the Maud Whalen camp.

1.3 Cross the creek and reach the Santos Trail junction. Stay right on the Abrigo Valley Trail.

1.4 Pass Wee-Ta-Chi camp; the pitch of the fire road steepens dramatically.

1.6 Take in Abrigo Falls from the fire road. Retrace your steps from here.

3.2 Arrive back at the trailhead.

Option: Make a nice lollipop loop by continuing the climb past the falls onto the Briones Crest, where panoramic views open eastward onto Mount Diablo, the Carquinez Strait, Suisun Bay, and the Sacramento River delta. Follow the Briones Crest Trail right (east) to the Mott Peak Trail and then descend from Mott Peak back to the junction with the Abrigo Valley Trail. Retrace your steps from the junction to the trailhead. This adds a little more than 1 mile to the hike distance.

77 Diablo Falls

Follow Donner Canyon up into a steep fold on the east face of Mount Diablo to view these ephemeral waterfalls.

Height: Four to five ribbons from 20 to 30 feet
Beauty rating: ★★★
Distance: 8.0 miles out and back
Difficulty: Strenuous
Best season: Winter and early spring
County: Contra Costa
Trailhead amenities: Picnic sites, visitor center, restrooms, and trash cans. Please do not bring dogs into undeveloped areas of Mount Diablo State Park (on trails); a hefty fine is charged for violation of dog restrictions.

Land status: Mount Diablo State Park
Maps: USGS Diablo CA; map at the trailhead; Mount Diablo State Park map available online. The Mitchell Canyon visitor center also has a detail map that you can take a picture of with a smart phone and use on the route.
Trail contact: Mount Diablo State Park, 96 Mitchell Canyon Rd., Clayton, CA 94517; (925) 837-2525; www.parks.ca.gov

Finding the trailhead: From I-680 in Concord take the Willow Pass Road exit. Follow Willow Pass Road east for about 0.7 mile to Gateway Road and turn right, then quickly left, onto Clayton Road. Follow Clayton Road east for 7 miles to Mitchell Canyon Road. Turn right onto Mitchell Canyon Road and go 1.6 miles to the park fee station. Pay the fee and then proceed another 0.1 mile to the parking area at the trailhead. GPS: N37 55.232' / W121 56.502'

The Hike

They don't call it Diablo for nothing. This iconic peak, the highest point on the east side of the San Francisco Bay Area, is lovely to look at, rising gold and green above the surrounding flatlands. But the mountain's temperament, like its geologic origins, can be volcanic. It tempts you with wildflowers and waterfalls, but wallops you with devilishly steep trails that, in rainy weather, can devolve into boot-sucking mud.

The falls at trail's end are tucked in a steep canyon along Donner Creek. Because I did the hike in a drought season, I can't personally vouch for how tall the falls are or how vigorously they flow, but the cluster of rain-fed plunges reportedly range from 20 to 30 feet in height.

You'll climb about 1,300 feet in 3 miles to reach the falls area, mostly on service roads that invite walking and talking. Hikers can follow a number of trails, both out-and-back routes and loops, to reach the falls. The route described here is a fairly straightforward out-and-back trek that begins in Mitchell Canyon, where you'll find ample parking and a visitor center where you can speak with a volunteer or park official about trail conditions. The hike takes 3.5 to 5 hours to complete, so work this into planning on short winter days, as the park closes a half-hour after sunset.

The steep, brushy slopes of Mount Diablo harbor a cluster of seasonal waterfalls.

The hike begins in the native plants garden behind the visitor center and climbs briskly through oaks into the rolling grasslands at the base of the mountain. Views are great, opening across the valley to the east and up onto the mountain to the west. Pass a number of well-marked trail junctions as you traverse the grassland, staying on Oak Road to Murchio Road, and then on Murchio Road eastbound to Donner Canyon Road. Trail signs are marked so that the trail you're on appears in small type at the top of the post and the destination appears in larger type vertically on the post.

The route is a straightforward roller coaster to Donner Creek. Once at the creek-side, the trail begins a gentle ascent shaded by oaks. Pass the Donner Cabin site; a section of the trail here is composed of flagstone pavers, and a jumble of concrete is on the right. The cabin, now in ruins, dates back to 1880 and belonged to rancher John Donner, who was, according to the Mount Diablo Interpretive Association, not related to the infamous emigrant party that suffered and perished on the Sierra pass that bears the same name.

Beyond the cabin site hitch back up onto the Donner Canyon Road, and the serious climbing begins. It's a steep ascent to the junction with Cardinet Oaks Road, followed by more steep, switchbacking climbing to the junction with the Falls Trail. Set your pace and slog on.

The Falls Trail, a singletrack path with brush and trees encroaching, traverses the mountainside back into the Donner Creek drainage/Wild Oat Canyon. The falls area is about 0.5 mile from the junction; this is where, depending on your timing, you'll

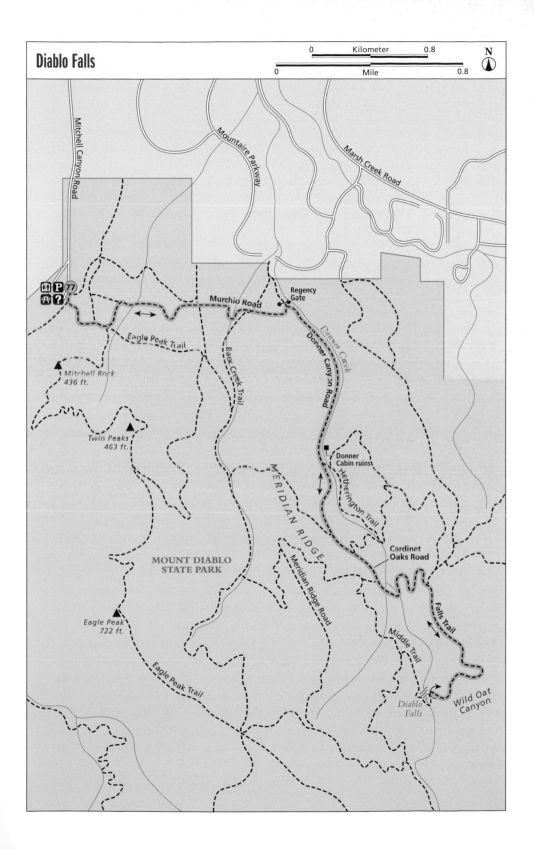

Diablo Falls

0   Kilometer   0.8

0   Mile   0.8

N

Mitchell Canyon Road

Mountaire Parkway

Marsh Creek Road

77

Murchio Road

Regency Gate

Donner Creek

Donner Canyon Road

Eagle Peak Trail

Back Creek Trail

Mitchell Rock
436 ft.

Twin Peaks
463 ft.

Donner Cabin ruins

Hetherington Trail

MERIDIAN RIDGE

MOUNT DIABLO
STATE PARK

Cardinet Oaks Road

Meridian Ridge Road

Eagle Peak
722 ft.

Falls Trail

Eagle Peak Trail

Middle Trail

Diablo Falls

Wild Oat Canyon

be able to catch your breath and enjoy a handful of falls fed by winter rains. Return as you came, enjoying the views north and east, out to Suisun Bay, as you descend.

Miles and Directions

0.0 Start behind the visitor center in the native plants garden, passing the information kiosk and following the split-rail fence up to Oak Road. Go left on Oak Road toward Murchio Road.

0.3 Pass three trail junctions in quick succession. At the first, with Watchtower Road, stay right and uphill on Oak Road. Less than a tenth of a mile farther, pass the junction with the Mitchell Rock Trail to Eagle Peak Trail, again staying on Oak Road. At the last, with Coulter Rim Trail, go left and downhill toward Murchio Road.

0.5 Go right onto Murchio Road, rolling briefly downhill.

0.9 At the junction of Murchio Road with Bruce Lee Road, stay straight on Murchio Road toward Donner Canyon Road.

1.2 A pair of trail junctions follow back to back. At the first, with the Back Creek Trail, stay straight. At the second, about 50 feet farther, stay right on the Murchio Road to Donner Canyon Road.

1.4 At the junction with Donner Canyon Road, go right. At the next junction, about 200 yards farther on, continue straight on Donner Canyon Road, tracing the creek bed upstream through the oaks.

2.0 Reach the junction with the trail to the Donner Cabin site. Go left on the side track, following the path past the cabin site.

2.25 At the Hetherington Trail junction, hitch right onto Donner Canyon Road. Go left and uphill on Donner Canyon Road toward Cardinet Oaks Road.

2.6 At the junction with the Tick Wood Trail, stay straight (uphill) on Donner Canyon Road.

2.75 Pass the top of the Hetherington Trail, staying on Donner Canyon Road.

2.9 Reach the junction with Cardinet Oaks Road. Turn left, descending across a culvert and Donner Creek before beginning a steep, switchbacking climb.

3.5 Turn right onto the signed Falls Trail, leaving the climbing behind.

4.0 Reach the falls area. Take in the sights; then return as you came.

8.0 Arrive back at the trailhead.

Options: There are a number of options that'll take you to and from the falls. You can shorten the route by starting at the Regency Gate and following Donner Canyon Road up toward the falls. This is a preferred route in a normal rainy season, when a good storm can turn the roads between Mitchell Canyon and Donner Canyon to mud.

From the Donner Cabin site, the Hetherington Trail offers a more winding alternative to reach the Cardinet Oaks Road junction, ascending through spindly manzanita and featuring a pair of creek crossings in the wet season.

You can also make a nice lollipop by continuing beyond the falls to the Middle Trail. Go right on the Middle Trail to the Meridian Ridge Road, then right again on Meridian Ridge back to the Donner Canyon Road, which leads down to the Regency Gate or Mitchell Canyon.

78 Little Yosemite Cascades

Alameda Creek steepens and gathers speed as it is funneled through the steep-walled Little Yosemite canyon, forming a series of rolling cascades.

Height: A series of short tumbles through boulders
Beauty rating: ★★★
Distance: 3.3-mile loop
Difficulty: Moderate
Best season: Winter and spring
County: Alameda
Trailhead amenities: Restrooms, doggie waste-disposal bags, picnic tables, and trash cans. Overnight camping facilities are available by reservation. Check out the Old Green Barn Visitor Center, where you'll find various historical and ecological displays and can pick up keys to identify the birds, butterflies, and wildflowers in the park.
Land status: Sunol-Ohlone Regional Wilderness
Maps: USGS La Costa Valley CA; East Bay Regional Park District brochure and map available at the trailhead and at www.ebparks.org
Trail contact: East Bay Regional Park District, 2950 Peralta Oaks Ct., PO Box 5381, Oakland, CA 94605-0381; (888) EBPARKS; www.ebparks.org

Finding the trailhead: From I-680 in Sunol take the CA 84 exit. Calaveras Road, which heads south to the park, departs from the east side of the interchange, opposite Paloma Road into Sunol. Follow Calaveras Road 4.1 miles south to Geary Road. Turn left (east) on Geary Road and follow it for 0.8 mile to the park boundary, and then for another mile to the entry kiosk and parking areas (1.8 miles total). A fee is charged. The trailhead is adjacent to the visitor center, which is served by the parking lot to the north (left) of the entry kiosk. GPS: N37 30.964' / W121 49.899'

The Hike

Soaring raptors and flitting butterflies, wildflowers and spreading oaks, serpentine rock outcroppings painted with lichen, and a lovely cascade tumbling through mossy creek boulders … this loop pretty much epitomizes an ideal Bay Area waterfall hike.

There is an easier way to view the cascades in the Sunol-Ohlone park's Little Yosemite gorge—you can simply follow the Camp Ohlone fire road out and back. But the loop described here tours a picturesque grassland dotted with serpentine rock outcroppings and archetypal oaks with canopies spread like mushroom caps forming pools of shade. The route tops out with an easy traverse offering excellent views in three directions before dropping to the falls on boulder-tossed Alameda Creek in Little Yosemite. The loop passes through an area grazed by lumbering bovines, but don't let the cow pies dissuade you. Watch your step and enjoy.

Start on the Indian Joe Nature Trail, which winds through a stretch of willow and alder along the creek. At the Indian Joe/Canyon View Trail split, head right (southeast) and uphill on the Canyon View Trail, passing through the gate and into Jacob's

Valley. The climbing is steep, but oaks shade rock outcroppings that sport coats of black and green lichen and offer great rest stops on the ascent.

Pass the McCorkle Trail intersection; the route traverses across open grassy hills. Views open south and then east onto the steep upper walls of Little Yosemite. Timbers span a muddy cattle track below a water trough in the shade of a sycamore tree. The trail then descends to an overlook of the Little Yosemite area. From the viewpoint the path drops to the junction of the Canyon View Trail and Camp Ohlone Road in Little Yosemite.

From the Camp Ohlone Road, take any of the side trails that branch down to Alameda Creek, where you can enjoy the cascades. The steep, dark valley walls overshadow the stream and its verdant riparian plant life. No swimming is permitted, and after rains, when the water is high, care should be taken when approaching the waterway.

To leave Little Yosemite follow the straightforward Camp Ohlone Road west and then north, back to the more developed portions of the park. The road traces the creek; again, a number of social paths lead to the streamside, but heed the posted cautions against swimming or wading. Cross the bridge that spans Alameda Creek at the Camp Ohlone Road trailhead; the last part of the loop follows an equestrian trail wedged between parking lots and picnic sites.

Miles and Directions

0.0 Start to the right (east) of the Old Green Barn, walking behind the park residence and adjacent picnic grounds to a bridge spanning Alameda Creek.

0.1 On the north side of the bridge, turn right (east) on the combined Indian Joe Nature/Canyon View/Ohlone Wilderness Trails. Pass Hayfield Road.

0.3 Pass a side trail and cross a seasonal stream. At the junction go left on the Indian Joe Creek/Canyon View Trails.

0.5 At the junction take the signed Canyon View Trail, which splits off right (southeast).

0.6 A steep ascent leads to a gate; close this after you pass.

0.8 Pass a trail marker for the Ohlone Wilderness Trail and then reach the McCorkle Trail intersection. Continue straight (southeast) on the Canyon View Trail.

1.0 Timbers bridge the cattle track at a water trough.

1.3 Drop to a gate and trail sign at the junction with the Cerro Este Road. Turn right (south) on the Canyon View Trail, skirting another water trough.

1.5 Reach the junction with Camp Ohlone Road in the heart of Little Yosemite, with picnic tables and a restroom. Alameda Creek and its falls are across the road; use side trails to check out the cascades. When you're ready, return to Camp Ohlone Road and go left, heading back toward the trailhead.

2.1 Pass a fence line and gate. A number of social trails drop left (south) to the creek; stay straight on Camp Ohlone Road.

◀ *Looking down into Little Yosemite from the Canyon View Trail.*

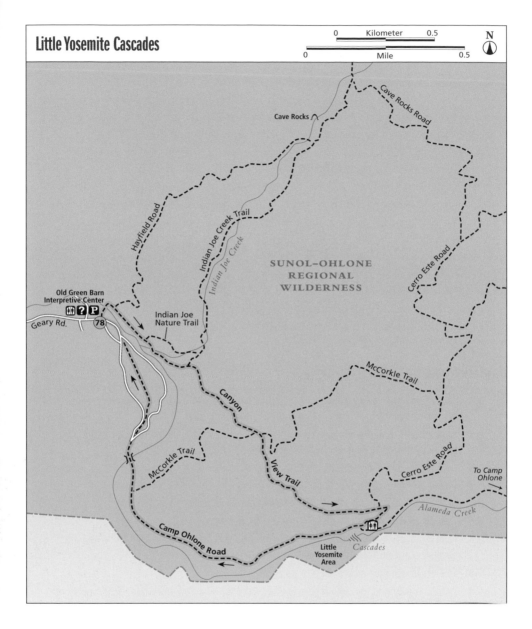

Little Yosemite Cascades

0   Kilometer   0.5

0   Mile   0.5

N

Cave Rocks

Cave Rocks Road

Hayfield Road

Indian Joe Creek Trail

Indian Joe Creek

SUNOL–OHLONE
REGIONAL
WILDERNESS

Cerro Este Road

Old Green Barn
Interpretive Center

Geary Rd.

78

Indian Joe
Nature Trail

McCorkle Trail

Canyon

McCorkle Trail

View Trail

Cerro Este Road

To Camp
Ohlone

Alameda Creek

Camp Ohlone Road

Little
Yosemite
Area

Cascades

2.7   Cross the bridge over Alameda Creek. The trail is paved on the far side, leading past trailhead information signs and restrooms into a large parking area. Pick up the equestrian trail that traverses the field inside the loop of the road.

3.1   The equestrian trail ends at the horse trailer parking lot. At the stop sign go left (north) on the paved park road toward the visitor center.

3.3   Arrive back at the trailhead.

Monterey and Big Sur

One of California's most photographed waterfalls is in Big Sur … but then again, a number of postcard-perfect destinations lie along the dramatic coastline that stretches from Monterey to Lucia. This is one of the few places in the state where driving from trailhead to trailhead is as pleasurable as the hiking itself. Monterey, Carmel, and Pacific Grove offer all the amenities, with Big Sur a more rustic destination. The waterfalls, with the exception of Garland Ranch Falls, all lie along scenic CA 1.

McWay Falls (hike 81).

79 Garland Ranch Falls

A lovely loop through a popular park strung along the Carmel River leads to a seasonal waterfall.

Height: 70 feet
Beauty rating: ★★★
Distance: 2.6-mile lollipop
Difficulty: Moderate
Best season: Late winter and early spring (best after heavy rains)
County: Monterey
Trailhead amenities: Information signboards and dog potty stations. Restrooms, water, and information are available at the nearby visitor center.
Land status: Garland Ranch Regional Park
Maps: USGS Seaside CA; map available online or from the park visitor center
Trail contact: Monterey Peninsula Regional Park District, 60 Garden Ct., Ste. 325, Monterey, CA 93940; (831) 372-3196; www.mprpd.org/index.cfm/id/19/Garland-Ranch-Regional-Park/

Finding the trailhead: From the junction of Carmel Valley Road and CA 1 in Carmel, head east on Carmel Valley Road for 8.4 miles to the signed park entrance on the right. Abundant parking is available in the gravel lot adjacent to the Carmel River. GPS: N36 30.596' / W121 45.981'

The Hike

This one's for the dogs. They are everywhere in Garland Ranch Regional Park, stretching their leashes (and, though they are not supposed to, romping off-leash through the grasses and brush). It's for the dogs' owners too: This is a neighborhood park, frequented by families, trail runners, and friends out for an afternoon walk-and-talk. The multiuse trails are wide enough for hikers to proceed side by side and to share with mountain bikers and equestrians, the large meadow at the base hosts a long loop that passes alongside the Carmel River, and the ridgelines of the Santa Lucia Mountains rise protectively to the south.

Oh … and there's a waterfall too.

This loop takes in everything but the ridgelines, coursing through the meadow at riverside, arcing up to the seasonal fall, and cruising through oak woodlands at the base of the mountains, with views, before returning to meadow and river. The fall is best viewed after winter rains have revitalized the watershed, an event that also causes the ferns to explode from the woodland floor and mosses to fatten up and display their most vivid greens. Winter also highlights the beauty of pale green lace lichens, which drape the bare limbs of buckeyes and deciduous oaks.

Start the loop by walking west from the parking lot. A wide path leads to the permanent bridge spanning the Carmel River and then curls back on the southern bank to the visitor center (a seasonal bridge may be in place, bypassing this section of the

The Lupine Loop follows the Carmel River toward the Garland Ranch waterfall.

route). From the visitor center the Lupine Loop traces the willow-lined river eastward, with the meadow opening on the south, stretching to the base of the mountains.

At the east end of the meadow, the route hitches up into the oaks, delving into a steep ravine where the waterfall descends. Even when dry, the 70-foot vertical cliff face is impressive, rising straight up from the edge of the trail bed. Ferns bloom on narrow ledges on the rock wall. When it flows, hikers stand a good chance of getting misted, or just plain wet.

A set of steep stairs leads farther up into the Santa Lucias, but this loop retreats from the waterfall to the Cliff Trail. This narrow singletrack winds through the woods along the base of the mountains, with ferns coating the slopes and views opening across the Carmel Valley at breaks in the trees. Enjoy superior views from a rock outcropping just before the Cliff Trail drops to cross the Mesa Trail.

Pick up the Buckeye Trail on the other side of the Mesa Trail, another traversing path lined with interpretive signs describing the surrounding flora. (Fun fact: The tannins in the buckeye seed are potent enough to stun fish in streams; the local Native people had to leach the seeds for a week before they were edible.) The Buckeye Trail drops back into the meadow; pick up the Lupine Loop on the flats and head back through the grasses to the year-round bridge and trailhead.

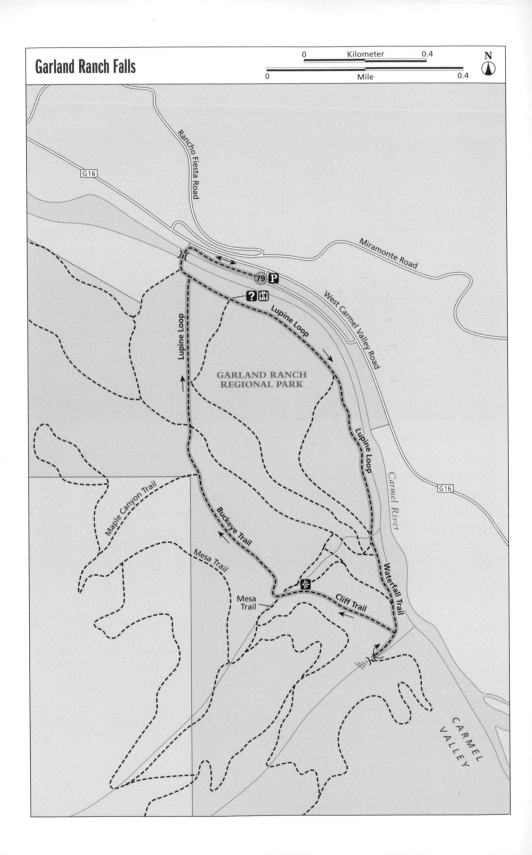

Garland Ranch Falls

Kilometer
0   0.4

Mile
0   0.4

N

Rancho Fiesta Road

G16

Miramonte Road

79 **P**

West Carmel Valley Road

Lupine Loop

Lupine Loop

**GARLAND RANCH
REGIONAL PARK**

Lupine Loop

Carmel River

G16

Maple Canyon Trail

Buckeye Trail

Mesa Trail

Mesa Trail

Waterfall Trail

Cliff Trail

**CARMEL
VALLEY**

Miles and Directions

0.0 From the parking lot follow the split trail west to the year-round bridge across the Carmel River at the entrance drive. Cross the bridge and turn left onto the broad Lupine Loop, toward the visitor center (signs point the way).

0.2 Pass the Lupine Loop trail junction; this is where you'll close the loop.

0.3 Reach the "plaza" at the visitor center, with all the amenities. Continue straight on the broad Lupine Loop, paralleling the river.

0.6 Pass the junction with the Sycamore Trail, staying left on the Lupine Loop.

1.0 At the junction of the Sycamore, Lupine, and Waterfall Trails, go left on the Waterfall Trail. Stay right and uphill on the broad trail at the signed path leading to private property.

1.1 Pass the junction with the Chamisal Trail; continue on the Waterfall Trail.

1.2 Pass the junction with the Cliff Trail; continue on the Waterfall Trail.

1.3 Cross a bridge, climb a couple of sets of stairs, and reach the base of the waterfall. Retrace your steps to the Cliff Trail junction.

1.4 Turn left onto the Cliff Trail, climbing switchbacks and stairs and then traversing the fern-clad slope.

1.6 Pass a rock outcropping that offers great views.

1.7 Drop onto the Mesa Trail. Cross the dirt track to the Buckeye Trail and ascend the stairs.

1.8 At the junction with the Siesta Point Trail, stay right (downhill) on the Buckeye Trail.

2.0 Exit the Buckeye Trail through a stile. At the trail Y just beyond, stay right toward the Lupine Loop.

2.1 At the junction with the Maple Canyon and other trails (with sign), stay left on the Lupine Loop. Stay left at the next junction as well, following the sign to vehicle parking.

2.4 Close the loop at the Lupine Loop trail junction near the year-round bridge. Retrace your steps from here.

2.6 Arrive back at the trailhead.

A picturesque staircase leads up and away from the Garland Ranch waterfall.

80 Pfeiffer Falls

Experience the interface between redwood forest and oak woodland on the trail to Pfeiffer Falls.

Height: 60 feet
Beauty rating: ★★★★★
Distance: 2.0 miles out and back
Difficulty: Moderate
Best season: Winter and spring
County: Monterey
Trailhead amenities: Restrooms, information, water, trash cans, picnic sites, camping facilities, and a lodge and cafe

Land status: Pfeiffer Big Sur State Park
Maps: USGS Big Sur CA; map available in the park brochure and online
Trail contact: Pfeiffer Big Sur State Park, 47225 CA 1, Big Sur, CA 93920; (831) 649-2836; www.parks.ca.gov

Finding the trailhead: From Carmel follow scenic CA 1 south for 27.5 miles to the signed entrance to Pfeiffer Big Sur State Park on the left. Finding parking can be problematic on busy spring and summer weekends. This route begins at the paved, signed trailhead in the parking lot at the Big Sur Lodge; your route at the outset may vary depending on where you are able to leave your vehicle. GPS: N36 15.067' / W121 47.177'

The Hike

Dramatic redwood groves, which flourish in the fog-shrouded ravines of Big Sur, bookend the trail to Pfeiffer Falls. The route begins in a stand of massive trees: The shade is thick, footfalls are muffled by a dense carpet of needles, and Pfeiffer Creek flows gently (most of the time) through on its final approach to its confluence with the Big Sur River. Trail's end is in another redwood stand, equally quiet and also bisected by the creek, but a 60-foot waterfall adds to the drama factor.

Between the redwoods the route climbs across a slope cloaked in oak woodland, the trees low and gnarled, throwing a spindlier shade across the landscape and allowing a thick chaparral, including coyote brush and poison oak, to thrive. Buckeyes, with their fragrant blooms, are among the first trees to leaf out in spring, and the smooth, deep burgundy bark of manzanita splashes color onto the gray and brown landscape.

Depending on where you park, you may travel a different route to the formal trailhead. From the restaurant at the Big Sur Lodge, a signed, paved path climbs gently to the to the trailhead proper. Beyond the information sign wire rails usher

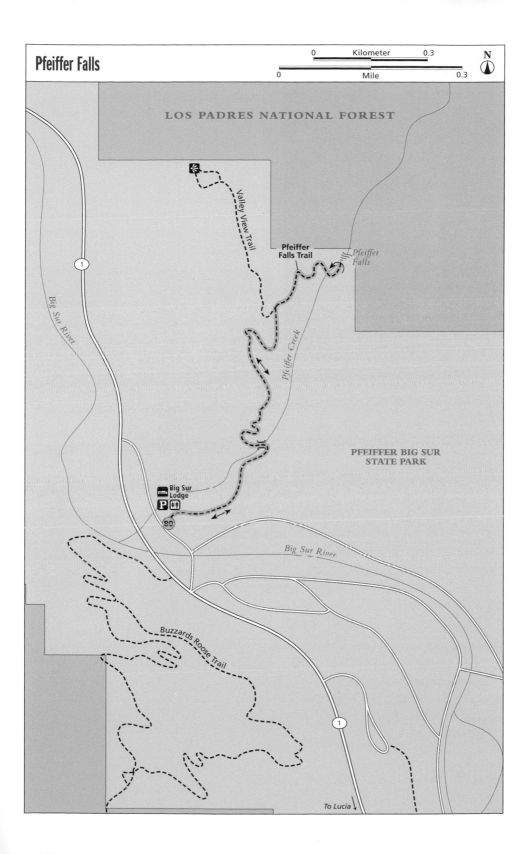

Pfeiffer Falls

0 — Kilometer — 0.3

0 — Mile — 0.3

N

LOS PADRES NATIONAL FOREST

Valley View Trail

Pfeiffer Falls Trail

Pfeiffer Falls

Pfeiffer Creek

Big Sur River

PFEIFFER BIG SUR STATE PARK

Big Sur Lodge

P

Buzzards Roose Trail

Big Sur River

1

1

To Lucia

Pfeiffer Falls splashes into a redwood-shaded pool.

you through the redwoods to the bridge across Pfeiffer Creek and then up onto the Valley View Trail. A short, switch-backing climb leads into the oaks, offer-ing views of the Big Sur valley.

The Valley View and Pfeiffer Falls Trails diverge at the top of the climb: Go right on the signed path to Pfeiffer Falls. The trail traverses the hillside, with views opening inland across the tops of the redwoods and onto the steep slopes of the Santa Lucias.

A switchbacking descent leads into the redwood grove at the base of Pfeif-fer Falls. Bear left on the path, climbing briefly to the overlook rocks at the base of the fall. The waterfall is tiered, with the middle section a sheet of whitewater when the creek is fully charged. Crane your neck to see the upper tier, high on the mountainside. Retrace your steps.

Miles and Directions

0.0 Start at the signed trailhead next to the Big Sur Lodge restaurant. Follow the pavement across the park road.

0.2 Reach the formal trailhead, with an information signboard. Head into the redwoods on the wide dirt track.

0.3 Cross the bridge and bear left onto the signed Valley View Trail.

0.6 Take in views from a switchback.

0.8 At the junction go right onto the Pfeiffer Falls Trail. The Valley View Trail heads left.

0.9 Descend switchbacks to a bridge in the redwoods.

1.0 Reach Pfeiffer Falls. Retrace your steps.

2.0 Arrive back at the trailhead.

Option: If you'd like to take in more vistas of the Big Sur valley and coastline, head up on the Valley View Trail. The rough singletrack continues climbing through the chaparral, passing benches along the way. The trail dead-ends at a lofty overlook; look north up the coastline, with the Santa Lucias forming an impressive rampart in the east and the world flattening into the Pacific in the west. Return as you came.

81 McWay Falls

The signature waterfall on the Big Sur coast, given its superlative setting, McWay Falls will not disappoint.

Height: About 80 feet
Beauty rating: ★★★★★
Distance: 0.8 mile out and back
Difficulty: Easy
Best season: Year-round
County: Monterey
Trailhead amenities: Restrooms, water, trash cans, information, picnic sites, and camping facilities. A fee is charged. Do not attempt to reach the beach at the falls; the cliffs are dangerous.
Land status: Julia Pfeiffer Burns State Park
Maps: USGS Partington Ridge CA; park map available at the park's entrance station or online
Trail contact: Julia Pfeiffer Burns State Park, Big Sur Station #1 / 47555 CA 1, Big Sur, CA 93920; (831) 649-2836; www.parks.ca.gov

Finding the trailhead: From Carmel follow scenic CA 1 south for about 38 miles to the signed entrance to Julia Pfeiffer Burns State Park on the left. The park is 11 miles south of Big Sur. There is a park fee, but the bend above McWay Cove is often congested with cars parking alongside the highway and using the secondary trail to reach the falls overlook. GPS (formal parking area). N36 09.570' / W121 40.107'

The Hike

McWay Cove, and the wisp of a fall that spills into it, is iconic. Waterfalls that spill directly onto a Northern California beach are few and far between—three are included in this guide. Each has a spectacular seaside setting, but McWay, with its inaccessible, untouchable crescent of beach and rugged Saddle Rock forming a protective break from the sea, stands apart. That it would become the focal point of an equally spectacular seaside home is no surprise: From the overlook among the foundations of the Waterfall House, the vistas are mesmerizing and inspirational.

A short, well-maintained, and well-traveled crushed granite trail leads from the day-use parking area to the waterfall overlook. Pass through the pedestrian tunnel under CA 1 and then turn right on the overlook trail, traversing the chaparral-coated slope above the cove. The path to the left leads up through a stand of eucalyptus to CA 1, providing access to visitors who've parked their vehicles alongside the highway. The waterfall comes into view as the trail curves gently westward, the spill arcing out from the tree-topped cliff face and freefalling onto the beach below.

The turnaround is at the overlook. Surrounded by the remnants of the Waterfall House, interpretive signs describe both the human and natural history of the park, including a synopsis of the life of park namesake Julia Pfeiffer Burns, who spent all her days on the Big Sur coast, and of Helen Hooper Brown, the heiress who, with her

Slender McWay Falls is a main attraction along the Big Sur coast.

husband, purchased Saddle Ranch in 1924 and built the house on the point, along with a funicular rail line to get to and from the site. There's also a description of the massive slide that took out CA 1 just north of the park in 1983; debris from the slide makes up the beach upon which slender McWay Falls makes landfall. The slide scar is still visible.

When you've taken it all in—if that's possible in a single visit—return as you came.

Miles and Directions

0.0 Start by descending the staircase and heading right on the Waterfall Overlook Trail. Pass the trail that leads left to the Pelton wheelhouse.

0.1 Pass through the pedestrian tunnel.

0.4 Reach the waterfall overlook. Retrace your steps.

0.8 Arrive back at the trailhead.

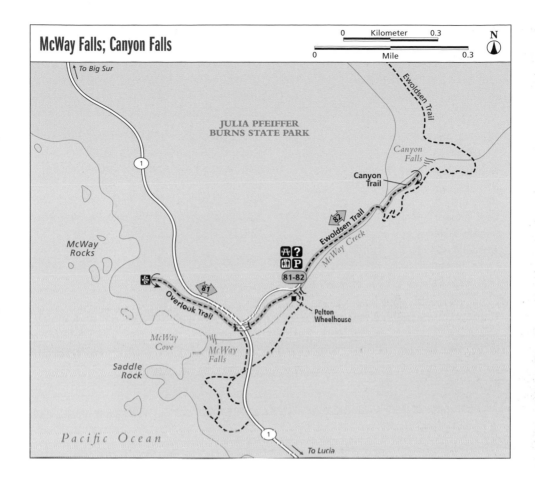

McWay Falls; Canyon Falls

JULIA PFEIFFER
BURNS STATE PARK

Option: As you near the trailhead on the return from the McWay Falls overlook, take a right turn onto the path leading down to the Pelton wheelhouse. The trail leads through a bower of willow down to the wheelhouse, where you can check out the wheel, sometimes called a "hurdy-gurdy," and read about how it was used to generate electricity from McWay Creek, which descended steeply enough out of the Santa Lucia Mountains to provide power for Saddle Ranch. The side trip will add about 0.1 mile to the hike.

82 Canyon Falls

Less than a mile inland from McWay Falls, Canyon Falls dances down a narrow gorge that seems a world away.

See map on page 281.
Height: About 80 feet
Beauty rating: ★★★★
Distance: 1.2 miles out and back
Difficulty: Easy
Best season: Year-round
County: Monterey
Trailhead amenities: Restrooms, water, trash cans, information, picnic sites, and camping facilities. A fee is charged.

Land status: Julia Pfeiffer Burns State Park
Maps: USGS Partington Ridge CA; park map available at the park's entrance station or online
Trail contact: Julia Pfeiffer Burns State Park, Big Sur Station #1 / 47555 CA 1, Big Sur, CA 93920; (831) 649-2836; www.parks.ca.gov

---

Finding the trailhead: From Carmel follow scenic CA 1 south for about 38 miles to the signed entrance to Julia Pfeiffer Burns State Park on the left. The park is 11 miles south of Big Sur. There is a park fee, but the bend above McWay Cove is often congested with cars parking alongside the highway and using the secondary trail to reach the McWay Falls overlook. GPS (formal parking area): N36 09.570' / W121 40.107'

The Hike

Follow McWay Creek downstream, and you can witness its final descent into the sea. Follow McWay Creek upstream, and you can watch it tumble down a steep gorge crowded with redwoods.

The trailhead is located at the uphill end of the day-use parking area, signed for the Canyon and Ewoldsen Trails. Pass through the picnic area, squeeze past a large boulder, and begin climbing into McWay Canyon. The creek is a boisterous companion, running in cataracts with drops 2 to 4 feet high. Redwoods tower overhead, and the sound of the sea recedes, replaced by the sound of flowing water.

At the Y-junction cross the creek on boards. Cables define the route as it switchbacks away from the creek and then traverses upstream through stands of redwoods. At the junction with Ewoldsen Trail, stay left on the trail to Canyon Falls.

The cataracts on the creek grow more lively, and the setting more magical, as the gentle ascent continues. The falls are not far above the junction, set in a sliver of canyon surrounded by redwoods, one of which has wrapped its exposed roots across the rock face beside the cascade like a gripping hand. A set of steep switchbacks leads up the hillside on the right side of the fall; then the trail drops to, and ends at, the pool at the base. If it's warm enough, the falls might provide a nice shower. Return as you came.

Less than a mile separates Canyon Falls from better-known McWay Falls, but the settings couldn't be more divergent.

Miles and Directions

0.0 Start at the uphill/inland end of the parking area on the signed Canyon/Ewoldsen Trails. Pass through the picnic area.

0.2 At the trail Y go right and cross the stream on boards. Cables delineate the route, which switchbacks up from the creek before continuing upstream.

0.4 At the junction with the Ewoldsen Trail, stay left on the Canyon Trail.

0.6 Reach Canyon Falls. Follow the steep switchbacks up and then drop down to the base of the falls at trail's end. Retrace your steps.

1.2 Arrive back at the trailhead.

83 Limekiln Falls

Leave the thunder of the Pacific surf behind on an easy trail that leads into the steep coastal canyon hosting Limekiln Falls.

Height: 100 feet
Beauty rating: ★★★★
Distance: 2.0 miles, including a side trip to the kilns
Difficulty: Moderate due to creek crossings
Best season: Winter and spring
County: Monterey

Trailhead amenities: Restrooms, water, trash cans, picnic sites, camping, and information. A fee is charged.
Land status: Limekiln State Park
Maps: USGS Lopez Point CA; park map available at the entrance station and online
Trail contact: Limekiln State Park, 63025 CA 1, Big Sur, CA 93920; (805) 434-1996; www.parks.ca.gov

Finding the trailhead: From Big Sur follow scenic CA 1 south for 24 miles to the signed turnoff for Limekiln State Park, on the south side of the Limekiln Bridge. The park is about 52 miles south of Carmel. Follow the entrance road for 0.1 mile to the entrance station, pay the fee, and park in the day-use parking area. GPS: N36 00.625' / W121 31.108'

The Hike

The Santa Lucia Mountains have an arid feel, washed in warmer winds that dry out the grasses earlier in the season than farther north. But slip back into Limekiln State Park, into the folds of the mountains, and you'll find moist ravines where redwood groves, ferns, and mosses thrive. Limekiln Falls is the prime attraction in one of these canyons.

The waterfall is a major draw, but the park's namesake limekilns, in the neighboring ravine, are equally engaging. The limestone deposit in the canyon was fed into the four towering metal furnaces that still stand alongside the trail in a dark hollow; the lime purified by fire in the kilns was shipped north and used to make concrete. The operation lasted for only three years in the 1880s, according to park literature, and aside from depleting the deposit, the processing also consumed the surrounding redwood forest. What stands in the hollows now is second-growth, but still statuesque.

This route takes in both the waterfall and the limekilns. It begins inauspiciously, passing through the park's linear campground. Cross the bridge over Limekiln Creek, however, and development slips away, as does the roar of the sea, overtaken by the sound of water flowing in Limekiln and Hare Creeks.

The trail forks immediately on the far side of the bridge, with the right fork leading up Hare Creek and the left following Limekiln Creek. Stay left, following Limekiln Creek and passing through named memorial groves. The forest floor is nearly clear of undergrowth, as if it had been carefully landscaped. Cross a second bridge and

Abandoned limekilns hunker in the forest near Limekiln Falls.

then bear right at the trail junction and cross the creek yet again, heading up the east fork of Limekiln Creek toward the falls.

The Falls Trail crosses the east fork several more times as it climbs toward the destination: Be prepared to do some keen balancing on rocks and wet logs or to get your feet wet—and be especially cautious when the flows are high. The last ford deposits you on the south side of the creek. Follow the path up to the overlook, where views of Limekiln Falls, cascading over a 100-foot cliff, are unimpeded. Take it in, then retrace your steps to the trail junction above the second bridge.

After wringing out your socks, turn right onto the Limekiln Trail and hike up into another stunning redwood grove, this one studded with tall, round, metal structures that are reminiscent of the helmets worn by the Knights Who Say Ni in *Monty Python and the Holy Grail*. Check out the massive kilns, with their brick-lined mouths, and then retrace your steps to the trailhead.

Miles and Directions

0.0 Start by walking from the day-use parking area up the road through the linear campground along Limekiln Creek.

0.1 Cross the bridge at the end of the camp to the trail Y. Go left on the unsigned trail along Limekiln Creek.

0.4 Cross a second bridge. The trail continues about 150 yards farther to another trail Y; go right to follow the trail to Limekiln Falls. The trail drops across the creek, with a board providing a narrow bridge.

0.7 Arrive at the falls overlook. Retrace your steps to the junction above the second bridge.

1.0 Back at the junction, turn right onto the Limekiln Trail.

1.1 Cross yet another bridge, proceeding up the north side of the west fork of Limekiln Creek.

1.3 Reach the four massive, antique limekilns. Retrace your steps.

2.0 Arrive back at the trailhead.

Yosemite

When it hits a landscape peppered with cliffs, what's a river to do? It must go with the flow; it must fall. In Yosemite National Park, the creeks and rivers doing the fall are epic. Most everything you'll need to support your waterfall explorations can be found on the Yosemite Valley floor, from camping to upscale accommodations at the historic Ahwahnee Hotel. Nearby towns include Groveland, Mariposa, and Wawona; highways leading into the park include CA 120/Big Oak Flat Road (coming from the north), CA 140 (coming from the west up the Merced River valley), and CA 41/Wawona Road (linking the valley to Wawona).

A perpetual rainbow arcs across the base of Vernal Fall (hike 97).

84 Rainbow Pool

A brief hike leads down to a perfect pool with a parklike fall on the South Tuolumne River.

Height: 20 feet
Beauty rating: ★★★★
Distance: 0.1 mile out and back
Difficulty: Easy
Best season: Spring and early summer
County: Tuolumne
Trailhead amenities: Restrooms, picnic sites, and trash cans

Land status: Stanislaus National Forest
Maps: USGS Jawbone Ridge CA
Trail contact: Stanislaus National Forest, Groveland District, 24545 CA 120, Groveland, CA 95321; (209) 962-7825; www.fs.fed.us (search for "Rainbow Pool Day Use Area")

Finding the trailhead: From Groveland continue east on CA 120/Big Oak Flat Road for about 13.5 miles to the bridge spanning the South Tuolumne River. Turn right at the sign and drive 0.1 mile down the access road to the small parking area. The pool and fall are located down a short trail opposite the restrooms. The access road is one-way; to leave the falls, follow the pavement for 0.6 mile, passing under the highway bridge, back to CA 120. GPS. N37 49.201' / W120 00.704'

The pool below the Rainbow Fall draws both swimmers and anglers.

Viewing the Falls

This one's sweet and easy, perfect for an outing with the kids, and sought after by early-morning anglers. A brief, easy staircase and footpath lead down to the rocky shoreline of the Rainbow Pool on the south fork of the Tuolumne River. Once at the riverside, scramble to an unspoken-for clearing alongside the pool and enjoy. The waterfall is short but, fed by the indefatigable south Tuolumne, is nearly always flowing.

Once a toll stop along Big Oak Flat Road, the Rainbow Pool was also the focal point of a resort that burned in 1958. Now the site lies in the midst of the infamous Rim Fire of 2013, which torched more than 257,000 acres (more than 400 square miles) and is currently the third-largest wildfire in California history. Mitigation in the wake of the fire, including taking down dead standing trees, was ongoing in 2015; check with the forest service to ensure the area is open when you choose to visit.

To reach the pool, head down a short staircase and footpath from the parking area opposite the restrooms. Take a swim, cast a line, and then return as you came. The round trip is less than a tenth of a mile long.

85 Carlon Falls

Follow a peaceful section of South Fork Tuolumne River to the jumble of river rocks and Carlon Falls.

Height: About 35 feet
Beauty rating: ★★★
Distance: 3.3 miles out and back
Difficulty: Easy, edging to moderate near the falls
Best season: Late spring and summer
County: Tuolumne

Trailhead amenities: Restrooms and picnic sites in the Carlon Day Use Area
Land status: Stanislaus National Forest
Maps: USGS Ackerson Mountain CA
Trail contact: Stanislaus National Forest, Groveland District, 24545 CA 120, Groveland, CA 95321; (209) 962-7825; www.fs.usda .gov/recmain/stanislaus/recreation

Finding the trailhead: From the Big Oak Flat Entrance to Yosemite National Park, follow CA 120 west for 1 mile to Evergreen Road. Turn right onto Evergreen Road (signed for Hetch Hetchy and Evergreen Lodge) and go 1 mile to the signed Carlon Day Use Area, at the bridge over the South Fork Tuolumne River. Parking is in the day use area or at the trailhead on the north side of the bridge. GPS: N37 48.875' / W119 51.755'

The Hike

In the wake of the 2013 Rim Fire, the hike to Carlon Falls has become a study in contrasts. Along the South Fork Tuolumne River a verdant riparian habitat thrives, with reeds, willow, alder, and primordial clusters of Indian rhubarb, with its giant umbrella-like leaves, cluttering the banks. But just a few hundred yards uphill to the east, the thick evergreen forest is scarred by the fire, the understory burned clear and the trunks scorched. The riverside is inviting and vibrant, the forest side is creaky and vaguely unnerving, and the juxtaposition makes the walk to the falls all the more invigorating.

Despite its proximity to Yosemite National Park and Hetch Hetchy, the route to Carlon Falls is less traveled. An easy walk, it begins by winding through the torched tree trunks adjacent to the Tuolumne, with short use trails offering access to fishing holes and swimming holes on the river. Foundations that cross the path are reported to be from buildings associated with the Carl Inn, which was built in 1918-19 by Dan and Donna Carlon and demolished by the park service in 1940.

The walking gets a bit more difficult beyond the 1-mile mark, when the path leaves the riverside and climbs up and over a steep but short ridge as the river bends eastward. Switchbacks drop into the narrower, rocky drainage that cradles the falls and the pools below. Route-finding can be tricky back at the riverside, depending on the

Fire and water: The devastation of the Rim Fire stops at the bank of the South Fork Tuolumne River downstream from Carlon Falls.

water level. But between the falls, the cascades, and the pools, there is plenty to see and enjoy year-round.

Miles and Directions

0.0 Start by walking up the day-use area access road to Evergreen Road. Cross the road and walk to the far side of the bridge to the signed trailhead proper.

0.2 Pass through a stile and into the Yosemite Wilderness. Signs advise caution when walking through the burn area, particularly in wind and rain, when dead or fire-damaged trees may fall without warning.

0.3 Concrete foundations crisscross the path.

0.6 A use trail breaks right to a particularly nice riverside beach.

1.1 The trail arcs away from the river, bending left.

1.2 Cross a streamlet and begin the short but steep climb.

1.6 Switchbacks lead down to the rock-strewn riverbed. Clamber through as water levels permit to the waterfall. Return as you came.

3.3 Arrive back at the trailhead.

86 Wapama Falls

The thrill of a hike to Wapama Falls is the stretch of trail that leads right through the fury. A boardwalk winds through the boulder field that catches the Wapama spill, while mist like spindrift swirls above.

Height: 1,400 feet
Beauty rating: ★★★★★
Distance: 5.2 miles out and back
Difficulty: Moderate
Best season: Late spring and summer
County: Tuolumne
Trail amenities: Parking and information signs at the trailhead. A fee is charged to enter the national park.
Land status: Yosemite National Park; Hetch Hetchy Valley

Maps: USGS Lake Eleanor CA; Yosemite National Park map available online and at the park entrance station
Trail contact: Yosemite National Park, Public Information Office, PO Box 577, Yosemite, CA 95389; (209) 372-0200 (dial ext. 3, then 5); www.nps.gov/yose. The website is extensive and should be every visitor's first stop for information on the park.

Finding the trailhead: From CA 120/Big Oak Flat Road 1 mile west of the Big Oak Flat Entrance to Yosemite National Park, take Evergreen Road toward the Evergreen Lodge and Hetch Hetchy. Follow Evergreen Road for about 7.2 miles to the stop sign at the junction with Mather Road and continue right on Evergreen/Hetch Hetchy Road. Pass the Yosemite National Park entrance station and continue to the parking area/trailhead at O'Shaughnessy Dam, which is a total of 15.9 miles from the junction with CA 120. GPS: N37 56.754' / W119 47.297'

The Hike

The destination is visible from the trailhead. Wapama Falls appears big, white, and relentless from a viewpoint on O'Shaughnessy Dam, but the distance minimizes its impact. And your focus will falter on the lovely walk that traces the shoreline of the deep, blue, quiet Hetch Hetchy Reservoir, with the falls mostly out of sight.

But there is sound and fury in Wapama. The roar strikes you first, rumbling around the rock face on the final approach. Climb onto the boardwalks at the base of the falls, and the mist and noise envelop you. Round the bend to near trail's end and crane your neck; the genesis of the falls is more than 1,000 feet above. The beauty, intimacy, and ferocity of these falls are unparalleled.

The hike to Wapama Falls showcases the spectacular Hetch Hetchy Valley and Reservoir. Legendary Yosemite champion John Muir waged his final conservation battle for this valley, taking on the city of San Francisco, which was rebuilding and burgeoning in the wake of the 1906 earthquake and firestorm. The City by the Bay had targeted Hetch Hetchy as the perfect place to sequester a secure water supply, regardless of the fact that the valley was within the boundaries of Yosemite National

Park. The city won: Today water from Hetch Hetchy travels 167 miles to San Francisco, powered only by gravity. But the controversy over flooding the valley has never entirely died out, and to this day wildland activists hope to drain the reservoir and restore what Muir called "one of nature's rarest and most precious mountain temples."

I am far too young to know what Hetch Hetchy looked like in Muir's day, but I can say that it remains a tremendous, evocative landscape.

Three waterfalls lie along the trail that passes Wapama. Wapama is a year-round event, unlike smaller Tueeulala Falls, which peters out as the summer season progresses. Rancheria Falls lies farther upvalley, and would be accessible via a 13-mile round-trip hike (best done as an overnight), but in spring 2014 about 16,000 tons of rock tumbled down the mountainside and obliterated a portion of the route. Plans call for the trail to be reopened … eventually. Check with the park to ensure access.

The route begins on the O'Shaughnessy Dam, authorized by the Raker Act in 1913, completed about 10 years later, and delivering water to San Francisco by the mid-1930s. Looking down into the narrow canyon beyond the dam face, you might see powerful jets of water discharging from outlets into the Tuolumne River. The dominant feature to the east, rising from the water, is Kolana Rock, rising to 5,774 feet, nearly 2,000 feet above the surface of the reservoir (depending on the water level).

On the other side of the dam, the trail passes through a long, dark, damp tunnel, emerging nearly 0.2 mile beyond in the shade of the valley wall. The path gradually narrows from road-width to singletrack, climbing via pavement and stairs to a trail junction. Stay right on the signed path to Wapama Falls and, eventually, the Yosemite Valley.

From the junction the route drops down to and across a granite apron with great reservoir views. The granite may be wet in early season; in fact, depending on the time of year and the quantity of snowmelt, much of the trail may be waterlogged. Stay left on the trail at about 1.5 miles and then veer right to cross more sunny slabs. Depending on the temperature, the shade of a stand of ponderosa pines at 1.9 miles will be welcome.

Tueeulala Falls is at about 2.1 miles, but may be little more than a black streak on the cliff face in late season or in drought years, even though neighboring Wapama Falls may be in full force. Swing up stony switchbacks and then drop onto the bridges that span the jumbled rock apron at the base of Wapama Falls. You'll want to walk to the very edge of the last footbridge to take in the entire spectacle.

Wapama Falls

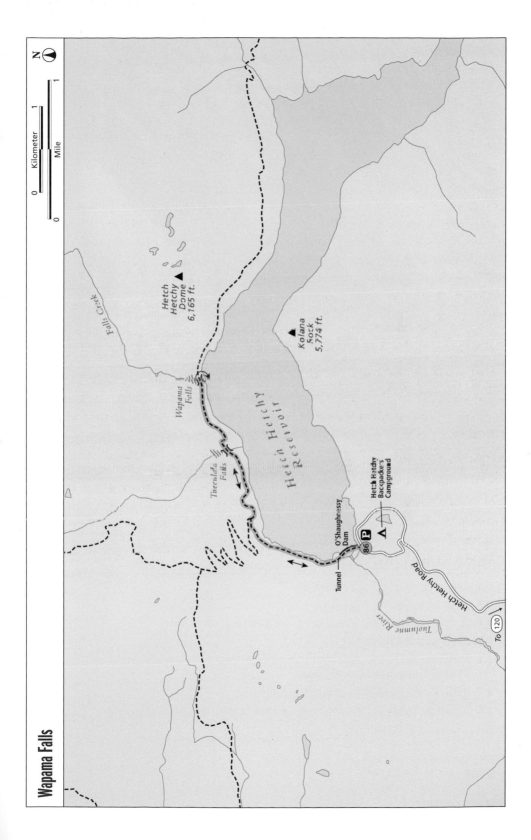

N

0   Kilometer   1

0   Mile   1

Falls Creek

Hetch Hetchy
Dome
6,165 ft.

Kolana
Rock
5,774 ft.

Wapama Falls

Tueeulala Falls

Hetch Hetchy Reservoir

O'Shaughnessy
Dam

Tunnel

86

P

Hetch Hetchy
Backpackers
Campground

Hetch Hetchy Road

Tuolumne River

To 120

Wapama Falls thunders into the boulder field at its base, then cascades into Hetch Hetchy Reservoir.

Miles and Directions

0.0 Start by crossing O'Shaughnessy Dam.

0.2 Enter the tunnel.

0.4 Emerge from the tunnel and traverse above the reservoir shoreline.

0.8 Cross a seasonal stream.

1.1 At the trail junction stay right on the signed trail to Wapama Falls. A left takes you to the Beehive, Laurel Lake, and Vernon Lake.

2.1 Cross the footbridge at the base of Tueeulala Falls.

2.6 Reach the boardwalks below Wapama Falls. Take it all in; then return as you came.

5.2 Arrive back at the trailhead.

87 Foresta Falls

This year-round waterfall and its upper cascades are surrounded by a haunting woodland burned in the historic Arch Rock Fire.

Height: About 50 feet
Beauty rating: ★★★★
Distance: 1.8 miles out and back
Difficulty: Easy
Best season: Late spring and summer
County: Mariposa
Trailhead amenities: None
Land status: Yosemite National Park; Stanislaus National Forest
Maps: USGS El Portal CA

Trail contact: Yosemite National Park, Public Information Office, PO Box 577, Yosemite, CA 95389; (209) 372-0200 (dial ext. 3, then 5); www.nps.gov/yose. The website is extensive and should be every visitor's first stop for information on the park. Stanislaus National Forest, Groveland District, 24545 CA 120, Groveland, CA 95321; (209) 962-7825; www.fs.usda .gov/recmain/stanislaus/recreation.

Finding the trailhead: Traveling east from El Portal on CA 140, pass through the Arch Rock gate of Yosemite National Park. Proceed toward Yosemite Valley to the junction with CA 120/Big Oak Flat Road. Turn left onto CA 120 and climb 3.3 miles to the junction with Foresta Road. Follow Foresta Road down through the small cluster of cabins, staying left on the pavement where the road forks. The road is barricaded at 2.3 miles (as of 2014); there is parking for about three cars alongside the dirt road at the barricade. GPS: N37 41.853' / W119 45.449'

The Hike

Foresta Falls is not an iconic Yosemite waterfall, nor is its setting classic Yosemite stunning. But it drops through a tortured landscape that is eerily moving and tells a story unlike any other.

It's the story of fire. This area has seen its share of fiery fury, as evidenced by the recovering woodland surrounding the community of Foresta. Fire blew through in 1991, devastating the area; the cabins now on the ground were built in the aftermath of that blaze. Fires threatened again in 2009 and 2011. The Rim Fire of 2013, historic in its size and ferocity, spared the hamlet but incinerated 402 square miles of Yosemite's backcountry. And in 2014 Foresta was evacuated twice, once in July for the El Portal Fire and again in October when the Dog Rock Fire crept close.

The closed dirt road that leads down along Crane Creek, offering views and access to the Foresta cascades and fall, winds through skeletal standing dead trees that groan when the wind flows through. I hiked to the fall between the two 2014 blazes. What struck me first was the smell of scorched pitch. Second was the sound of woodpeckers knocking on the trunks for their breakfast. Large, ash-filled holes checkered with chunks of coal lined the trail—all that remained of trees completely consumed or removed. The burned trees were scarred with char and stripped of needles; with

Foresta Falls is out of the way but evocative, tucked in a landscape repeatedly touched by fire.

no canopy, the views opened down and away, into the Crane Creek ravine and toward the Merced River valley far below. It was a brown-and-black landscape, but signs of life were erupting from the ash—an understory of ferns, grasses, and wildflowers matted the forest floor like gauze, filmy but enduring.

Because of the burn, little impedes views of Crane Creek's slides, cascades, and waterfall. The slides and cascades come into view within a quarter mile of the trailhead: a double spill with a cascade about 25 feet high dropping into a pool, which in turn feeds a slide about 30 feet long. The road provides an easy walk-and talk descent; to reach the slides and swimming holes, you'd have to break left and downslope cross-country toward the creek. While no signs prohibit this, I'd advise against it: This is a fragile, recovering ecosystem and trampling the mountainside will only cause erosion, not to mention that it could be hazardous. Practice Leave No Trace ethics by staying on the trail.

Beyond the cascades the roadway curves away from the creek, traversing the hillside to a switchback and then cutting back toward the waterway. The final fall is at the bridge, which, while not passable to motor vehicles in 2014, was sturdy enough to support hikers. The fall drops from about 50 feet above, fanning out across the dark slab before being scattered in a mash of boulders and deadfall at its base. The year-round creek then rumbles under the bridge, through a cataract created by more deadfall on the downhill side. This is an upside-down hike, so be prepared for the uphill on the return; as a bonus, views of the cascades and slides are better on the way back.

Miles and Directions

0.0 Start just beyond the last cabin on Foresta Road (at the barricade forbidding vehicle traffic). The wide dirt roadway/trail heads downhill.

0.2 The cascades and slides come into view on the left.

0.3 Pass the sign designating the McCauley Ranch Addition.

0.5 Round a switchback.

0.9 Reach the bridge and the 50-foot fall. Return as you came.

1.8 Arrive back at the trailhead.

88 The Cascades and Wildcat Falls

Two gateway waterfalls located just outside the Yosemite Valley proper are linked by a short roadside walk.

Height: About 750 feet for Cascade Fall; 700 feet for Wildcat Fall
Beauty rating: ★★★★
Distance: Less than 1.0 mile out and back
Difficulty: Easy
Best season: Late spring and early summer
County: Mariposa
Trailhead amenities: Restrooms and trash cans. An abundance of amenities—from gift shops to restaurants to tent cabins and more—not to mention the basics, such as restrooms,

water, and trash cans, are available farther up the road in Yosemite Valley.
Land status: Yosemite National Park
Maps: USGS El Capitan CA; park map available online and at park entrances. No map is needed.
Trail contact: Yosemite National Park, Public Information Office, PO Box 577, Yosemite, CA 95389; (209) 372-0200 (dial ext. 3, then 5); www.nps.gov/yose. The website is extensive and should be every visitor's first stop for information on the park.

Finding the trailhead. Traveling east from El Portal on CA 140, pass through the Arch Rock Entrance Station of Yosemite National Park. From Arch Rock proceed 2.8 miles to the Cascade Fall pullout on the left side of the highway, with parking for about eleven vehicles. The Cascade picnic area is about 200 yards west of the Cascade Fall pullout; parking may be available here as well. GPS: N37 43.438' / W119 42.726'

The Hike

Cascade and Wildcat are Yosemite's gateway falls. They are glorious when full with snowmelt, turning the heads of drivers following scenic CA 140 through the Merced Gorge toward Yosemite Valley proper. A quick stop and a short walk link the two plunges, which can run year-round but fade to ribbons in late season.

Begin in the pullout below the Cascades, with limited parking (there's more, potentially, across the road in the Cascade picnic area). When the Cascades are full, you need go no farther than the low stone wall that encircles the parking area to enjoy, though short social paths lead behind and closer to the creek. Interpretive signs in the parking area point out the staggering growth in popularity the park saw in the twentieth century, with 5,000 people making the 2-day train journey from San Francisco in 1900, and 4.1 million people traveling 5 hours by car to visit in 1995. They came to see, among other wonders, falls like the Cascades, a spectacular tiered plunge fed by Cascade and Tamarack Creeks. The longest drop, and the one most visible from the CA 140 as you travel toward the valley, is 500 feet.

To reach Wildcat Fall, tumbling down Wildcat Creek, follow the highway back to the west, toward Arch Rock, for a little less than a half mile and then follow an

Neighboring Wildcat Fall and the Cascades are the first falls visitors may see as they drive toward Yosemite Valley on CA 140.

obvious social trail into the woods, walking toward the northern wall of the gorge. The evergreens grow thickly here, encroaching on the fall and hiding its height. But Wildcat is different in that it is a major fall less visited. Particularly later in the season, you may have the verdant alcove at its base to yourself, an uncommon experience in this wildly popular park. Retrace your steps to the parking area.

Miles and Directions

0.0 Start at the Cascade Fall parking area, checking out Cascade Fall. When ready, head west alongside CA 140 toward Wildcat Fall.

0.1 Pass the Cascade picnic area parking lot on the left (south) side of the highway.

0.4 At an unsigned parking pullout, go right on the narrow, unsigned use trail toward Wildcat Fall.

0.5 Reach the base of Wildcat Fall. Return as you came.

1.0 Arrive back at the Cascade Fall parking area.

89 Bridalveil Fall

Drive into the Yosemite Valley proper, and Bridalveil is the first fall you'll see, spilling over the shadowy cliff wall nearly opposite El Capitan. While many visitors simply stop alongside the road to view the waterfall, a short paved trail leads closer to its base.

Height: 620 feet
Beauty rating: ★★★★★
Distance: 0.5 mile out and back
Difficulty: Easy
Best season: Late spring and early summer
County: Mariposa
Trailhead amenities: Restrooms and trash cans. An abundance of amenities—from gift shops to restaurants to tent cabins and more—not to mention the basics, such as restrooms, water, and trash cans, are available farther up the road in Yosemite Valley.

Land status: Yosemite National Park
Maps: USGS El Capitan CA; park map available online and at park entrances. No map is needed.
Trail contact: Yosemite National Park, Public Information Office, PO Box 577, Yosemite, CA 95389; (209) 372-0200 (dial ext. 3, then 5); www.nps.gov/yose. The website is extensive and should be every visitor's first stop for information on the park.

Finding the trailhead: From El Portal take CA 140 east into Yosemite Valley via the Arch Rock entrance Station—or find your way into the valley via CA 120/Big Oak Flat Road or CA 41/Wawona Road. Take Southside Drive (one-way) to the signed junction with Wawona Road/CA 41. Turn right onto Wawona Road and then turn immediately left into the signed parking area for the Bridalveil Fall trailhead. There is a large lot, and overflow parking is available alongside the Wawona Road. GPS: N37 42.988' / W119 39.076'

The Hike

When Bridalveil Fall is fully charged, its spray washes over viewers gathered on the tiered platforms at trail's end. Expect to jostle with fellow hikers for the best camera angles during late spring and early summer, when the valley begins to clog with seasonal tourists. But regardless of whether the overlook is teeming or empty, the up-close views of the fall, the roar of its descent, and the thrill of its proximity will satisfy any waterfall aficionado.

Later in the year Bridalveil fades away, though it hosts a year-round flow. Even when thinned by summer heat, however, the fall is still an iconic gateway element of the Yosemite Valley.

The trail is short and simple. From the trailhead follow the paved path up to a trail Y. Stay right on the signed route, climbing relatively steeply alongside a segment of Bridalveil Creek to the small overlook. Gaze upward at the long, slender spill of Bridalveil; then, if it's early in the season, turn around and look across the valley at

Bridalveil Fall plunges toward the valley floor.

Ribbon Fall, which drops more than 1,600 feet from the cliff top west of El Capitan to the valley floor. Return as you came.

Miles and Directions

0.0 Start on the signed paved trail at the east end of the parking lot.

0.1 At the Y stay right on the signed path to Bridalveil Fall.

0.25 Reach the overlook. Retrace your steps.

0.5 Arrive back at the trailhead.

90 Ribbon Fall

Heralded as the tallest uninterrupted waterfall in the United States, Ribbon Fall slips down the cliff just west of El Capitan.

Height: 1,612 feet
Beauty rating: ★ ★ ★ ★
Best season: Spring
County: Mariposa
Trailhead amenities: An abundance of amenities—from gift shops to restaurants to tent cabins and more—not to mention the basics, such as restrooms, water, and trash cans, are available farther up the road in Yosemite Valley.

Land status: Yosemite National Park
Maps: USGS El Capitan CA; park map available online and at park entrances. No map is needed.
Trail contact: Yosemite National Park, Public Information Office, PO Box 577, Yosemite, CA 95389; (209) 372-0200 (then dial 3, then 5); www.nps.gov/yose. The website is extensive and should be every visitor's first stop for information on the park.

Viewing the Fall

With no trail leading either directly to its base or directly to its summit, Ribbon Fall is best viewed from Bridalveil Fall or from the pullouts alongside the meadows on Southside Drive at the base of Bridalveil Fall. Fed by Ribbon Creek, the waterfall is just what its name implies: a ribbon of water streaking more than 1,600 feet down one of the valley's steep ramparts. The fall is ephemeral and typically disappears just as the summer season in Yosemite kicks into full gear.

Ephemeral Ribbon Fall is visible cross-valley from the Bridalveil Fall overlook.

91 Horsetail Fall

Site of Yosemite's famous February firefall, Horsetail Fall is an ephemeral drop off El Capitan that lights up with setting sun in late winter.

Height: 1,575 feet
Beauty rating: ★★★★★
Best season: Late winter and early spring (mid to late February for the firefall)
County: Mariposa
Trailhead amenities: An abundance of amenities—from gift shops to restaurants to tent cabins and more—not to mention the basics, such as restrooms, water, and trash cans, are available in the Yosemite Valley.

Land status: Yosemite National Park
Maps: USGS Half Dome CA; park map available online and at park entrances. No map is needed.
Trail contact: Yosemite National Park, Public Information Office, PO Box 577, Yosemite, CA 95389; (209) 372-0200 (dial ext. 3, then 5); www.nps.gov/yose. The website is extensive and should be every visitor's first stop for information on the park.

Finding the trailhead: From the Yosemite Lodge on Northside Drive, head west to the El Capitan picnic area. GPS (picnic area): N37 43.695' / W119 37.238'

Viewing the Fall

You'll have to time this just right: Not only is Yosemite's Horsetail Fall short-lived, but the window for viewing the spectacle of firefall is even shorter. For a few weeks in February, conditions permitting, this narrow fall catches the light of the setting sun just right and lights up. It has been described by witnesses (myself not among them … yet) as like a flow of lava down the east face of El Capitan. The fall cannot be approached via trail, but can be viewed from the El Capitan picnic area on the valley floor, west of Yosemite Lodge, or from points along Northside Drive.

Horsetail Fall lit by the February sun. ▶

92 Sentinel Fall

Though the tiers of Sentinel Fall can be seen the easy way, looking up from Sentinel Beach or other locations on the Yosemite Valley floor, this loop takes you to the funnel at the top, as well as to the awesome 360-degree views from the summit of Sentinel Dome.

Height: About 2,000 feet
Beauty rating: ★★★★★
Distance: 4.8-mile loop
Difficulty: Moderate
Best season: Early summer
County: Mariposa
Trailhead amenities: Restrooms and trash cans
Land status: Yosemite National Park

Maps: USGS Half Dome CA; park map available online and at park entrances
Trail contact: Yosemite National Park, Public Information Office, PO Box 577, Yosemite, CA 95389; (209) 372-0200 (dial ext. 3, then 5); www.nps.gov/yose. The website is extensive and should be every visitor's first stop for information on the park.

Finding the trailhead: From El Portal take CA 140 east into Yosemite Valley via the Arch Rock Entrance Station—or find your way into the valley via CA 120/Big Oak Flat Road or CA 41/Wawona Road. Take Southside Drive (one-way) to the signed junction with Wawona Road. Turn right onto Wawona Road and follow it for about 9 miles, through the tunnel and up to the junction with Glacier Point Road (open late May to October or November, snow permitting). Turn left onto Glacier Point Road and follow it about 13 miles to the signed trailhead and parking area for Sentinel Dome and Taft Point. The roadside parking lot fills quickly in high season; you may need to park at Badger Pass Ski Area. GPS: N37 42.749' / W119 35.187'

The Hike

While the trail to Sentinel Dome sees a lot of traffic, the longer loop etched along the lip of the valley wall is relatively less traveled and well worth experiencing. The route, which crosses Sentinel Creek above where it begins its abrupt drop to the Merced River, offers tree-shaded views across the valley to El Capitan, the Three Brothers, and Yosemite Falls. Tack on the ascent to the summit of Sentinel Dome, with its unimpeded views of the summits of the High Sierra, and the Sentinel tour is complete.

While viewing Sentinel Fall in its entirety is best done from the valley floor, either from Sentinel Beach on Southside Drive or from the north side near Lower Yosemite Fall, standing at the top, where Sentinel Creek is funneled into a dark crevasse of rock and drops out of sight, is thrilling (and not for those with a fear of heights). Glacier Point Road may open only after the ephemeral waterfall is past its snow-fed prime, so this is an excellent choice for a late-season experience.

The route begins by heading west from the trailhead toward Taft Point. The trail meanders through woodlands, passing a striking outcropping of white quartz that

Looking down the Yosemite Valley past El Capitan from the top of Sentinel Fall.

stands out like statuary against a background of brown forest duff. Roll downhill to a signed trail split in the woods and take the right fork toward Sentinel Dome (the left fork heads to Taft Point and the Fissures).

The trail continues a downhill run through pine and fir, breaking into an open area dotted with big ponderosas and granite erratics (a boulder garden) with views to the right (east) and up to Sentinel Dome. A brief passage through woodland again leads to the brink of the south valley wall, with the granite base dropping abruptly away and views opening across the void to El Capitan on the distant north side. Several granite perches offer great vista points as the trail arcs eastward and continues to follow the rim.

Drop across Sentinel Creek at just about the halfway point; depending on the season, the water may flow fairly swiftly. A use trail leads left out to the brink, with more views of El Cap, the Three Brothers, Yosemite Falls, and the winding Merced River on the valley floor. This is also the brink of Sentinel Fall; the drop is abrupt and breathtaking. It's all breathtaking.

From the creek crossing the trail begins to climb through the woods, rounding three switchbacks before reaching the junction with the signed route to Glacier Point and the trail leading up to Sentinel Dome. Head right and up toward the dome, passing radio towers and following the road-wide trail as it crosses a service road twice.

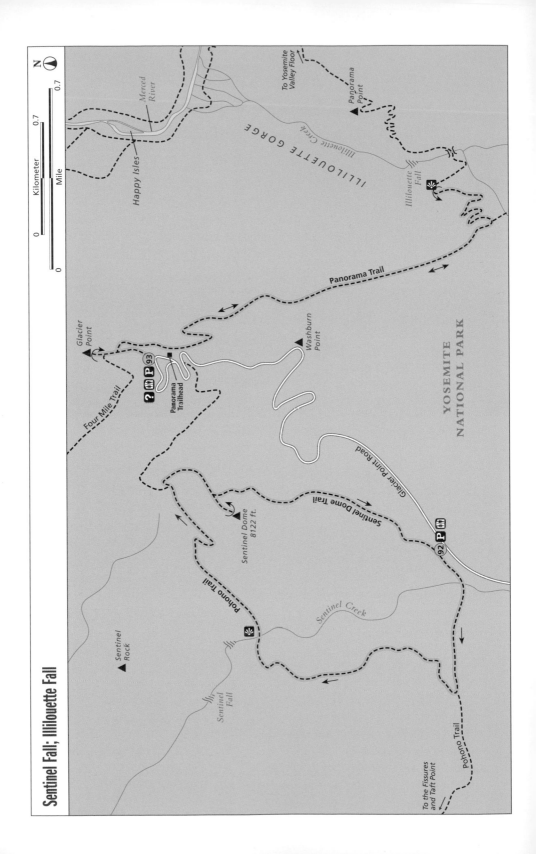

Sentinel Fall; Illilouette Fall

Bear right on the track as it arcs toward Sentinel Dome. Two access trails meet the trail to the summit of the dome as you approach the polished granite slabs, which are visible through the trees. There's no marked route to the summit: Pick your line and climb the low-angle rock to the top.

Views from the summit of Sentinel Dome are staggering. The Cathedral Rocks, Half Dome, El Cap, the distant glacier-sculpted peaks and ridges of the High Sierra—a compass rose helps you name them all, including distant Mount Conness, Mount Ritter, and Banner Peak. A few weathered pines find purchase on the windy dome top, as gently curved as a shallow, upside-down bowl. It's tough to leave.

But when you do, head down to the first signed junction and turn right, heading back toward the trailhead. The route appears paved for a stretch. At the junction follow the signed trail leading to the Sentinel Dome parking area. Cairns and trail signs keep you on track as you descend more slabs. Back in the woods, cross a plank bridge over a seasonal stream before ending the loop at the trail junction near the restrooms and parking lot.

Miles and Directions

0.0   Head down the signed trail behind the restrooms for about 200 yards to the fork. Go left on the wide path signed for Taft Point. The trail to the right, signed for Sentinel Dome, is the return route.

0.3   Pass a striking white quartz outcropping and cross a seasonal stream.

0.7   At the signed trail split, go right toward Sentinel Dome (the left-hand trail leads to Taft Point).

1.1   Emerge from the woods briefly, looking to the right toward Sentinel Dome.

1.5   Reach the rim of the valley, where the trail curls eastward and offers fabulous views.

1.8   Cross Sentinel Creek and head left to the vista point at the top of Sentinel Fall. Return to the creek to pick up the main trail, which begins to climb. (Avoid the narrow use trail that leads uphill/northeast from the viewpoint.)

2.6   Round three switchbacks.

2.8   Climb to a three-way junction. Go right on the signed trail to Sentinel Dome; the left trail leads to Glacier Point. Beyond the radio towers stay on the middle track leading uphill, crossing the service road a couple of times.

3.4   At the first signed junction with the trail to the summit of Sentinel Dome, continue straight; the polished granite slabs rise ahead.

3.5   Pass a second junction and keep heading up, climbing onto the granite east face of Sentinel Dome.

3.6   Reach the top of Sentinel Dome. Take in the views; then descend to the first signed trail junction and turn right, heading toward the trailhead.

4.0   At the junction stay right on the dirt track signed for the Sentinel Dome parking area. Cairns and trail signs mark the route across the slabs beyond.

4.7   Cross the plank bridge.

4.8   Arrive back at the trailhead.

93 Illilouette Fall

Follow the Panorama Trail past classic views of Half Dome to a sheltered overlook of one of Yosemite's more remote falls.

See map on page 306.
Height: 370 feet
Beauty rating: ★★★★★
Distance: 5.4 miles out and back
Difficulty: Strenuous
Best season: Late spring and early summer
County: Mariposa
Trailhead amenities: Restrooms, water, information, a cafe and gift shop, trash cans, maps, and information signboards

Land status: Yosemite National Park
Maps: USGS Half Dome CA; park map available online and at park entrances
Trail contact: Yosemite National Park, Public Information Office, PO Box 577, Yosemite, CA 95389; (209) 372-0200 (dial ext. 3, then 5); www.nps.gov/yose. The website is extensive and should be every visitor's first stop for information on the park.

Finding the trailhead: From El Portal take CA 140 east into Yosemite Valley via the Arch Rock Entrance Station—or find your way into the valley via CA 120/Big Oak Flat Road or CA 41/Wawona Road. Take Southside Drive (one-way) to the signed junction with Wawona Road. Turn right onto Wawona Road and follow it for about 9 miles, through the tunnel and up to the junction with Glacier Point Road (open late May to October or November, snow permitting). Turn left onto Glacier Point Road and follow it about 13 miles to its end in the Glacier Point parking lot. Despite its expansiveness, this lot fills quickly in high season and can be clotted with buses. You may need to park at Badger Pass Ski Area. The trailhead is opposite the visitor center and gift shop. GPS: N37 43.633' / W119 34.507'

The Hike

Just about every waterfall in Yosemite National Park could be called bucket list. For Illilouette Fall it's not only because of the fall itself—which, don't get me wrong, is spectacular as only a Yosemite fall can be—but also because of the journey. Let's put it this way: The trail's not named Panorama for nothing.

As you traverse below the Illilouette Ridge, heading southeast into Yosemite's backcountry, views open in an arc before you. First, from Glacier Point, look down into Yosemite Valley onto El Capitan and the Brothers, Yosemite Falls and the Royal Arches, and North Dome. As you head south and east, Half Dome dominates the frontcountry, and then the eye is drawn down to Vernal and Nevada Falls in the Merced River Gorge. The white-capped summits, sharp and shining in the sun, mark the skyline: Watkins, Hoffman, the Echo Peaks, and more.

The hike to the fall starts and ends at storied Glacier Point. Before or after heading out on the Panorama Trail, tour the often packed paved paths that lead out to the various vista points. With any luck you'll visit on a less busy day, when you can find a

The Panorama Trail leads to an overlook of Illilouette Fall and offers spectacular views of Half Dome and other Yosemite landmarks along the way.

spot along the rail and thrill in the edge-of-the-void views. The out-and-back route described here incorporates that tour at the outset.

After taking in the Glacier Point sights (be sure to check out the information signboards, including one that describes McCauley's Mountain House and the Glacier Point Hotel, which burned in 1969, and another that identifies landmarks in the foreground and on the horizon), pick up the signed Panorama Trail, directly opposite the gift shop, and set off on the relatively gentle downhill run toward Illilouette Creek and Illilouette Fall.

The route begins by switchbacking down through stands of evergreens settled on the stone with parklike precision. Within half a mile the woods end and the trail ramps with relative gentleness (for Yosemite) across a scrubby mountainside. Pockets of trees and tall deciduous shrubs thrive in shallow gullies carved by seasonal streams, but none are serious enough to screen the amazing views. If hiking on a hot day, however, be sure to carry lots of water, bring a hat, and wear sunscreen. Half Dome dominates the views for the first mile or so, and then the shadowy canyon cradling Vernal and Nevada Falls comes into play.

The one and only trail junction on this out-and-back hike is just beyond the 2-mile mark; head left on the trail signed for Illilouette Fall, Nevada Fall, and the valley floor. While still in the scrubland, views are dead-centered on Half Dome. Cross a streamlet and then drop into the woodlands surrounding Illilouette Creek. The overlook, which is the turnaround for this hike, is at a break in the trees directly opposite the Illilouette Fall.

The fall runs year-round. When fully charged, it plunges off the cliff into the shadowy gorge below; later in the season, when the flow mellows, Illilouette Creek drops about 30 feet into a pool and then splinters and falls hundreds of feet into the gorge, crashing into a steep, narrow cleft where the sun seldom shines. Trees shelter the rock slabs at the overlook, but depending on the time of day and time of year, those sitting rocks may bake in the sun. If you want to check out the top of the falls, continue down the path and cross the creek.

From the overlook retrace your steps to the trailhead. It's all uphill from here. Though never painfully steep, the hike back is a slog, albeit a slog with phenomenal views. Set your pace, stay hydrated, and enjoy.

Miles and Directions

0.0 Start with a tour of the paved paths on Glacier Point at the gift shop.

0.3 Complete the short Glacier Point loops at the signed Panorama trailhead opposite the gift shop. Head left on Panorama Trail, staying left at the Y and climbing briefly before traversing into trees.

0.5 Leave the trees for the long traverse down toward the Illilouette Creek drainage.

2.1 At the trail junction at a switchback, go left on the signed trail to Illilouette Fall, Nevada Fall, and the Yosemite Valley. The trail to the right leads to Mono Meadows, Buck Camp, and other points in the backcountry.

2.6 Cross a seasonal creek in the woods.

2.7 Round a switchback and arrive at the Illilouette Fall overlook. This is the turnaround; retrace your steps. (You can also drop another tenth of a mile or so to cross the creek near the top of the fall.)

5.4 Arrive back at the trailhead.

Option: A number of hikers continue past Illilouette Fall on a moderately strenuous one-way day hike to the valley floor. The route takes in a section of the John Muir Trail, includes views of Nevada Fall and Vernal Fall, and, depending on the route you chose, incorporates the stairs of the Mist Trail. The route is not all downhill; it negotiates a significant uphill section between Illilouette Creek and the John Muir Trail. And don't discount the difficulty of the final downhill run: The Mist Trail can be brutal on the knees. The one-way distance is about 8.5 miles.

94 Lower Yosemite Fall

An easy paved trail leads to the base of Lower Yosemite Fall, where Yosemite Creek completes its dive onto the valley floor.

Height: 2,425 feet total (1,430 for the upper fall; 675 for the middle cascade; 320 for the lower fall)

Beauty rating: ★★★★★

Distance: 1.0-mile loop

Difficulty: Easy

Best season: Late spring and early summer

County: Mariposa

Trailhead amenities: Restrooms, trash cans, shuttle stop, and information signboards. An abundance of amenities—from gift shops to restaurants to tent cabins and more—not to mention the basics, such as restrooms, water,

and trash cans, are also available elsewhere on the Yosemite Valley floor.

Land status: Yosemite National Park

Maps: USGS Half Dome CA and Yosemite Falls CA; park map available online and at park entrances.

Trail contact: Yosemite National Park, Public Information Office, PO Box 577, Yosemite, CA 95389; (209) 372-0200 (dial ext. 3, then 5); www.nps.gov/yose. The website is extensive and should be every visitor's first stop for information on the park.

Finding the trailhead: Though you can start at a number of nearby valley attractions in Yosemite Village or at Yosemite Lodge, the trailhead for this route is at shuttle stop 6/Lower Yosemite Fall, located between the two. Parking is available along Northside Drive, with additional parking available at Yosemite Village. Parking fills quickly during high season. GPS: N37 44.768' / W119 35.536'

The Hike

One of the park's premier attractions in spring and early summer, Yosemite Falls features three tiers that drop more than 2,400 feet from rim to valley floor. The upper fall is the tallest at 1,430 feet; the middle cascades are the most difficult to see; and the lower fall, at 320 feet, attracts the hordes. For good reason: The paved path to Lower Yosemite Fall leads into the spray itself when the flows are at their peak, and the experience is sublime.

From the trailhead the paved Lower Yosemite Falls Trail heads north, toward the falls, passing benches and interpretive signs that describe one of Yosemite's nineteenth-century accommodations, James Hutchings's boardinghouse. As you'll discover as you continue reading the interpretive plaques alongside the pleasant, wandering path, Hutchings would hire a young John Muir to work in his sawmill in the valley, sparking a career that would alter the ethos of wilderness preservation in the West. Muir would go on to fight for preservation of Yosemite as a national park, and to cofound the Sierra Club, still a potent wilderness advocacy organization.

Lower Yosemite Fall is a popular and often crowded destination on the valley floor.

Stay right at the junctions as you continue toward the lower fall, enjoying forest and meadow watered by a peaceful stretch of Yosemite Creek. The path climbs to a junction with the Valley Loop Trail; go left toward the falls.

When the flow is at its peak, the mist hits before you reach the bridge that spans the rock-tumbled base of the fall. The bridge is broad, but this section of the route is commonly congested. The slowed pace allows more time with the spectacular sights.

Beyond the Lower Fall, the paved route continues past the Spider Caves (on the right). At the Y stay right on the broad path, passing benches and interpretive signs as the trail loops back toward the restrooms near the shuttle stop/trailhead. You can end the hike here or continue along the Valley Loop Trail past Yosemite

Lower Yosemite Fall; Upper Yosemite Fall

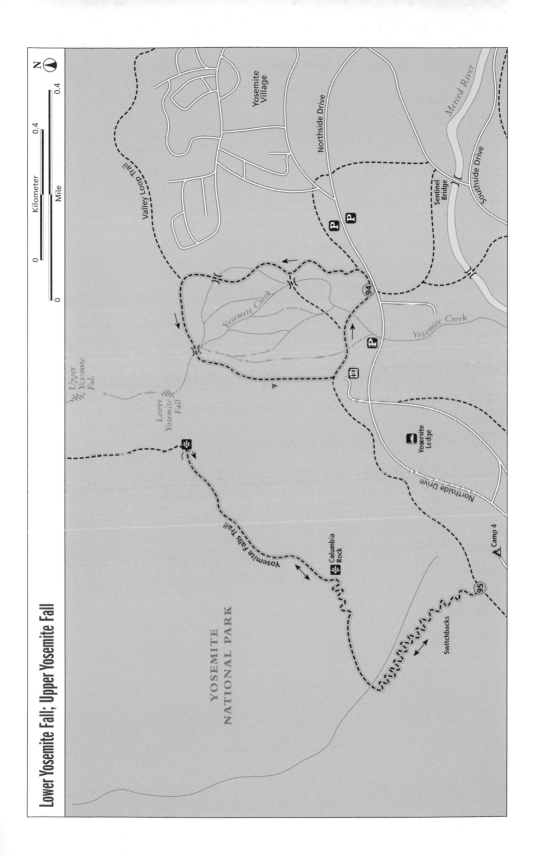

Lodge and into Camp 4, haunt of Yosemite big-wall climbers for more than half a century. A parallel dirt track cruises through the woods above the roadside, leading past a monument to the Ahwahneechee people, and boulders where climbers learn or hone their techniques.

Miles and Directions

0.0 Start at the information signboard on the signed paved path.

0.1 Stay right on the paved path.

0.2 Stay right on the paved path. The left path leads to a falls overlook.

0.3 Cross a boardwalk.

0.4 At the junction with the Valley Loop Trail, go left on the trail to Lower Yosemite Falls.

0.6 Reach the base of Lower Yosemite Fall. Capture the sight in your mind and in pictures; then continue along the paved loop.

1.0 Close the loop near the restrooms at shuttle stop 6. You can end your hike here or pick up the Valley Loop Trail, heading right (west) on the paved path that follows Northside Drive past Yosemite Lodge.

95 Upper Yosemite Fall

Reaching views of Upper Yosemite Fall involves a demanding hike accompanied by outstanding vistas of the Yosemite Valley.

See map on page 313.
Height: 2,425 feet total (1,430 for the upper fall; 675 for the middle cascade; 320 for the lower fall)
Beauty rating: ★★★★★
Distance: 3.0 miles out and back
Difficulty: Strenuous
Best season: Late spring and early summer
County: Mariposa
Trailhead amenities: Restrooms, trash cans, shuttle stop, and information signboards. An abundance of amenities from gift shops to restaurants to tent cabins and more—not to mention the basics, such as restrooms, water, and trash cans, are also available elsewhere on the Yosemite Valley floor.
Land status: Yosemite National Park
Maps: USGS Half Dome CA and Yosemite Falls CA; park map available online and at park entrances.
Trail contact: Yosemite National Park, Public Information Office, PO Box 577, Yosemite, CA 95389; (209) 372-0200 (dial ext. 3, then 5); www.nps.gov/yose. The website is extensive and should be every visitor's first stop for information on the park.

Finding the trailhead: Begin at shuttle stop 7/Camp 4, located along Northside Drive west of Yosemite Village and Yosemite Lodge. Limited day-use parking is available at the camp, along Northside Drive, and at Yosemite Lodge; parking fills quickly in the high season. GPS: N37 44.768' / W119 35.536'

The Hike

One of the park's premier attractions in spring and early summer, Yosemite Falls features three tiers that drop more than 2,400 feet from rim to valley floor. The upper fall is the tallest at 1,430 feet; the middle cascades are the most difficult to see; and the lower fall, at 320 feet, attracts the hordes. The trail to Upper Yosemite Fall, given its steepness, doesn't attract quite as many visitors as the trail to the base of the lower fall, but still sees plenty of traffic. An alpine excursion not suitable for those who don't like exposure, the trail climbs the south-facing wall of the valley, past Columbia Rock, to a falls overlook, and then on to the top of the fall on the rim. You can break it down any way you choose: The route described here leads to the falls overlook and back, but you can also turn around at Columbia Rock, or continue past the falls overlook turnaround to the top of the upper fall, as weather, daylight, and stamina permit.

The signed Upper Yosemite Falls Trail begins behind Camp 4, haunt of Yosemite big-wall climbers for more than half a century. If you happened to follow the Valley Loop Trail from Yosemite Village to the camp, you'll likely have passed climbers dangling from boulders alongside the trail, either learning or honing their skills. The

trail itself is a devious Yosemite ascent, with sixty switchbacks carved into the mountainside leading up to the Columbia Rock overlook. No doubt the switchbacks ease the climbing (as the sign says), but this is not a trail for wimps. Thankfully the sharp, steep curves are shaded by an oak woodland.

The switchbacks are separated by longer traverses as the route nears the Columbia Rock overlook. A long stretch across an open slope leads up to the overlook, where views open east across the valley floor to Half Dome and the granite summits that surround it.

The viewpoint is a turnaround option, but the Upper Fall overlook is the target, and it's only about 0.5 mile farther. Continue up a staircase carved into the slope, traverse around the mountainside, and then make a downhill run around switchbacks, stepping through spring-fed gullies. A final curve, and the upper falls are in sight. The vista is thrilling: You won't be immersed in mist, but the suddenness of the waterfall's appearance and the thunder that it emits are guaranteed to thrill.

This is the turnaround: Take it all in; then return as you came.

Miles and Directions

0.0   Begin at Camp 4. The signed Upper Yosemite Fall trailhead is on the north (back) side of the parking area; there are restrooms in the campground.

1.0   Reach the Columbia Rock overlook. Enjoy the magical views and then continue up the staircase toward the fall overlook.

1.5   Reach the Upper Yosemite Fall overlook. Take in the amazing view; then retrace your steps.

3.0   Arrive back at the Upper Yosemite Fall trailhead.

Option: The Upper Yosemite Fall Trail continues to the top of the upper fall, climbing switchbacks along the left (west) side of the cliff for a total of 2,700 feet. This is a challenging day hike, requiring both leg strength and lung power; it's 7.2 miles round-trip from the Camp 4 trailhead.

◀   *Upper Yosemite Fall plummets from the valley rim.*

96 Staircase Falls

This ephemeral waterfall is easy to miss, both because its season is short and because other falls in Yosemite Valley are showier. It is viewable from Curry Village and the boardwalk in Stoneman Meadow.

Height: 1,300 feet
Beauty rating: ★★★★
Distance: Minimal; less than 1 mile within Curry Village or into Stoneman Meadow
Difficulty: Easy
Best season: Spring
County: Mariposa
Trailhead amenities: An abundance of amenities—from gift shops to restaurants to tent cabins and more—not to mention the basics, such as restrooms, water, and trash cans, are available on the Yosemite Valley floor. Park

officials don't recommend approaching the base as there are a lot of rockfalls in the area.
Land status: Yosemite National Park
Maps: USGS Half Dome CA; park map available online and at park entrances. No map is needed.
Trail contact: Yosemite National Park, Public Information Office, PO Box 577, Yosemite, CA 95389; (209) 372-0200 (dial ext. 3, then 5); www.nps.gov/yose. The website is extensive and should be every visitor's first stop for information on the park.

Finding the trailhead: From the Arch Rock entrance, follow CA 140 into Yosemite Valley, and then Southside Drive to Curry Village. Find parking alongside Southside Drive/Happy Isles Road near the Curry Village tent cabins. Stoneman Meadow opens north of Curry Village. GPS: N37 44.393' / W119 34.234'

Viewing the Falls

Checking out Staircase Falls does not require a significant hike. A walk through Curry Village reveals the lower part of the spill, which runs in rivulets down the cliff face behind the tent cabins. A more impressive view of the falls, which scatter across the cliff face as an unnamed creek drops from near Glacier Point into the Yosemite Valley, can be had from the boardwalk in Stoneman Meadow, which begins opposite the road leading into Curry Village. The short walk through the meadow also offers great views of Half Dome and other Yosemite monoliths as well.

Staircase Falls

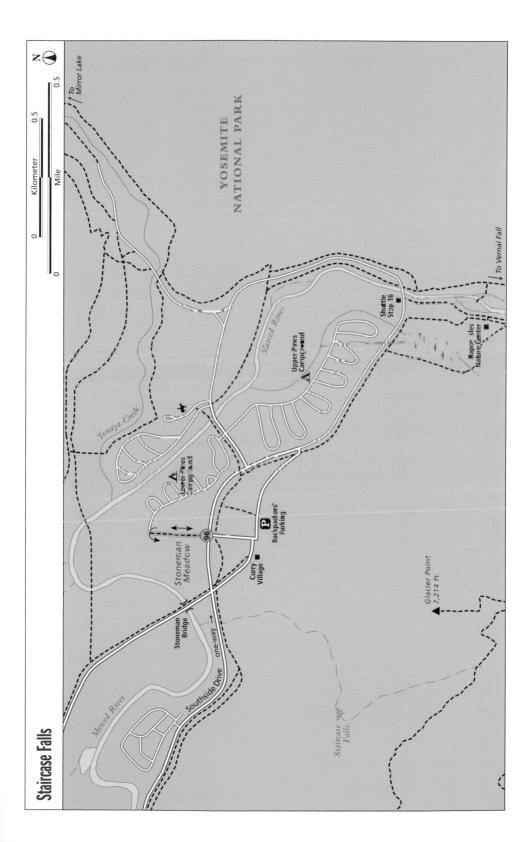

N

0   Kilometer   0.5
0   Mile   0.5

To Mirror Lake

YOSEMITE NATIONAL PARK

Merced River

Tenaya Creek

Stoneman Meadow

Stoneman Bridge

Southside Drive

one-way

Merced River

Curry Village

Lower Pines Campground

Backpackers' Parking

Upper Pines Campground

Shuttle Stop 16

Happy Isles Nature Center

To Vernal Fall

Staircase Falls

Glacier Point 7,214 ft.

96

97 Vernal Fall

The Mist Trail to Vernal Fall is one of Yosemite's most popular, for good reason. It follows the thundering Merced River up to and then alongside the spectacular fall, topping out on a sun-washed slab that offers stellar views down valley past Grizzly Peak.

Height: 317 feet
Beauty rating: ★★★★★
Distance: 3 miles out and back
Difficulty: Moderate to the bridge; strenuous to the top of the falls
Best season: Late spring and early summer
County: Mariposa
Trailhead amenities: Restrooms and information at Happy Isles (shuttle stop 16). An abundance of amenities—from gift shops to restaurants to tent cabins and more—not to mention the basics, such as restrooms, water, and trash cans, are available on the Yosemite Valley floor.
Land status: Yosemite National Park
Maps: USGS Half Dome CA; park map available online and at park entrances. No map is needed; just follow the crowds.
Trail contact: Yosemite National Park, Public Information Office, PO Box 577, Yosemite, CA 95389; (209) 372-0200 (dial ext. 3, then 5); www.nps.gov/yose. The website is extensive and should be every visitor's first stop for information on the park.

Finding the trailhead: The nearest parking for the Happy Isles trailhead is opposite the Upper Pines Campground at the east end of the valley floor. If parking is available (which may not be the case in the summer season), follow the roadside path south and east to the Happy Isles trailhead. If you find parking elsewhere in the valley, take the shuttle to stop 16. Cross the bridge to the trailhead on the right. GPS: Upper Pines parking lot, N37 44.129' / W119 33.935'; Mist Trail at Happy Isles, N37 43.993' / W119 33.466'

The Hike

The Mist Trail is a bucket list hike. It's simply that good. Yes, it's steep, and the footing can be treacherous, but the experience is quintessential Yosemite, full of granite and spray and views that soar heavenward.

The trail begins gently, following the relatively quiet Merced River through a boulder garden. But the river gains vigor as the trail gains elevation, starting within 0.1 mile of the trailhead. The ascent is unbroken from the base to the bridge below the falls but is mitigated by the river cascading alongside, whitewater crashing among boulders as it completes the final flight of its Giant Staircase.

One of the most popular trails in Yosemite, given its moderate length and elevation gain (by comparison to its cohorts), the Mist Trail is often packed with people. Patience and courtesy are as necessary as good walking shoes. If you are in a group, walk single file and stay right so that faster hikers can pass.

The route flattens briefly at the Vernal Fall bridge. The waterfall is picture-perfect at this spot, framed in evergreens and backed by granite peaks. A water fountain and

Vernal Fall; Nevada Fall

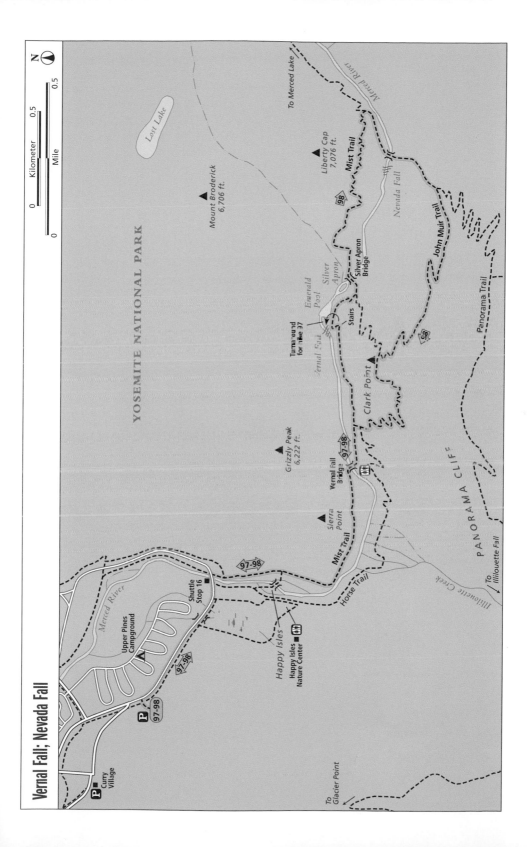

restroom are on the far side of the bridge. This is a good turnaround point for those who aren't in shape; the length is 1.6 miles round-trip.

To continue to the top of the fall, follow the trail past a junction with the John Muir Trail, the return route if you choose to take in Nevada Fall and make a loop. The pavement of the treadway is broken here, and the falls flicker in and out of view as you continue to climb.

Below the final ascent alongside the fall, several wide spots in the path allow you to pull aside and put on rain gear. What's generated by the fall when it's flowing full force hardly resembles mist; it can be drenching. Likewise, the mighty Mist Trail stairs—more than 600 of them—are perennially drenched. If the sight of the fall and the wind being sucked from your lungs by altitude aren't enough to slow your pace on the staircase, taking time to climb carefully will.

The turnaround is at the top of the fall on a sunny granite apron. The Merced appears calm above the cliff, gathering in the spectacular Emerald Pool before taking the plunge. Don't be fooled: This is a swift mountain stream, especially when swollen with snowmelt. Heed signs cautioning against wading and swimming. A railing near the top of the fall offers a great vantage point down the river valley, with a rainbow or two arcing in the mist and sunshine. Enjoy your lunch; then return as you came.

Miles and Directions

0.0   Start by taking the Mist Trail from Happy Isles.

0.1   Begin climbing up the paved path alongside the tumbling Merced.

0.8   Arrive at the bridge below Vernal Fall. Water from the fountain on the far side of the bridge is delicious. Continue up the path, now on the other side of the river. (**Option:** If you're not going to the top of the fall, this is a good turnaround point for a 1.6-mile hike.)

1.1   At the junction with the John Muir Trail, stay left and riverside on the Mist Trail.

1.5   Ascend the Mist Trail stairs to the top of Vernal Fall. Return as you came.

3.0   Arrive back at the Happy Isles trailhead.

Options: If you'd like to visit Nevada Fall, continue up the Mist Trail; the route is described in the next entry. You can also loop back to Happy Isles and the valley floor from the top of the fall via the John Muir Trail. Take the trail to Clark Point, which leads up from the top of the falls to connect with the Muir Trail. The Muir Trail offers great views across the valley as it switchbacks down to meet the Mist Trail above the Vernal Fall footbridge; from there retrace your steps to Happy Isles.

◄   *Vernal Fall is the lower of two iconic falls on the Merced River.*

98 Nevada Fall

The famous Mist Trail arguably serves up the best views of Nevada Fall, with the backward vistas of the whitewater plunge from the John Muir Trail pulling a close second.

See map on page 321.
Height: 549 feet
Beauty rating: ★ ★ ★ ★
Distance: 6.9-mile lollipop
Difficulty: Strenuous
Best season: Late spring and early summer
County: Mariposa
Trailhead amenities: Restrooms and information at Happy Isles (shuttle stop 16). An abundance of amenities—from gift shops to restaurants to tent cabins and more—not to mention the basics, such as restrooms, water, and trash cans, are available on the Yosemite Valley floor.
Land status: Yosemite National Park
Maps: USGS Half Dome CA; park map available online and at park entrances
Trail contact: Yosemite National Park, Public Information Office, PO Box 577, Yosemite, CA 95389; (209) 372-0200 (dial ext. 3, then 5); www.nps.gov/yose. The website is extensive and should be every visitor's first stop for information on the park.

Finding the trailhead: The nearest parking for the Happy Isles trailhead is opposite the Upper Pines Campground at the east end of the valley floor. If parking is available (which may not be the case in the summer season), follow the roadside path south and east to the Happy Isles trailhead. If you find parking elsewhere in the valley, take the shuttle to stop 16. Cross the bridge to the trailhead on the right. GPS: Upper Pines parking lot, N37 44.129' / W119 33.935'; Mist Trail at Happy Isles, N37 43.993' / W119 33.466'

The Hike

You can't get to Nevada Fall from the Yosemite Valley floor without passing Vernal Fall. Unless you approach from behind—the long, long way—this is a two-waterfall hike. If you choose, you can catch views of the lower fall from the Vernal Fall bridge and then leave it behind, hiking out and back to the Nevada Fall via the John Muir Trail ... but that omits half the wonder. This loop, heading up to the top of Nevada Fall via the Mist Trail and back down on the John Muir Trail, immerses you in double the excellent views and drenching mist.

Begin on the paved, often crowded Mist Trail, which climbs alongside the Merced River. The path ascends to the Vernal Fall bridge in less than a mile, where picture-perfect views of Vernal Fall are framed by woodland. Take a sip of sweet water from the fountain on the far side of the bridge and then proceed up the Mist Trail staircase, composed of more than 600 granite steps washed in spray from the fall that spills alongside.

At the top of Vernal Fall, check out rainbows in the spray from the railing and then take a breather on the sunbaked granite apron. The Mist Trail to Nevada Fall

Nevada Fall as viewed from an ascent along the Mist Trail.

continues beyond the apron alongside the now reasonably placid Merced, which fills the Emerald Pool and wets the Silver Apron. Social trails weave through the woods at the riverside; stay left of the restroom and follow the most obvious path. At the signed trail junction, stay left and proceed over the footbridge. The trail winds up a gentle incline through the forest.

Views of Nevada Fall open at a small granite overlook near the base of the 500-plus-foot cliff. In full swell it's a powerful sight. This makes a good turnaround should you decide not to take on the thigh-burning, switchbacking climb to the top of the cliff.

If you decide to make the climb, set your pace and keep your head up. It's not a brutal ascent, as the switchbacks make the steepness tolerable, but it's stiff enough to elicits comments like "This is the longest 1.3 miles ever" from fellow hikers.

The trail tops out at a junction with the John Muir Trail, which leads to the top of the falls in one direction and farther into the Yosemite backcountry in the other. Turn right on the Muir Trail and walk out to the granite platform at the top of Nevada Fall, basking in views of Liberty Cap and the mighty Merced as it is funneled over the precipice.

You can return as you came, but connecting with a descent on the Muir Trail makes for a great loop hike. Wander over the slabs to the footbridge spanning the

river and cross to the far side, following the John Muir Trail gently downhill through the woods.

A section of the Muir Trail is etched into the canyon wall as you leave the Merced behind, the granite face leaking moisture early in the hiking season. Turn around to take in views of Liberty Cap and Mount Broderick backing Nevada Fall. The exposure is exhilarating.

The Muir Trail presents a steady but moderate descent, with switchbacks and plenty of shade. Drop to Clark Point, where you can turn right to return to the top of Vernal Fall and then back to the valley floor via the Mist Trail. This loop continues on the John Muir Trail, beginning a steeper descent toward the Yosemite Valley. Switchbacks ease the grade, as do views across the valley. Drop to the junction with the Mist Trail above the Vernal Fall bridge, then retrace your steps to the trailhead.

Miles and Directions

0.0 Start by taking the Mist Trail from Happy Isles.

0.1 Begin climbing up the paved path alongside the tumbling Merced.

0.8 Arrive at the bridge below Vernal Fall. Water from the fountain on the far side of the bridge is delicious. Continue up the path, now on the other side of the river.

1.1 At the junction with the John Muir Trail, stay left and riverside on the Mist Trail.

1.4 Ascend the Mist Trail stairs to the top of Vernal Fall. Take in the views; then continue on the most obvious path along the riverside, passing the Emerald Pool. Do not swim in Emerald Pool, as inviting as it may be. Several people have died after being swept over Vernal Fall just downstream.

1.75 At the signed trail junction, go left on the Mist Trail to Nevada Fall.

1.9 Cross the footbridge.

2.25 Take in the view from the small granite overlook at the base of the fall.

2.9 Arrive at the junction with the John Muir Trail and other backcountry routes at the top of the climb. Go right on the John Muir Trail toward the top of the fall.

3.0 Reach the granite slabs at the top of the fall. Cross the footbridge over the Merced and begin to descend on the John Muir Trail.

3.5 At the signed junction stay right on the John Muir Trail; the trail to the left leads to Illilouette Fall.

4.6 At the signed junction at Clark Point, stay left on the John Muir Trail. Long switchbacks break up the descent.

6.1 Reach the junction with the Mist Trail above the Vernal Fall bridge. Turn left and retrace your steps.

6.9 Arrive back at the Happy Isles trailhead.

◀ *The John Muir Trail offers great views of Nevada Fall.*

99 Chilnualna Fall

A short, easy hike leads to the bottommost plunge of Chilnualna Fall outside Wawona.

Height: About 695 feet
Beauty rating: ★★★★
Distance: 0.8 mile out and back
Difficulty: Easy
Best season: Late spring and early summer
County: Mariposa
Trailhead amenities: Trash cans and an information signboard

Land status: Yosemite National Park
Maps: USGS Wawona CA; park map available online and at park entrances
Trail contact: Yosemite National Park, Public Information Office, PO Box 577, Yosemite, CA 95389; (209) 372-0200 (dial ext. 3, then 5); www.nps.gov/yose

Finding the trailhead: Chilnualna Fall is located in the southwestern reach of the park. From Yosemite Valley's Southside Drive, take Wawona Road/CA 41 for about 21 miles to Chilnualna Fall Road, just outside "downtown" Wawona. Turn left onto Chilnualna Fall Road and go 1.7 miles, winding through a neighborhood of cabins and more extravagant homes, to the signed falls parking area on the right. GPS: N37 32.859' / W119 38.063'

The Hike

This is the easy way out: A nearly flat walk of less than a mile leads to what could be called the tail end of Chilnualna Fall, the last plunge on Chilnualna Creek before it cascades into the South Fork Merced River. It's a pleasant lowland Yosemite excursion, nice for an afternoon stroll after a visit to the Mariposa Grove.

Chilnualna Fall, composed of five cascades along more than 4 miles of Chilnualna Creek, flows year-round, though in late season (or drought) the watercourse and waterfall thin to streams. This may not be what waterfall lovers crave, but even when the water slows up, the last plunge of the long fall fills a lovely, shaded pool suitable for wading and toe-dangling.

A short jaunt up the paved Chilnualna Fall Road leads to the signed trailhead proper on the left. A sign at the trail split at the outset denotes the stock trail and the foot trail; stay right on the foot trail. The route starts out wide and then narrows to singletrack as it traverses the mountainside under cover of a mixed oak forest. Chilnualna Creek, clotted with boulders, runs alongside down and to the right.

It's a gentle climb to the base of the first staircase, where side trails lead down to the pool at the base of a wall of rock about 50 feet high. Climb the stone steps on the left to reach another side trail and fall overlook; these steps are a continuation of the longer route that climbs several more miles to the upper Chilnualna cascades. A smattering of trees find purchase on the cliff, clinging like rock climbers to the wall, a

Though drained by drought, Chilnualna Fall still musters enough of a flow to fill a pool at its base.

remarkable feat considering the pummeling of the fall, especially when charged with snowmelt. When ready, retrace your steps to the trailhead.

Miles and Directions

0.0 Start by climbing the paved Chilnualna Fall Road to the right toward the trailhead proper. At the split head right on the designated foot trail.

0.4 Arrive at the base of the final section of Chilnualna Fall. Chill for a bit; then retrace your steps.

0.8 Arrive back at the trailhead.

Option: The trail to the top cascade, designed by the same trail builder, John Conway, who constructed the devious yet brilliant switchbacking trail to Upper Yosemite Fall, dates back to the turn of the twentieth century. It's a strenuous, 8.2-mile round-trip day hike to the top cascade and back, with an elevation change of 2,400 feet.

Resources

Waterfall lovers have written guidebooks and created websites that provide abundant information on falls to visit in Northern California. Check them out.

Books

Brown, Ann Marie. *California Waterfalls*, 4th ed. Berkeley, CA: Moon Outdoors, 2011.
Danielsson, Matt, and Krissi Danielsson. *Waterfall Lover's Guide to Northern California*.
Seattle, WA: Mountaineers Books, 2006.

Publications

Greene, Linda Wedel. Historic Resource Study. *Yosemite: The Park and Its Resources, vol. 1, Historical Narrative*. Washington, DC: US Department of the Interior/National Park Service, 1987. www.nps.gov/yose/historyculture/upload/greene1987v1.pdf.

Websites

www.parks.ca.gov; search for "waterfalls" and select "Wet Winter Strengthens Cascading Waterfalls in California State Parks
www.worldwaterfalldatabase.com
www.waterfallswest.com
www.world-of-waterfalls.com/california.html
http://hikemtshasta.com
http://visitredding.com
http://chicohiking.org

Hike Index

About the Author

Tracy Salcedo-Chourré has written guidebooks to a number of destinations in California and Colorado, including *Hiking Lassen Volcanic National Park, Best Hikes Near Reno-Lake Tahoe, Best Hikes Near Sacramento, Best Rail-Trails California, Exploring California's Missions and Presidios, Exploring Point Reyes National Seashore and the Golden Gate National Recreation Area,* and Best Easy Day Hikes guides to San Francisco's Peninsula, San Francisco's North Bay, San Francisco's East Bay, San Jose, Lake Tahoe, Reno, Sacramento, Fresno, Boulder, Denver, and Aspen. She lives with her family in California's Wine Country. You can learn more by visiting her website at www.laughingwaterink.com.

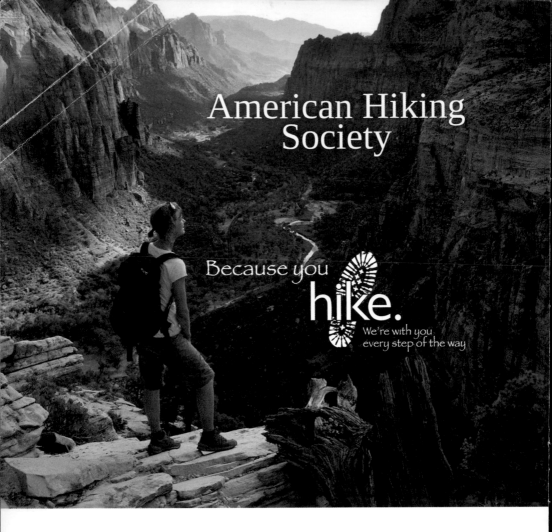

American Hiking Society

Because you **hike.**
We're with you
every step of the way

As a national voice for hikers, **American Hiking Society** works every day:

- Building and maintaining hiking trails
- Educating and supporting hikers by providing information and resources
- Supporting hiking and trail organizations nationwide
- Speaking for hikers in the halls of Congress and with federal land managers

Whether you're a casual hiker or a seasoned backpacker, become a member of American Hiking Society and join the national hiking community! You'll enjoy great member benefits and help preserve the nation's hiking trails, so tomorrow's hike is even better than today's. We invite you to join us now!

American Hiking Society